Parenting for Life

Consciously Creating
Your Lifetime Relationship
With Your Child

NINA SIDELL, M.A.

Parenting for Life

Consciously Creating Your Lifetime Relationship With Your Child

Nina Sidell, M.A.

For permission requests, information and inquiries contact the author/publisher at:
www.LiveInspiredwithNina.com.

Printed in U.S.A.

Design and editing by Doug Munson

First Printing 2015

ISBN-13: 978-1506175584
ISBN-10: 1506175589

Library of Congress Control Number: 2015900115
CreateSpace Independent Publishing Platform, North Charleston, SC

This book is dedicated to my two beloved children,

Matthew and Daniel,

whom I love with my whole heart.

They are wonderful people in their own right,

and they teach me, because of who they are,

about unconditional love, respect, acceptance,

and how to continually learn and love.

I hope I do the same for them.

Acknowledgements

Thank you to my parents for a lifetime of love and care and the skills you have given me, your youngest child. To Jessie, my 2nd mama, big sisters, and all of my wonderful friends and family for your love, inspiration, support, and encouragement as I was writing this book. Thank you to my children for your creative and editing input in my writing process. Thank you to my closest friends and my "sisters and brothers of the soul" for believing in me and being like family to me. I appreciate your unending care, our wonderful times together, and the special moments that draw us close. Thank you all for your wisdom, guidance, and patient support. Thank you to my former agent who believed in me and my vision. Thank you to my editor for helping me fine tune and clarify my message as a guide and friend and for making me laugh during tough writing transitions. Thank you to my artist who put my vision into form and was a joy to work with as we co-created the manifestation of this book. Thank you to my proofreader and friend who made sure that my written words and messages were expressed skillfully. To all of you, I appreciate your support in helping me find my voice.

Table of Contents

Author's Preface xii

Introduction xiv

— *Growing Your Relationship* —

1. **Attachment: A Lifetime Proposition** 2
   Emotional Bonding: From Pregnancy to Old Age 2
   The Formative Years: Dependency 5
   The Self-Reliant Years: Independence and
       Interdependency...11
   "Family Wellness"...14
   Homework Assignment #1: Discover Your Life's
       Parenting Purpose 17

2. **Create Sanctuary in Your Home**...................................19
   Home as a Safe Harbor 19
   Create Family Wellness: Work on Your Attitude......................23
   Build Trust 25
   Keep it Real 27
   Start With One Person 29
   Create an Environment of Freedom, Respect, and Peace 34
   Homework Assignment #2: Take a Physical,
       Mental, and Emotional Inventory.. 40

3. **Clarify Your Parenting Style and Parenting Goals**......41
   Who Are You as a Parent?...41
   What Is Your Parenting Style?...43
   Define Your Parenting Purpose 49
   Question Authority: You Know Your Child Best 52
   Homework Assignment #3: Parenting Style Checklist................. 54

4. **Once a Parent, Always a Parent**....................................56
   A Permanent Truth..56
   Set the Stage for All Future Relationships.....................................57
   Constant Opportunities for Mutual Growth and Healing,

at Every Age 61

Homework Assignment #4: Expand Your Vision 67

5. Family: The Ultimate Chance for Belonging 69

A Basic Human Need: From Birth to Death and All the Stages
In Between..69

Individual and Group Identity Starts Here 74

Emotional Health for a Lifetime 76

Homework Assignment #5: Reach Out to Family Branches 78

— *Evolving Your Relationship* —

6. Let Everyone Evolve: Learn Life Lessons....................80

Be a Student of Life...80

How Personal Growth Heals Relationships........................85

Factor in Regular Self-Care 85

Allow Yourself and Your Child to Evolve 87

Homework Assignment #6: Evolve Your Love.......................89

7. Recognize and Nurture Your Child's Gifts 91

Meet Your Child Where He or She Is 91

A Singular Voice 92

Learn Well 93

Release Comparison 94

Support Your Child's Right to Blossom 96

Homework Assignment #7: Be a "Behavior Detective" 99

8. Learn to Re-Parent Yourself.............................100

Get to Know Yourself Better...................................100

Be Honest With Yourself: Pay Attention to What You Truly
Need 104

Allow Your Inner Parent to Take Care of Your Inner Child 108

Homework Assignment #8: Your "Inner Child" Creative
Visualization 114

9. Live in the Moment with an Eye on the Future 116

Stop, Look, Listen, and Breathe—Focus Your Attention 116

Raise Your Awareness 118

When You Mess Up, Fess Up 120

Be Open and Aware in the Moment 121

Wisdom From Other Places 123

Welcome the Future 125

Homework Assignment #9: "The Doorway" Creative
Visualization 127

10. Conscious Parenting and Conscious Living 129

Your Choice: Be Awake or Asleep 129

Free Yourself and Commit to Parent With Awareness 133

Awaken to Endless Opportunities to Learn Life Lessons
and Heal 134

Enjoy Your Time Together 135

Homework Assignment #10: Meeting and Befriending Your
"Inner Guide" Creative Visualization 138

**11. The Best Deal: Parents in Charge; Children Have a
Voice 140**

The Need for Structure, Leadership, and Democracy
at Home 140

Hold Family Meetings 142

Promote Healthy Communication 145

Find a Balance Between Limits and Compromise 147

Homework Assignment #11: Family Meeting Practice Run 153

12. Question Your Role Models (History/ Her Story) 155

Where Did Your Parents Come From? 155

Insight Moments and Lifetime Insights 156

How Did You Benefit and Struggle With Your Role Models? 159

Rewrite the Script, Take the Best and Leave the Rest 161

Homework Assignment #12: History Lesson—A Timeline of
Family Adjectives 165

13. Know Who Your Child Is 167

Accept Your Child Today, Embrace Their Potential
for Tomorrow 167

Get to Know Your Child's Temperament, Learning Style,
and Spirit.. 172

Allow for Trial and Error in Your Child's Learning Process 173

Homework Assignment #13: Parent Coaching Session—
Examine Your Perceptions of Your Child 176

14. Listen Well: There Is No Substitute............................ 178

What Do Butter, Sugar, and Good Listening Have in
Common?.. 178

To Listen Well is to Learn Well 180

The Best Present of All 183

How to Process New Information Heard 184

Homework Assignment #14: Practice Active Listening 188

**15. Pay Attention: Understanding Derived from
Observation..190**

Be an Archaeologist or Behavioral Scientist.......................... 190

Showing vs. Telling: How Feelings and Needs Are Expressed.... 194

Strive for Emotional Neutrality, Working Things Out in the
"Home Zone" 195

Invite Each Interaction, Positive or Negative, to Draw You
Both Closer 196

Homework Assignment #15: Heightened Awareness 199

—*Resolving Your Relationship*—

16. The Power of Positive Relationships 202

Positive vs. Negative Energy and How it Affects
Relationships 202

Invite Gateways for Personal Growth and Healing in All
Your Relationships 207

Continue to Do What Works, Let Go of What Does Not
Work 211

Homework Assignment #16: Parent Credos 215

17. Essential Forgiveness: The Potential for Healing...... 217

Feel Your Feelings 217

Appreciate Someone Else's Vantage Point..................................222

Let Go of the Pain . . . for Yourself...224

Homework Assignment #17: Forgive and Live 228

18. What Happiness Is and What It Isn't..........................229

Love the Beauty and Potential of Each Moment.....................229

Where Does Happiness Come From?..231

You Have a Right to Be Happy; Your Child Has a Right to Be
Happy...236

Enjoy That Which Gives You Joy, Seek Inner Peace...................240

Homework Assignment #18: Happiness Requirement Chart 244

19. Know When to Hold On and When to Let Go 246

Know Where Your Child is Developmentally 246

A Reciprocal Relationship..250

Remember What It Felt Like to Be a Child, and Then
Grow Up...253

Knowing When to Hold On and When to Let Go
Brings Benefits...255

Lead With the Power of Your Heart..258

Let Go and Learn: Invite Understanding and
Resolution... 260

Homework Assignment #19: Hold On, Let Go! 264

20. Create a Lifetime Relationship with Your Child 266

Treasure Every Moment, Every Stage...266

Remember That Knowledge is Limitless....................................271

Trading Places: What Your Child Can Teach You About
Yourself... 274

Your Heart Knows No Bounds 276

Define Your Legacy, Your Ultimate Message 278

Homework Assignment #20: Your Final Words of Wisdom 281

Afterword **282**

What's Next? **283**

Bibliography/References **284**

Author's Preface

*T*he SUV struck me as a pedestrian and I stood there, the victim of a hit and run on Broad Street in Philadelphia. Everything around me was so still. It seemed as if even time itself ceased to exist. In that moment of stillness, there was clarity. I thought of my two children. I needed to talk to them, listen to them, and connect with them. Since the accident, my parenting purpose and life purpose clarified and crystalized. My devotion to my children as their lifetime advocate strengthened. I reinforced my commitment to being the best lifetime parent I could be. After healing from my physical injuries, I emerged eager to write my first book, hoping to share some pearls of wisdom that worked for me as a mother with my children and my clients. I have always been very perceptive, intuitive, and observant as a lifetime learner. As an Expressive Arts Therapist, I enjoy using creative tools, combining insight and action in life. As a therapist, life coach, speaker, and writer, I have always sought to help empower others and strengthen the relationships in their lives. However, this miraculous event renewed my higher purpose. I wanted to inspire others with the insight and emotion instilled in me the instant I was hit and share what I have learned in my professional and personal life.

After careful consideration, it became clear to me that the right topic to explore was parenting. I had expertise in this professionally and it was the closest subject to my heart. As a devoted mother and child advocate, I was compelled to discuss this topic. I realized that parenting with awareness throughout one's lifetime is potentially the most mutually life-affirming, beneficial path toward self-awareness, self-development, and empathy. I recognized the core significance that parenting well has as an endless process needing attention in our current world. With all else going on in society, families need support.

Mothers, fathers, and children deserve the chance to be better than their parents in a real sense and on a multitude of levels. Parents lend support and guidance and do the best they can with the information and skills they have at the time. Due to this reality, I wrote this parenting manual for parents to follow as they become better acquainted with themselves and their child or children for life.

A parent's job is to nurture, reward, and support a healthy bond while reinforcing the child as separate with a growing positive sense of self in the world. Another role is to support the child to be or become better than themselves. Therefore, a parent must recognize the importance of autonomy, be intentional, open, and self-aware while getting to know his or her child.

We live in a digitalized world and it is time for us to get back to living a more humanized one. The opportunity for mutual growth and healthy love is always possible between parent and child and does not diminish as children become adults. A vital long-term parent-child relationship sets the stage for greater happiness, health, and life success. This relationship holds within it potent expressions of love, conflict, growth, and resolution. It can benefit both parents who are raising and relating to their children, and adult children who need to find understanding and healing. Young children need their parent(s) for specific emotional and developmental requirements. As this relationship matures into adulthood, needs change. Roles may reverse.

This mindful parenting program honors both parent and child. Focus on each individual child in your family separately. Take the time you need to process each chapter and homework assignment. Create a *Parenting Journal* to work on each of the 20 homework assignments. By applying the principles and practices of this book, you can personalize your own inspirational parenting journey.

This is a parenting book with heart, a relationship book with purpose, and a lifetime parenting plan for everyone. You and your child will be happier for it. Manifest the best life possible. You both deserve it! Live your best life yet!

Live Inspired! ®

Nina~

Introduction

*P*arenting is a journey of love. Because your relationship with your child lasts a lifetime, honor and nurture it as a growing, living, and evolving process. You parent for a lifetime and have at your disposal great power and responsibility to use love, care and wisdom as your guide. The impact of your role helps your child to eventually fly free, and yet maintain the capacity for you to share a lifetime of closeness.

For a parent, no matter how young or old your child is, raising your offspring is a humbling and awesome experience. The practice of lifetime parenting is a privilege and responsibility that does not end when your child grows up. What you bring to the table matters. Your history and parenting attitudes steer the ship into the future. Your past colors the way you see your role, your responses, your child's individuality, and his or her self-expression. Parenting brings you to your knees, raises your spirit forward, enlightens your mind, and captures your soul. It is with this awareness and intention that *Parenting for Life* has been written.

As the parent you teach and learn the basis for real and healthy intimacy: being able to genuinely connect with and honestly relate to others.

You can grow with your child, at every age and stage. Part of the gift of this relationship is recognizing the beautiful opportunity at every turn. You can parent yourself while you parent your child. Learn and grow as you go. Opportunities to express unconditional love, acceptance, patience, and respect are available in each moment, year, and stage. These values are highlighted in the basic parenting principles, homework, affirmations, and more which are described in this book.

This new way of seeing the responsibilities of parenting will transform your parent-child lifetime relationship forever. You will learn that positive movement naturally evolves each person in a relationship; mutual love and respect, and empathy keep you close and are always possible.

Since all life's stories begin at home, the characters and plot are written over a lifetime. Children are products of their parents and their early environments. They become adults who often live out early roles, scripts, relationship patterns, unmet needs, and expectations. Early relationships plant seeds for later ones. Therefore, it is natural (at appropriate times) for both parent and child to examine their roles as family members so they can learn, grow, heal, and thrive over time. *Parenting for Life* holds parents accountable, helps children forge their own paths, and strengthens the parent-child bond through love, respect, and empathy.

Although the meaning of family has remained relatively the same, the configurations of family have changed in these times. This book speaks to mothers and fathers. There are single, married, divorced, straight, gay/lesbian, intergenerational, adoptive, and foster parents raising children. *Parenting for Life* speaks to all parents who are engaged in the art of growing, evolving, and resolving a lifetime relationship with their child or children. What matters is the commitment to raise and relate to each child with conscious intent and humane actions across a lifetime. *Parenting for Life* follows a structure that supports this lifetime approach to the parent-child experience by stressing three crucial phases: Growing Your Relationship, Evolving Your Relationship, and Resolving Your Relationship. Success in these phases helps ensure successful lifetime parenting. Actions, sometimes natural events, individual development, and chronology determine what stage of the parent-child relationship you are in.

So often parenting books explore what is wrong with a child, where the parent-child relationship gets stuck, how to remedy behavioral maladjustments and tendencies, or how to understand partial aspects of a child. Predominantly, the essential opportunities for mutual learning and growth present within the parent-child relationship, and what the parent brings to the table, are left out. All parenting books mean well and hold value and focus, however the individuals and development of the parent-child relationship are often overlooked.

Most books leave out the significance of the parents' history in creating and influencing their child's life and their shared life together. This element is a missing key that will unlock a happier and healthier lifetime relationship moving forward. You are a parent for as long as your child is your child. Just because your child eventually grows up does not mean that he or she is no longer your child. You become interdependent, healthy as autonomous people, and learn to balance changing times and roles. You have a lifetime role and responsibility to fulfill as your child grows and matures.

Find ways to help your child move from dependency to eventual independence. You are in it for life, no matter what. Therein lies great continuous opportunities for lifelong growth, love, and learning between you and your special kid.

Do you worry that you will "mess up" your child? No parent is perfect. Do your best. So much is about your relationship and its lifetime impact. A good, secure relationship between you fosters greater self-esteem and success in other relationships and in life for your child. If your relationship and your child's (potential) sibling relationships are cohesive, and your child is developing well, then you did not mess up. Focus on the overall positives.

Parenting for Life offers back-to-basic values, new insight, and a chance for a healthy, healing relationship between you and your child. It examines the lifelong dynamic and potential for true healing, mutual self-discovery, and a lifetime of conscious relating. Each chapter examines aspects of your lifetime relationship. The potential for ongoing positive growth between and within you is examined within each chapter subsection. All sections of the book share a set of basic tenets that are designed to help you succeed in the practice of mindful lifetime parenting. They are as follows:

- Enjoy your child—every age and stage.

- Let your relationship with your child inspire you.

- Exercise empathy toward your child and others.

- Choose to parent with consistent respect and love.

- Set healthy limits while encouraging freedom of expression.

- Recognize the importance of everyone's needs on the family team.

- Be responsible for your own attitudes, behavior, history, and self-care while you take care of your child.

- Allow for your child's individuality and personal evolution as well as your own.

- Learn from your mistakes as a parent and be open to change.

- Apply the power of positive thinking to your relationship with your child.

- Always remember that parenting is a privilege that lasts a lifetime.

There are homework assignments for each chapter to help practice this program. The exercises included in the homework assignments are meant to support tenets that constitute the core of the book. You may not complete each exercise or each homework assignment and that is okay. You may choose to come back to an assignment later. Work at a pace that is appropriate for you. You may also find that your responses to some of the earlier exercises have changed after you finish the book. Revisiting your old assignments can be a helpful way to mark your growth or remind you of areas in your parenting skill set that still need attention.

Since this book is intended to personalize the parenting journey for you, its terms include parenting both genders and these genders (his or her and he or she) alternate throughout the book. Keep your child (and each of your children individually) in mind when reading this book. Keep yourself in mind when healing your relationship with your parent, too.

Parenting for Life draws the necessary connection for you to remain open, clarify your parenting identity, parenting goals, and embrace natural opportunities in each moment to connect in a positive way. *Parenting for Life* inspires you to grow closer and bond well for a lifetime with each individual child in your life. You can heal your own childhood issues and grow to be your child's best parent. Believe and await the natural miraculous learning opportunities that shine through your relationship and see your other relationship dynamics improve.

Keep the door of dialogue open between you and your child as you walk your lifetime path. Start wherever you both are now. See wonderful growth happen as your guiding love, healthy limits, and unconditional support lead the way. *Parenting for Life* is intended to educate, encourage, and inspire you to be the best parent you can be, all the days of your life. There is no time like the present to take charge and be the best parent you can from this moment forward. Work to grow your parental toolbox. So dig in and put these principles to work now, so you can enjoy the blessings of connecting and reconnecting with "your baby," each and every day, even when he or she is all grown.

Growing Your Relationship

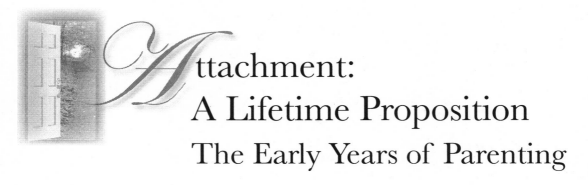ttachment:
A Lifetime Proposition
The Early Years of Parenting

It is only with the heart that one sees rightly; what is essential and invisible to the eyes.

—Antoine de Saint-Exupéry from *The Little Prince*

Emotional Bonding: From Before Birth to Old Age

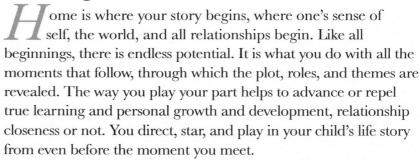

> You direct, star, and play in your child's life story from even before the moment you meet.

Home is where your story begins, where one's sense of self, the world, and all relationships begin. Like all beginnings, there is endless potential. It is what you do with all the moments that follow, through which the plot, roles, and themes are revealed. The way you play your part helps to advance or repel true learning and personal growth and development, relationship closeness or not. You direct, star, and play in your child's life story from even before the moment you meet.

Home, in this sense, incorporates the everlasting place of emotional attachment that parent and child return to. The practice of parenting for a lifetime is like any other practice that you commit to. Decide to embark on your parenting journey knowing that you may stumble and fall. Yet know that you will always return to the humility of the practice, the discipline, and the art of the goal. With consciousness you understand that when you practice lifetime parenting, it is an ongoing process. The dynamics between you and your parental responsibilities change over time, yet your relationship continues during (and even after) your shared lifetime ends.

As a parent, you inspire intellectual, emotional, and spiritual revelations for yourself and your child by the way you parent. Whether you use one predominant parenting style or another, (which will be discussed later) your attitude about parenting will convey everything. You learn as you experience real time together, when you unplug or silence all the gadgets and simply connect. You find out about yourself and about someone else. You attach emotionally and sometimes detach the connection. Your child does the same since as in any relationship, time and space are required for a person to fully bloom.

Naturally, you hold on and learn to let go as your child feels, thinks, and forms her own opinions, independent of you when the time comes. Think about that truth for a moment. For most of us, family begins with the creation, presence, and acceptance of a new individual life joining the person, couple, or group. You make room for this new person and accept him or her into the fold. Home and family life, no matter who comprise the family, set the blueprint for a person's future. The love and support present at home are what cradles an individual's soul, body, and mind. Each life's story germinates from the seeds of innate potential and interpersonal relationships between family members. You are let into a family. Let someone else in and create a healthy cycle of dependency, interdependency, and ultimately, independence emerge. Learn to hold on and let go all at the right times. As you evolve as a parent, you feel more peaceful in your relationship. When you feel more peaceful, so does your child. The cycle is continued.

Learn how to make peace with yourself—and your child—for life!

The quest for a happy and healthy family life revolves around meeting everyone's needs as best as possible. However, your little one's needs often trump yours in the early years. What mother has not had her most basic needs, such as using the bathroom, interrupted by tiny prying eyes or the demands of itty-bitty fists battering the door? How often has your morning shower or family laundry waited until 11:00 at night, when you are completely ready to collapse? Self-sacrifice comes with the territory. Over time, mutual respect, personal responsibility, individual self-

> You are let into a family. Let someone else in and create a healthy cycle of dependency, interdependency, and ultimately, independence emerge.
>
> Learn to hold on and let go all at the right times. As you evolve as a parent, you feel more peaceful in your relationship. When you feel more peaceful, so does your child. The cycle is continued.

expression, a cooperative home environment, and effective communication design the patterns of the parent-child relationship. Your child becomes less "self-absorbed" and you are required to make fewer sacrifices; you begin to listen, empathize, and negotiate and the relationship becomes more balanced. Everyone's needs matter; hopefully they get worked out over time. You cannot keep the scales perfectly balanced, only keep everyone in mind.

> Your job is to provide the anchor that stabilizes your child's sense of safety and security, and the wings that give him freedom to explore his environment and his identity.

You discover that your needs will incrementally come back into view once your child is developmentally ready to become more self-reliant over time. When you have done your job well, you have helped to instill a sense of security that will eventually give your child the confidence to step out, know himself, feel secure with you, and be bold and self-directed in the world as a young adult. Your job is to provide the anchor that stabilizes your child's sense of safety and security, and the wings that give him freedom to explore his environment and his identity. Your child's self-worth and self-perceptions grow under your care as you present your best self and encourage him to do the same. Ultimately, *Parenting for Life* holds parents accountable, helps children forge their own paths, and strengthens the parent-child bond through love, respect, and empathy.

You have the responsibility and honor to consistently parent your child with love and respect. Be remorseful for your wrongdoings and learn from your mistakes. Reinforce this valuable lesson in your words and actions in the home you run now. The predominant parental figure whether mother or father, grandparent or foster parent, serves as the authority figure and role model whom a child will rebel against or follow. The parent leader establishes the family tone and structure. The mother is typically considered the first teacher in a child's life and is also the first woman in a child's life. There is a lot of power to bond emotionally and establish healthy intimacy, unending acceptance, and support. Parental personalities, histories, and social roles combine teachings about inner and outer life. Parents teach the many life skills needed to succeed in today's world with ongoing changing political, gender, and family roles. Take the responsibility of your job as parent seriously, and then remain flexible enough to know when to relax and have fun.

The lens through which you see your child and the feedback you give her informs her of who she is and teaches her the beginnings of self-knowledge. This is especially true for young children. This lens brings into focus your child's abilities and areas of developmental need. Widen your vision by seeing your child's perspective; enjoy her individual unique talents, gifts, and strengths. Allow your child's story to unfold and be told in her way. Honor and respect who your child is as a whole person, her thoughts, ideas, needs and feelings. She will eventually learn to honor and respect you as a person in return, and see you more clearly through her own lens.

The Formative Years: Dependency

Your child must depend on you for all he needs in the first year of life. By age two years, your child discovers independence and needs to test how much he can do without you. At age three years, and some say up to seven years, your child's basic personality is cemented and offers a more cooperative interdependence between you, allowing you to work together moving forward as a team. In most cases, the mother is the primary parent and caregiver. This is true in both the human world and in most animal kingdoms. In every case, a young child needs someone close to depend upon.

When a mother prepares to create (or adopt or foster) and raise a new life and bring that life into her world, she is faced with emotional needs that fulfill her maternal instincts. Those instincts revolve around her needing to care for, protect, and love her little one. She seeks to create, love, and bond emotionally and physically as protector, caregiver, and nurturer. The baby needs a secure emotional attachment to feel safe, secure, and cared for. The baby responds to this love and requires the strong connection to the nurturer in order to survive. This is when the two interrelate intimately and deeply, biologically, symbiotically, almost as one, mother caregiver and infant.

The symbiotic relationship, comprising the early bond where mother and child are as one, keeps the child nurtured by and dependent upon the mother. This is natural until it is time

> The lens through which you see your child and the feedback you give her informs her of who she is and teaches her the beginnings of self-knowledge.

for the child to separate and symbiosis ends.[1]

Deepak Chopra and Rudolph Tanzi in their book, *Super Brain*, remind us that, "by the mother cradling, cooing and cuddling with her baby, the limbic-emotional brain (which effects future love relationships and a physical response to love) is developed."[2] A baby is genetically programmed to need its mother—to connect, be nurtured by, empathized with, draw life from, mimic, and to be as one. It is at this initial stage of development that the parent-child relationship is born, initializing the seeds of a close, growing lifetime relationship. This relationship example impacts all future relationships for your child. Mother and child exist within the same physical body during pregnancy. They share the same food system and experience a closeness that defines the essence of life itself: a relationship intertwined, beginning with unequivocal, incomparable care and love. The bonding process occurs as parents and other primary caregivers find nurturing ways to deeply connect with their little one. Primary caregivers include natural, adoptive, foster, or inter-generational parental figures.

> Since love is at the core of good parenting, be committed to loving with awareness and respect. It is through this deep bond that healthy love can grow, benefitting both parent and child.

Since love is at the core of good parenting, be committed to loving with awareness and respect. It is through this deep bond that healthy love can grow, benefitting both parent and child. Both mother and child are a part of one another. A baby's cells remain in the mother's body long after birth while the mother's hormones slowly return to normal regulation after birth. They need one another and need to love and be loved until the need to separate becomes inevitable. Ironically, separating from this deep emotional attachment enables emotional health when you emotionally and physically separate; it is what also makes your child stronger so that she can begin to stand alone as an individual. This bonding allows for integrated emotional and brain development and sets the foundation for future relationships, including your child when she becomes a parent herself. All the days of your lives, keep the love alive by putting into action the essential components that keep your relationship strong. Your relationship with your child has such strong lifetime significance and will follow you both throughout your time when together and apart. It starts between you and is a viable starting point for healthy intimacy. "Intimate relationships cannot substitute for a life plan. But to have any meaning or viability at all, a life plan must include intimate relationships." Harriet Lerner pointed out in her book, *The Dance of Intimacy*.[3] It is with this understanding that you realize the importance of consciously parenting for life.

Many studies and literature in psychology demonstrate that disruptions to attachment and bonding can absolutely negatively impact emotional and psychological development. Family loss experiences and separation have been clearly identified as a definite risk factor for mental health problems in childhood and adulthood. High intelligence coupled with faulty bonding can increase these odds. Keep in mind that genetics, temperament, and the way a person processes experiences all play key roles. However, children who have had interrupted relationships with primary caregivers are more likely to have compromised mental health. Separation and loss can be more traumatic depending on the circumstances and timing, how many needs have already been met or not, and how the child learns to cope.

Ironically, separating from this deep emotional attachment enables emotional health when you emotionally and physically separate; it is what also makes your child stronger so that she can begin to stand alone as an individual.

If bonding with the biological mother or mother figure is stifled or impeded during the first three years of life or on a consistent, long-term basis, proper emotional and perhaps mental health development will suffer later. Severe, dysfunctional maladaptive bonding could create a future mental illness or personality disorder in adulthood. Dr. Dan Kindlon and Michael Thompson who wrote *Raising Cain—Protecting the Emotional Life of Boys* relay the numerous studies that show that "disordered attachment, such as an insecure or disorganized mother-child bond, contributes to later problems in the child, such as disruptive behavior in school, depression/anxiety, and poorer cognitive functioning."[4] It would be harder for a child to find relationship intimacy, and if they stumbled upon it, may not recognize a healthy, close relationship. Otherwise, he will just have to work a whole lot harder to learn that he deserves healthy love. Create a strong and positive attachment. It will follow your child all the days of his life.

Your job as parent is to care for, protect, nurture, model, and help shape and encourage your child to be healthy and happy and strong enough to eventually feel safe enough to fly the coop. Your child's job is to depend upon your protective efforts. Your child absorbs wisdom through cues and messages, and imitates you. Remember, to her, you are as powerful as God or as close to being God-like as anyone can be. As time passes, you both learn and grow while your love remains the same.

The mother or mother figure model and demonstrate how to act and how to love while the baby (child and teen) mirrors and copies expressions, mannerisms, emotional feelings, and other behaviors of her mother. In operant conditioning and child rearing, reinforcement for how one feels about themselves and his or her own environment comes from a psychological and behavioral process called shaping. Children are shaped by their environment and all that encompasses that. Imitation, positive and negative reinforcement, a sense of belonging, emotional attachment, learned skills, coping and defense mechanisms set the tone for later expression. You may have already figured this out, but understand that you are being watched more than you are being listened to.

Often when we hear the word "bonding" we do not necessarily think of its origins. It refers to the act of forming attachments. The idea of "bonding" has been discussed in recent years, mostly focused upon men with each other and single fathers with their children. Bonding occurs between parents and children, friends, lovers and in some business alliances. Strong bonds also develop as behavior patterns are observed, identified and learned in childhood with the caregivers. Recognize the power of what it means to truly connect with another person. Your life is enriched as you are accepted for who you are while you accept another person. You find a comfortable and safe meeting place for your common interests or values and personalities. When you bond as healthy individuals coming together, and keep your negative tendencies or patterns in check, you create mutual advancement and the highest good for each of you.

A young child depends upon his or her parent for

> Create a strong and positive attachment. It will follow your child all the days of his life.

> As time passes, you both learn and grow while your love remains the same.

connection, staying physically and emotionally safe, and being intellectually dependent for literal and symbolic survival. Older kids and teens sometimes lash out, express their individuality and need to separate, sometimes harshly forcing space for their own right. As a parent of a "tween" or teen, you may sometimes wish that your child had his own space…in someone else's house…in another state…on the opposite coast. Sometimes feeling so lovey-dovey is a laborious task when you are pretty sure that your tween or teen has been invaded by an alien being. Either way, thank goodness your child is becoming an individual. That is what children are supposed to do, grow as a separate person. As grown adult children, autonomy and independence reign supreme while your lifetime relationship is set-up over time. Then, it is up to the two adults who relate at this point, still *parent and child*, to negotiate the agreed terms of your future relationship.

> When you bond as healthy individuals coming together, and keep your negative tendencies or patterns in check, you create mutual advancement and the highest good for each of you.

The best way to promote a strong bond that lasts a lifetime is to develop trust, provide consistent love and support, and be accountable. Express and model the building blocks of trust and emotional safety. By being accountable, you are in charge of yourself and take complete responsibility for your attitudes, words, and actions. Without accountability, insensitivity and excuses reign. What was once unacceptable can become tolerable, and thus acceptable. With personal accountability you model honesty and strength. You display a willingness to improve and take pride in yourself by telling the truth, exhibiting trustworthiness, and being responsible for your actions. These principles must be initiated when your child is young and continue over time. If trust is broken, whichever party fractured the trust is responsible for correcting and building a trust repair plan, even if done in small steps. It is easier to build from the ground up then to regain a sense of safety and confidence in another that has been torn down.

She has less separation anxiety when entering preschool when she feels secure with her attachment with you. By knowing you will return, she can learn to trust a new caregiver and make new friends. By feeling the strength of your caring and devoted presence, it is easier for your child to say "So long," explore independently, and trust that you will reunite.

Without a deep sense of security in your presence, your child can experience episodic separation anxiety that may grow into emotional insecurity over time and last the rest of his life. This can continue over a lifetime if the impact of an early uncomfortable separation or series of separations are perceived as too intense or too negative for him. Being afraid to be close or to love and be loved, being afraid to leave or be alone can show up years later in other relationships. It is in the early, formative years that your child learns by your behavior whether to feel a deep sense of security and trust or deep insecurity and distrust.

Since safety, respect, and trust are the cornerstones of all good relationships, focus on building them with your child. The good news is that beyond the early years, again with love, respect, consistency, and accountability, you can offer him increased opportunities to build trust between you. These "do-over" moments offer a chance to develop greater inner security and personal responsibility by teaching the value of being honest and vulnerable by acknowledging your history, owning your mistakes, and committing to parent better the next time. A good example is if you find that you are overreacting in conversation or getting increasingly impatient with your child for being irresponsible or having made a mistake, stop and gain some perspective.

> With personal accountability you model honesty and strength. You display a willingness to improve and take pride in yourself by telling the truth, and being responsible for your actions.

Check in with yourself and ask what your "parenting intention" (more on Parenting Style in Chapter 3) is for the day or that moment with your child. Put your issues, pressures, worries, dreams, and needs aside to respond with more emotional neutrality than reactivity. This outer security translates emotionally into a feeling of internal security. Your child does not doubt the depth of your love and care; it is felt, seen, heard, and understood. Your child emotionally internalizes your love and care and assimilates it into his psyche.

The gift of giving unconditional love and respect (which go together), acceptance and support is the best present you can ever give. The ribbon that wraps it all together is the indisputable underlying core bond that lovingly binds you as family for life. What connects you for life best is the safety, respect, and trust that you create every day.

The Self-Reliant Years: Independence and Interdependency

As your child grows, you want to ensure that she knows, loves, and respects herself and others and makes wise choices to reflect that. When she transitions to new developmental stages, initial awkwardness is replaced by learned responses, however bumpy or smooth. In your child's formative years, those between early childhood and late adolescence (birth to age 18 years), her dependency needs are met. From childhood and beyond the teen years, parts of your child's drive to individuate strengthen and cause her to resist, rebel, and break free. Ego development (a part of the psyche that helps to fuel unique self-perceptions) keeps your child working toward gaining personal gratification with others and in the world. Your child becomes more independent and your job is to encourage this. She is increasingly motivated more by socializing, experimentation, dealing with peers, learning how to deal with conflict, and exploring external role models than by pleasing you. That being said, your role and presence in assuring your child who she is, that immediate connection and feedback will help remind her who she is and to make the best choices possible.

As you love, learn, and grow together, independence and healthy interdependency forms your best, most mature eventual relationship. You take stock of your personal autonomy and shared responsibilities. You see who your child is and can sense when important, sometimes life-changing choices are necessary.

A client family I worked with had a teen who was becoming addicted to drugs and alcohol, got into fights, and had some academic setbacks during high school. The mother trusted her instincts and confronted her son to help him take responsibility and get help for his increasing problems. In time and with the right knowledge and support, the young man chose to accept

> The gift of giving unconditional love and respect (which go together), acceptance and support is the best present you can ever give.

> As you love, learn, and grow together, independence and healthy interdependency forms your best, most mature eventual relationship.

11

the right care to get him clean, sober, and healthy. With the right structure, he learned to take better care of himself and practice self-discipline. The communication between the two grew from then on between mother and son. In another client family scenario, during the parents' divorce, a high school boy chose to bully his younger brother incessantly, both emotionally and physically, out of their parents' view. The younger son's school work and friendships suffered. The parents did not seem to notice the misdirected anger and abuse as they were dealing with their own issues. This left the younger brother feeling beaten and ignored. It took him time to honor his feelings and learn how to stand up for himself with his family. Eventually, he felt stronger and able to have a voice within the family. Members of the family system transitioned into a new way of life, with better choices being made by everyone. With some counseling for the divorcing parents, happier feelings were shared and more understanding and closeness began to develop between parents and children.

When you understand and communicate to your child at the right times in your lifetime relationship that it is safe to be close and safe to be separate, you are doing a good job! Give your child the secure feeling that he is safe to be with you and relate to you. Equally give him the confidence to feel empowered, believing in himself enough to know that he can be smart and safe in the world. Communicate that life is about learning, loving, sharing and when to hold on and when to let go. You teach and he will learn on his own, when to stay, when to move onto something else, and when to follow his dreams—still connected, but away from you. When ready, your little bird can spread his wings and fly away from the gilded cage. Let him go with confidence and encouragement. Believe in him; encourage him to believe in himself. Your child appreciates your belief in him at every age and stage and he cannot hear it or feel it enough. Communicate in words and actions that your child's original home is with you while he finds his transformative home in the world. You both mature a little more when you learn to let go. You continue to love, guide, relate, then release as your child expands and individuates which ironically, brings you closer.

> When you understand and communicate to your child at the right times in your lifetime relationship that it is safe to be close and safe to be separate, you are doing a good job!

This lifetime connection between you helps set the stage for positive connections with people and is at work outside of your relationship. Remember, parenting is an awesome lifetime responsibility. Continue to build your lifetime relationship of love, respect, trust and safety, by being aware, accountable, accepting and mindful all the days of your lives.

Interestingly, comparisons are drawn between toddlerhood and the teenage years. Both stages of development require that the individual search their identity, rebel against the world, including authority figures, and become highly inner- and self-focused. Toddlers and teens need to explore, question, and express their own personhood and feel their own power. They need to test the limits of external boundaries and seek instant gratification and unique identities as they separate themselves from controlling influences. An essential stage that toddlers and teens face is to begin to master self-awareness and self-control skills while also recognizing the need for approval and guidance from parental figures. The push-pull between child and parent, the murky, sometimes heated power struggles during those tough times is a healthy outward expression of this necessary internal struggle toward independence.

While the inevitability of power struggles or conflicts arising may bother you at the time, resolving the conflict can be a positive learning experience for both of you. Be mindful of these necessary phases of life, natural misunderstandings and your child's need to push and pull against you. Be aware of your natural reactions, personal history, unresolved pain and pre-conceptions running you. Clearly, be aware of your part in the power struggle or conflict and if you are projecting unrealized or unresolved conflicts from your earlier life. Notice your attitudes and desire to ignore, negate or control. Your young child may test you to learn boundaries and play games. At that older teen/young adult stage, your child looks older but acts younger and often cannot help it. Be mindful that your child's journey includes all of who she is, at every turn. Her emotional landscape, personality, tendencies, lessons and even mistakes, serve to make her stronger when she goes out on her own. When

Believe in him; encourage him to believe in himself.

The push-pull between child and parent, the murky, sometimes heated power struggles during those tough times is a healthy outward expression of this necessary internal struggle toward independence.

she settles into a strong sense of herself, owning all the parts that make her who she is, the inner and outer power struggles will begin to subside.

If you experience long-term or repetitive power struggles, you may need to learn new ways to respond and communicate to diffuse the pattern and resolve the underlying issue or wound. Since you are the parent, with inherent power beyond your child's control, be aware not to overuse it. As Martin Hoffman identified, "Power is an ingredient in many social situations. If we consider power as the potential and individual has for compelling another person to act in ways contrary to his own desires, we can see that there are a variety of situations in which power exists. The parent-child relationship is one of these."[5] Make sure that the division of power, freedom and skills available to each of you is just.

A father I worked with learned he needed to play racquetball to unwind when he was stressed. He realized that when triggered and under great work and marital pressures already, if a conflict arose at home he would become more rigid, dogmatic, hostile, and ineffective in the conversation. His behavior gave rise to the escalating conflict. The attempt at wielding all the control and feel a sense of his own power in his life was evident. However this attempt at forcing his authority did not address or resolve the conflict, nor invite a solution.

He was clearly a part of the escalation, not the solution at that point. This man learned that both he and his two teenage sons each in their own ways contributed to their cycle of conflicts. He essentially took ownership that he was part of both the problem and the solution and was able to calm down, listen, and regroup. The family's communication style softened and was marked by the positive lessons learned. The family tone of near-constant conflict focused on blame or shame shifted to one of healthy communication, relaxation, and democracy.

Family Wellness

"Family wellness" is an overall state of well-being for every family member. It is not necessarily focused on any one person, only some, or the "identified patient" (if one of the

> "Family wellness" includes the emotional, intellectual, physical and spiritual components that make family members feel happy, healthy, loved and balanced.

14

group is troubled, sick, or struggling). Mutual love, respect, empathy, and accountability are what each member strives for and deserves within the family. It is characterized by the goal of meeting physical, intellectual, emotional, and spiritual needs of each person in the family unit.

Ensure "family wellness" by employing your ability to live in the present moments. Employ your memories, feelings, observations, understanding and empathy with your child to remain clear in the role of parent. "Family wellness" includes the emotional, intellectual, physical and spiritual components that make family members feel happy, healthy, loved and balanced. You are parenting your child's emotional, social, and spiritual, as well as physical and intellectual life. Know who you are and were, remember what mattered to you most when you were growing up. Reflect on your own childhood experiences during that period. You can learn a great deal about your sense of internal security, self-knowledge, and current attitudes when looking back at how you felt while growing up, particularly during times you distinctly needed either connection or space.

If you felt safe, loved, respected, and accepted by your primary caregivers, a strong foundation was laid for your future. You received the message that it is safe to be close and when expressing a need, it would be met. You also learned that it is safe to stand on your own, that someone believed in you to survive and thrive as an individual, yet stay emotionally connected. If that was not your experience, you know the importance of providing this for your child. You may have gone without the emotional or affection connection with a parent or two. You may have been abandoned, overpowered, not believed in, not supported to be yourself, not had your needs met, or not have been encouraged to reach for your goals and dreams. You might relate to having parents with a similar family history. You may need to heal this within yourself. You may need to understand that your parents had limitations and negative, unsatisfying histories that accompanied their love and they simply acted from their vantage point and skill set.

Open your awareness; become familiar with, resolve

> When you practice lifetime parenting, you create the space later for your adult child to want to come back to you, not because they have to.

and separate out your past from your current family. Notice similarities in pattern or tone and choose to create wellness in your home now. Give more than you got. These personal reflections will make you a better parent; your child will appreciate your wisdom to develop your "family wellness" so that overall wellness is felt and encouraged at home.

When you practice lifetime parenting, you create the space later for your adult child to want to come back to you, not because they have to. This is accomplished slowly over a long period. As mentioned earlier, another interesting comparison between the toddler and the teen years is the increased need for self-reliance. Obviously, a teenager can become literally more self-reliant while a toddler does so in a smaller and less dramatic way. This must be done in steps, both holding on to the needs of childhood while embracing the new skills of adulthood. Parental caregivers can recognize the duality of childhood in this sense. It is best described as a parent "giving her child roots and wings," which means giving a child the healthy balance of security and skills to eventually grow away from you and into her own happy life. For a teenager to feel ready to spread her wings, she must feel that she is rooted in love, safety, and security. It is in this relationship born of safety and attachment that your child can eventually become who she truly is, independent of you and happy to call you her parent.

Search for what drives and motivates you as a parent. Get to know your parenting style, goals and purpose overall (see Chapter 3). It is important to keep in mind that your child "learns what they live." When living in a home environment that supports emotional closeness and growth and the needs of your family team are met, your child's life improves overall. Be willing to invest your love, time, awareness, and commitment to this most precious relationship, no matter how busy or stressed you are. Invest in a lifetime of love, mutual respect, and achievable goals with your child; find common ground to walk together and apart for years to come.

> Invest in a lifetime of love, mutual respect, and achievable goals with your child; find common ground to walk together and apart for years to come.

Homework Assignment 1

Discover Your Life's Parenting Purpose

This exercise is designed to help you clarify who you are as a parent. It will also help you to re-define any aspects of your parenting practice that you wish to identify as part of your parenting purpose.

- Take the time to find a safe, peaceful and quiet physical space. Have a notebook or journal handy to be used as your *Parenting Journal*. You will write down your images and insights after the exercise.

- Allow your body to rest comfortably in a favorite chair or sofa. Take a few slow, deep breaths and close your eyes. Feel supported by the solid foundation of the furnishing and let your body sink into it completely. Get comfortable and relax. You can write in your journal when you need to.

- Think of this exercise as a recording of *you* across time.

- Go back in time and remember the first impressions, thoughts and feelings you had about being a parent. You may have been a little child, perhaps a young or older teen or became ready just recently. You may have imagined life as a parent, and some of its reality, whether prepared or surprised by eventual parenthood. You may have positive aspirations or negative reactions to the way you were parented. Let your mind wander; visit moments from your past as you ponder your role as parent.

- Be open to recalling words, phrases, images, feelings, and anything else you can remember and write them down. If you have mostly nonspecific impressions, do your best to record the impressions accurately and fully. Make a list of your parenting ideals from the past and write them down.

- Next, go back to what you have written and notice what reflects your parenting style and goals at this time.

- Put a star next to each description that matches you now.

- Place a line through those that no longer represent your parenting ideals. Relax. Be in the moment. Think of your role and personal identity as a parent. Focus on who you are, how you think, feel, express yourself as your child's guardian, guide, teacher, protector, and role model. This can work if you are a parent now or planning to be a parent in the future.

- Make a list of your current parenting ideals with as much clarity as possible. Know that you can go back to your list, add, subtract, and rethink what you need to later.

- Allow your descriptions to match your values, attitudes and actions as your ideal parent now. Take some time with this; write down your impressions as they come to you. Do not censor, simply record your inner parent's voice. Take time to fine-tune this list so that it accurately reflects you as your child's parent. Once you have done that, you have identified your true *Life's Parenting Purpose*. This clarity will help you to be authentic in your role as parent all the days of your life, as you practice this program of inspired lifetime parenting.

CHAPTER TWO

Create Sanctuary in Your Home

There's no place like home.

—Dorothy Gale from *The Wizard of Oz* by L. Frank Baum

Home as a Safe Harbor

When you think of creating a lifetime family environment, you think of home and all the parts that make it special. Whether real or fantasized, images of home conjure feelings of safety and peace. Home or its ideal image is a place where you can be yourself. It is a place of love, vulnerability, comfort, beauty, reality, and familiarity. A home that is filled with love fills up the giver and the receiver. Contained within a home are the original seeds for all present and future relationships and expectations for life experience to come. Its effects start an important journey that last a lifetime.

Imagine parenting across a lifetime knowing up front that you can provide a constant safe harbor for your child. Lead the way by creating sanctuary in your home. Remain open and ready to nurture your child's needs. Hear his feelings and be emotionally and physically available and responsive. Create inner security for your child and convey that he will always matter. Knowing home is safe a harbor provides shelter from the storms of life, reassuring your child that he is not alone. Living in a safe home offers your child a place to be himself and feel emotionally nourished and supported. Living in a home that is

A home that is filled with love fills up the giver and the receiver. . . . Knowing home is safe harbor provides shelter from the storms of life, reassuring your child that he is not alone. Living in a home that is treated as a sacred place is the best way to start the day and the most reassuring way to end the night.

treated as a sacred place is the best way to start the day and the most reassuring way to end the night.

Nurture the goal of personal peace for all and home as sanctuary above all else. Set aside specific areas of your home for relaxation, contemplation, and meditation. Separate this area from areas meant for eating, sleeping, and recreation. Another approach is to create a sanctuary in each room, places set aside for calm retreat, reflection, and regeneration. Your sanctuary room or areas need to feel calm and serene and encourage comfort for all of your senses. Add creative color, design, or Feng Shui elements that please your sense of comfort, harmony, and beauty. There should be no disruption of that feeling and it should feel like a safe haven to enjoy again and again. It is best to have colors and objects that are soft and comfortable and that feel welcoming to your body, soul, and mind. Your home is available not only for physical nourishment, but it is the safe haven from the rest of life. The home that you create offers the vital growth environment necessary for real and long-lasting personal nourishment. The home your child lives in stays a part of who he is, even when he leaves home and becomes your grown child, making a home elsewhere. Your child takes the good feelings with him wherever he goes, feeling and spreading the love and peace he knows.

What kind of energy is felt inside your home? What do family members and guests notice when spending time there? All too frequently, the emphasis is placed more on beauty and functionality rather than on how people treat one another and the energetic qualities that occupy a home. A sense of love, respect, and kindness contribute to the unseen beauty felt within your home. These signs of conscious love show onlookers visiting your household a story worth noticing, too.

The emotional and sensory appeal of home includes its smell, visual delights, the people inside, and your associations to those people. Where and how you live can be just as important as who you live with. Feeling welcomed, included, and safe draws you in. Physical warmth, safety, and comfort inspire a relaxed

> Your home is available not only for physical nourishment, but it is the safe haven from the rest of life. The home that you create offers the vital growth environment necessary for real and long-lasting spiritual nourishment.

feeling. Energy is felt, attitudes are perceived, and behaviors then follow. You can create and re-create your home environment, both physically and interpersonally, anytime you wish. It is your space and you have the power to create special places that invite relaxation, comfort, and revitalization—your own personal and family sanctuary.

When designing a home environment in which to raise your child, be cognizant of what you are creating both directly and indirectly. Establish your home and know that a true sense of home transcends far beyond the physical necessities, comfort, and accoutrements. A home is designed to be a safe space; above all else it is a "family sanctuary" where safety and respect for all are expected. Home is safe and open—a sacred learning and loving environment. Nothing less is tolerated. Intolerable behavior is not supported or accepted. Mistakes are accounted for without heavy blame or shame while a focus on solutions and resolutions prevail. In a safe home, attitudes of love and mutual respect, sharing, fun, cooperation, and learning are encouraged. You can agree to disagree.

Diplomacy and kindness are hallmarks of this kind of home. A team spirit that exemplifies fair authoritative leadership and inspires cooperative participation over time is the best way. All family members feel comfortable in their shared space; they know they deserve to thrive in shared living conditions. A mutually loving and respectful place contributes to a feeling of safety for those who live there. Your attitude as family leader and adult in charge trickles down to your child who is watching, listening, and following your lead. Life feels loving and nurturing, stable, predictable, fun and fair. You and your child communicate in many ways. The tone, body language, and underlying messages you express come through loud and clear. What you convey both verbally and non verbally tells your child everything she needs to know. Your personal impact and the climate you set at home, whether you live in a beautiful palace or modest bungalow, is part of the lesson you teach and the life legacy you leave. As the parent, you are accountable for yourself and chiefly responsible for the environment you provide.

A home is designed to be a safe space; above all else it is a *"family sanctuary"* where safety and respect for all are expected. Home is safe and open—a sacred learning and loving environment. Nothing less is tolerated.

Think of your home as a sanctuary, or at least a place where everyone feels safe, loved and respected deep down inside at all times. A sanctuary can be the whole environment, or it can be specific places, spots to go chill out, meditate, create or relax. For a sanctuary to exist there must first be physical safety. Physical safety comprises the basic needs of being fed, clothed, protected from harm, being given appropriate affection, and never being touched in anger. Next is the assurance of emotional safety. A home that is emotionally safe offers shelter, not ongoing storms or battlefields that rock everyone off course. When storms arise, they should be dealt with quickly and fairly with everyone's needs in mind.

Home represents all that is safe, nurturing, stable, and supportive. Home is a place where examples are set; conditions are tolerated, rejected, or negotiated; human expression is accepted; and internal politics are tested. The world seeps into a home, but does not define it. It is the one place where you retreat from everything that does not really matter or that which could crush you in an instant. It is a place that can protect you and keep you from harm. An idealized healthy family is proportionally balanced with physical and emotional safety.

> Now it is your turn to parent what you know, or if necessary, parent what you feel to be right for you and your child.

Your child's basic needs are met consistently and your separate personal needs also are met. The feeling in the house is generally easy, energetic, and free-flowing, not stifling or consistently tense. When issues or emotions erupt, effective communication tools are used and fine-tuned to deal with and resolve problems. The home is democratic, not run like a dictatorship or left to dissolve into anarchy. You may have been raised in a dictator-like home environment. Your parents may have been, too. That is what they learned and passed down to you. Now it is your turn to parent what you know, or if necessary, parent what you feel to be right for you and your child. Even coming from a champion of the automotive industry, for whom the financial bottom line and turning around companies were king, Lee Iacocca in his book, *Iacocca: An Autobiography*, said, "No matter what you have done for yourself or for humanity, if you cannot look back on having given love and attention to your own family, what have you really accomplished?" [6] The way you relate to your child conveys the ultimate message you send. Make it safe; be responsive and nurturing to guarantee your child's best knowledge of what home really is.

Most people either replicate the way they were parented or go in the opposite direction. There can be a combination for specific key issues or trigger points. When a child is raised in too rigid, harsh, or one-sided of an environment, she learns that her voice is not heard. The parent is always right, and issues become unfair, inconsistent, and mostly result in negative consequences, even when the parent is actually wrong. That can be a damaging blow to a child's forming ego and self-worth, as well as to her inevitable future relationships. As a parent, you are empowered to trust your instincts while you look for times to positively reinforce and empower your child. There should be a sense of "parents in charge, children have a voice" happening. This concept is discussed further in Chapter 11. When this message is spoken in words and repeated with behavior, it both comforts and empowers everyone, keeping everyone at home happy in the process. Say it, do it, and see what happens.

Create Family Wellness: Work on Your Attitude

Attitude is indeed everything. Your attitude creates or destroys everything you do, everyone you come in contact with and especially your "family wellness" (as described in Chapter 1). As stated earlier, family wellness encompasses the emotional, spiritual, social, physical, and intellectual well-being of all your family members. Home can feel like a roller-coaster ride, a wasteland, a war zone, or a secure and happy place. It could also be a combination of these. The energy generated is felt by all and internalized by each family member in his or her own way.

The way you feel at home and the energy there makes you behave in certain ways. Your responses and expressions vary depending on how you feel and what your attitudes are. Your

> Attitude is indeed everything. Your attitude creates or destroys everything you do, everyone you come in contact with and especially your "family wellness."

personal history, family environment, what happened (or did not happen) and how you processed and coped with it, dictate your current attitudes and behaviors. If you have a bad attitude or a chip on your shoulder or try to over-control and micro-manage others, you will not enhance "family wellness." If you act like your child's friend and forget to create guidelines, rules, structure, or natural consequences like a permissive parent, you will fail as family leader and diminish "family wellness. It is only when you carry the proper attitude as consistent family leader that you serve as teacher, student, guide, protector, and occasional friend that your family wellness will blossom and thrive.

> It is only when you carry the proper attitude as consistent family leader that you serve as teacher, student, guide, protector, and occasional friend that your family wellness will blossom and thrive.

You lead and your family follows. Your attitude affects your relationship with your child today and in the future. By choosing to live consciously, you will see a clarified vision of your safe haven; your family sanctuary will be kept alive and consistently modified. You have the power in every moment to see yourself and become aware of your attitudes, feelings, and reactions. Review and re-affirm your goals, re-negotiate, self-correct, and create a home of peace, love, and inspiration in which you and your child live, love, and learn. Your physical-emotional space will be tweaked and become clarified and un-cluttered as your attitudes reveal the need for change. When you realize that your attitudes contribute directly to the whole family feel, then you have stopped the domino effect dead in its tracks. You will parent with more awareness, self-honesty and a better plan. This will help you relax, cope, and get back to creating a safe, cooperative, and loving home environment for all.

Open your heart and be conscious. Personal responsibility and accountability are highlights of mature adulthood. When you "mess up," "fess up." Use every opportunity to learn and grow. Replace a "kick the dog" mentality with a "kiss the dog" approach in your home. Take care of yourself when you need to. Protect your child from unnecessary emotional, verbal, or physical fallout from past or current intense, explosive situations in your life. Find ways to diffuse the bombs and alleviate anything that contributes to a war zone versus a love zone at home. Know that your child picks up on your tone, mood, emotions, attitudes, and expressions. You find ways to realize your wrongdoing or limited belief and consciously self-correct. When you parent with the attitude of taking personal responsibility and accountability for your part, you are inspired to be the best parent and best person you can be. When you do this, your child has a better chance of growing up to be a healthy, happy, and responsible adult.

Just like you can count on the sun rising in the morning, you will make mistakes. At those times you need to step back, take a breath, and start over just like you tell your child to do. Take responsibility for your mistakes. Make a heartfelt apology and consider the situation a lesson learned. Often times, when you practice self-correction, especially when under pressure, that is the greatest skill you can teach. When you parent for life, be humble and grateful that you can learn from your mistakes and stop repeating them with your child.

Build Trust

You teach by example, through the way that you act and the things that you say. This basic early learning teaches trust, or the lack thereof. The basis of trust starts early and continues without end. Your presence, availability, consistency, or lack thereof teaches your child if he can trust you or not. A young child, growing older over time needs to learn that his caregiver is worthy of being believed and counted on time and again. Keeping your word and behaving consistently with care and responsibly regarding important obligations and sensitive issues builds trust. Being accountable and re-negotiating when it is needed builds trust, too. Teaching the value of trustworthiness through your words and actions makes a great impact upon your child. Keep your word. Only make agreements that you can keep or renegotiate. You offer a felt sense of greater security with you and model safety in creating trust, thus affecting all of your child's future relationships. "It is an equal failing to trust everybody, and to trust nobody,"[7] as an English proverb states. Teach the value of trustworthiness. You cannot go wrong as you share that important gift.

Often times, when you practice self-correction, especially when under pressure, that is the greatest skill you can teach. When you parent for life, be humble and grateful that you can learn from your mistakes and stop repeating them with your child.

Since trust (and respect) is a two-way street, you teach what you also expect in return. When your child can trust you, chances of his feeling betrayed lessen. Once betrayal rears its ugly head, it is a big job to make things between you pretty again. As a therapist, I worked with a woman who was carrying a great deal of extra physical weight. Worry, regret, and guilt overwhelmed her every day.

She was riddled with despair about feeling betrayed by significant people in her life. She knew she had not kept promises to herself or to her children. She had a compulsive personality, and her life and relationships were dramatic and conflicted. It had turned out that she had not been able to trust her parents on basic emotional and physical levels while growing up. This lack of trust in her caregivers devastated her. Yet, without knowing it, she, in turn, replicated the same mental-emotional-behavioral patterns of not being fully present or accountable. She had to learn to do what she said and make promises she could keep in order to stop the negative cycle. Over time, her marriage, children, and self-worth improved because of healing the hurt of others' betrayals, as well as the hurt her betrayals caused. She learned how to stop the unconscious cycle of destructiveness and invited constructive family agreements instead. When your child learns that he is worth being tended to, both in private and in public, he feels secure. When trust is strong, your child is proud to be with you at home or around others. Your child knows that you will always be there for him and reunite after times of separation. How you treat your child and other people in front of your child either strengthens or weakens trust between you. It is a primary way your child learns to feel about himself, and how to behave and relate to others.

Only make agreements that you can keep or renegotiate.

Keep it Real

Parent your child with intention, clarity, and vision. Be aware while you are relating to your child in the present about the days to come and how current modes of relating and patterns between you will affect the future. Ask yourself if what is happening now is what you envision between you later. When you change or improve your attitude and mode of relating, your child's attitude will improve as well. As the family leader, set the tone and ground rules and teach how to share unconditional love and respect in your family. If tension or conflicts arise, do what you can to promote relaxation at home again. Be willing to talk about what went wrong without blame, shame, or rigid role assignments. Your focus and ability to return to sanity leads the way.

Allow healthy expressions of joy, sadness, anger, fear, anxiety, frustration, and disappointment to exist freely in your home. Do not take your child's expressions of feeling as a personal affront or threat. Choose to see these expressions as honest displays of your child's joy or pain. Notice how your child's legitimate emotions and expressions trigger your own. In this way, your child becomes your teacher quietly and profoundly. You learn from each other as you both grow.

Your job is to exhibit love, respect, understanding, empathy, and healthy limits for your child; by doing so with loving generosity, you promote wellness between you. She will feel loved, respected, understood, and protected, all of which are the cornerstones of healthy self-esteem and emotional security. To parent well for a lifetime, understand that love and respect go hand-in-hand as you walk the path of life with your child. Find a place in your heart that is always open to caring about what she is experiencing. Teaching empathy and lending unconditional support trains your child to give these gifts to her children later on. You give and set limits with consistency. Your values and priorities, over time, return to you as your adult relationship with your child unfolds.

When your child is having a bad day or dealing with difficult issues or transitions, try to remain calm when receiving your upset child; a neutral emotional position works best. If you are feeling upset, stressed, or vulnerable at the same time and are having difficulty staying centered in a calm state, do your best to be a loving parent. Take care of both of you at the same time. Take a little "time-out" if you need to regroup, and then

Be aware while you are relating to your child in the present about the days to come and how current modes of relating and patterns between you will affect the future. Ask yourself if what is happening now is what you envision between you later.

27

return to your child in need. Find appropriate people to talk with and healthy outlets to keep you and your boundaries strong when dealing with negative feelings. You may have to exercise or practice other forms of self-care at a different time of the day or change the day or dinner plans to adapt. Be flexible, break things up, and start anew. Your job is to be present and responsive. Parent accordingly.

Notice how your child's legitimate emotions and expressions trigger your own. In this way, your child becomes your teacher quietly and profoundly. You learn from each other as you both grow.

Many single and coupled parents know the value of reaching out to other parents, friends, therapists, life coaches, and clergy when they need a sounding board or a strategy. Encourage and model an open mind, consistent love, mutual respect, happiness, joy, enthusiasm, courage, faith, and personal accountability. Find healthy outlets, people to talk to, and ways to deal with and release your negative emotions. Scheduling regular self-care time also helps you to keep your head and heart ready for tricky parenting moments. Make feelings and learning from mistakes acceptable in your household as a part of each person. These feelings are a natural extension of the person, not the whole enchilada. Do what you have to in order to make a calm state easy to return to; make calm your default setting. Reach out to your support network when you need to, so that you have more to give and increased clarity to help guide your child.

Start with One Person

The way to keep balance in your family sanctuary is to start with one person—yourself. Take responsibility for whatever ails you. Get the support you need to improve current conditions or old, unresolved feelings, pain, patterns, and issues. Recognize unmet childhood needs, learn to rise above your past and meet the current needs of your child. Be courageous and choose to perpetuate an environment of love, peace, honesty, openness, and acceptance at all costs. Do what you can to mend and heal disagreements and power struggles. Be the adult, anticipate and end conflicts after (or even before) they begin. Be willing to admit when you are wrong. Listen more than you talk and establish a balance between the two. Learn from your mistakes. Learn to be a better parent despite and because of your history, humanity, parenting successes, and mistakes. Essentially, be accountable for yourself as leader of the pack. Thank your child for her honest feedback about how you parent her and what your child needs from you, all the days of your lifetime relationship. See your child's feedback as a valuable gift for you to be your very best. Whether you receive verbal or non-verbal feedback, it is all helpful and worth noting. Find sanctuary in yourself, your life, and your home.

Whether your day goes well or not become aware that your child still needs your love, affection, and attention—so you will have to juggle. If you are having a bad day or do not know how to handle an outside situation, someone else's behavior can make you feel unbalanced, overwhelmed, or distressed. It is always best not to blame the person or what they did that triggered you or attack them personally. Simply identify the wrong behavior, your part in it, and any subsequent feelings. Your separateness and taking personal responsibility is essential for both you and your child to grow as people and for your relationship, if it is to continue. It is your responsibility to comfort yourself and to comfort your child, not the other way around. If your child is comforting you, make sure it is kept in check and that the scales balance more in your child's favor.

Remember that you are the parent and you are in charge of the core mood of the household. Rather than deny yourself, seek support with friends, family, and professionals outside of the parent-child relationship and open up your heart and mind when you are with your child. Loving, playing, laughing, and sharing can improve physical and emotional health while bolstering this precious relationship. The same is true for adult relationships when you use the power of love, empathy, understanding, and forgiveness to heal conflict, misunderstanding, and hurt feelings. Learn to resolve your problems in safe places without turning and dumping, displacing or projecting them onto the people around you.

> The way to keep balance in your family sanctuary is to start with one person-- yourself. Take responsibility for whatever ails you.

Remember your child is watching which choices you make (over and over again); her sense of self-worth is largely defined by how you treat her. Be willing to learn from your mistakes, be accountable, and examine parenting moments that do not make you feel proud. Be proud of all of your parenting successes and be confident that you are doing your best with what you know now. Learn how to create new, healthy ways of living rather than continue old patterns that no longer serve you and your child's emotional hunger. Your mood leads the way; it either feeds or deprives everyone around you.

Conflicts often arise in loving relationships. Within the core of the conflict being resolved, healing, understanding, and great life lessons can be discovered. You love your child when you are with him and also when giving or taking time and space, if either person needs to resolve issues or emotions internally. Equally vital is returning home to the parent-child connection after the issue has been resolved. The air has cleared, emotions are tamed, minds and hearts return to rational focus, and you are back to the business of connecting with your child and what matters most. Resolve each conflict with loving dialogue and positive, forward-moving actions in order to strengthen the cord that binds you. Your desire to relate in healthy ways surpasses the core of the conflict that dragged you both down.

Remember that you are the parent and you are in charge of the core mood of the household.

By practicing the art of age-appropriate, specific, and timely positive reinforcement, you are deepening a feeling of emotional sanctuary in your home. Tailor expectations and consequences appropriate for your child's developmental stage. This translates to emotional safety for your child because she will feel known and understood. Start with the present moment. Think about the kind of a family you want for you both. Use your influence to move your family forward in that direction. In an increasingly chaotic and unsafe world where everybody's disconnecting from each other and plugging into something electronic, sleeping less, and stressing more, you both need an oasis of sanity and safety. Use your clear intentions, loving support, and feedback to row your family to a safe, calm, and dependable shore.

Your intention is paramount for the manifestation of your dreams and desires. Next, your thoughts, the conscious and subconscious ones, come into play. Be aware of what you are thinking, whether your ideas are new or ones that repeat old belief systems and outdated patterns. Be aware of your intention behind every action. Make it a practice to step aside and observe yourself, your thoughts, and actions. Be truthful with yourself in your observation. As you pay attention to each step along the way, develop a greater awareness about your motivations. In essence, you can learn to train your brain, and then you can go beyond your wildest dreams and create a reality that works well for yourself, your home environment, and everyone around you. As Anthony Robbins observed, "It's not what's happening to you now or what has happened in your past that determines you who become. Rather, it's your decisions about what to focus on, what things mean to you, and what you're going to do about them that will determine your ultimate destiny." [8]

What you consciously intend and intentionally work toward helps create a better reality.

> Conflicts often arise in loving relationships. Within the core of the conflict being resolved, healing, understanding, and great life lessons can be discovered.

Beneath all other riches lay the precious wealth that love, family, and emotional connectedness within a safe home supplies. Mutual respect and self-empowerment are also worthy goals for your family as your older adolescent and teen comes into his own, gradually relating to you more and more as an adult. Love and the consistent expression of love in your home is the silken string tying the eternal gift of your parent-child relationship together forever. With love comes respect in this system of parenting. With mutual love and respect, any subject can be discussed, any problem solved, compromised, released, or negotiated. The tie between you and your child is permanent and deep and will travel with you both through time. In a home where growth and healing are valued, there is beauty in the truth that you can continually find yourself and each other over time. Build a sacred space for each person living and growing in your family home and keep re-connecting through each cycle of life.

You can start from any point in time, any state of household, and any stage and state of your parent-child relationship. It is never too early or too late to return to the heart of your family and your relationship. After all, what better gift is there than to continually enjoy an everlasting lifetime relationship full of love, respect, and learning with your growing child? What matters is the unfolding of both of your lives and how you uphold each of your personal rights and dignity while always keeping the lines of communication open. Communication is ongoing and cyclical, chugging alongside your child's developmental train. Your lifetime relationship depends on being available, loving, firm, and consistent. Know that, at every age, your words and actions are almighty in your child's eyes, ears, and heart. You are the teacher and the student as you allow your child's special presence in your life to be almighty as well.

Your child needs to be like you, be unlike you, and push against you to become her own person.

She needs the dance of connection and disconnection and to know that you understand that need. Building this level of deep trust is a never-ending process. In time, you will see your adult child reflect your influence back to you.

When your child has the early life experience of a relationship built of trust and respect, he will be better prepared to accept the same standard for future relationships. With repeated exposure and consistent positive reinforcement over time, your child learns. Teach by example what it sounds, looks, and feels like to be in a safe, trusting, and nurturing relationship. This is also true as your child sees you relate well with the other parent or parent figures and other people. Your child grows to expect the best treatment, and deserves fair treatment. Give him proof that he deserves to be treated well. If trust has been broken, self-correction and communication tools are needed to repair the damage. When the seeds for emotional safety and mutual trust have been planted properly, your adult child will know that he deserves and will only accept high personal

> With mutual love and respect, any subject can be discussed, any problem solved, compromised, released, or negotiated.

standards for his significant relationships. Teach your child the acceptable baseline for meeting his own relationship needs by guiding the way for a secure, happy, and fulfilled future.

All children, no matter their age, need the consistent care, unconditional love, acceptance, and support of their parents. Over time, maturing into the teenage years and early adulthood, a healthy individual seeks independence. That means limits and consequences set by you and sharing your values, attention, approval to help define the direction your child will go. Being the parent in charge is a continual part of your role. Engage your child. Help her to think, choose, and emerge on her own, to help learn lessons by knowing when to step back and observe and when to create natural consequences as she enters adolescence and beyond. Your actions of love and acceptance speak a thousand words. Just remember that your child is listening. Accept your child well so that she can then accept herself.

Parenting for Life philosophy and system uses momentary opportunities from early on and as your child grows up to practice unconditional love, respect, support, and empowerment. As the parent in charge who listens well to your child's voice, know that each momentary opportunity matters. While your growing child matures into adulthood, he needs his space, independence, and the ability to choose wisely but will still need you. He lives in between the place of childhood and adulthood which can be a tricky proposition. Separate lives are in motion, not necessarily separate hearts. When you give your child consistent, unconditional love and support across a lifetime, he will grow to want to stay close with you. Separate with independent and sometimes inter-dependent lives, a close lifetime relationship remains in reach. A miraculous by-product of loving your child well over time is that your relationship evolves into a higher functioning one, as you eventually relate as equal adults. When your adult child calls to talk, hang out, ask your advice, catch up, and share his life with you, you can be pleased and proud. That is a blessing and the natural outcome of a well-nurtured lifetime relationship. *"I will always love you, be*

When your child has the early life experience of a relationship built of trust and respect, he will be better prepared to accept the same standard for future relationships.

here for you and believe in you, no matter what" becomes more than a mantra; it becomes a way of life.

Create an Environment of Freedom, Respect, and Peace

Love is a two-way street; feeling loved and respected offers the freedom to be oneself. Feeling safe to be oneself offers acceptance, peace, and creates happy, healthy, individuals and mutually satisfying relationships.

> **A miraculous by-product of loving your child well over time is that your relationship evolves into a higher functioning one, as you eventually relate as equal adults.**

Check in with what attitudes and expectations you have running in the background of your behaviors. Decide if your thoughts and actions are working, and, if not, re-think your parenting plan to reflect your highest purpose. What you expect, think, believe, focus on, and say (whether positive or negative) affect the outcome. As a parent, this is a very powerful awareness and an equally powerful tool when applied. Your attitude, self-talk, and expectations have so much power for both you and your child. The universe will provide what you expect, believe, think and talk about. Your beliefs, repeated expectations, and words attract similar outcomes as described in The Law of Attraction principles. You have the choice to open your mind to seeing that, in many cases, you create what is directly in front of you. You create what you believe and expect, and what you think and express. Therefore you create your own reality, and attract more of the same to you. Daily life can be felt as treacherous or miraculous, depending on your point of view.

> **Decide if your thoughts and actions are working, and, if not, re-think your parenting plan to reflect your highest purpose.**

Every moment and every interaction has the potential to become a lesson, a new opportunity to create more of what you and your child want and need in your relationship. How amazing is it that you can actually steer your own course, as a person, a parent, every day, every moment by what you tell yourself and your child? What you honestly believe and expect controls life experience and outcomes. The simple truth is that you choose to evolve your thoughts, beliefs, and attitudes when you focus on your goals and your child's goals and design a safe haven accordingly. Home, when designed as a place that

34

provides sanctuary for all, is ever-expanding when you realize that your home represents and expresses who you are as a parent and a person, how you accept and support your child's authentic self, and how you make manifest your family vision.

You can see all experiences as cosmic opportunities to learn life lessons, serving to better your capacity to love and to learn. This process of continual lifetime learning is both practical and spiritual. You better your attitudes and actions and serve as a stronger teacher, protector, guide, and caregiver. As you grow, you mature emotionally and reconcile your life. Your heart and soul evolve to the next level of your personal and spiritual development. You then improve your life, your child's life, and your relationships and begin to live your parenting purpose and your personal life's purpose. That message consistently role-modeled by you is a priceless commodity to your child and teaches an invaluable life skill. Allow your vision and the feedback you receive to lead you sure-footed on your path. As you continue to travel together, ask your child regularly, "What do you need from me?" and listen to the answers you receive.

While your child is developing stage by stage, you have reached your own stage of maturity. Your both continue to grow in different ways. Your child grows every day on the outside and the inside while you are capable of growing every day on the inside. You have already grown physically and face the reality of aging while your child is still in his growing mode. You have no choice there, but can choose to continue learning and growing in other ways, no matter your age. Speak and behave comfortably in ways that are consistent with these messages.

Where your child is concerned, at every age and throughout adulthood, you can learn from her, learn for yourself, and enjoy your blooming relationship. While you relate differently at different ages and stages, learning is a choice, not an obligation. Nothing is too big or too small to deal with and potentially, heal in your relationship with your child.

When you focus on a necessary issue or goal, you stimulate

> Every moment and every interaction has the potential to become a lesson, a new opportunity to create more of what you and your child want and need in your relationship.

new courses of thought or action and are inspired to learn and grow in your personal development. Your mind is illuminated and your intention clarified, by first envisioning then taking positive new thought and action to make it so. As a result, you both learn and grow from the experience. This is an outcome of natural progression. Remember, your child is watching you and will likely follow in your footsteps somewhere along life's path.

As the parent-team leader, you are in charge of inspiring your child-team player whose voice you hear, along with your own so that you take appropriate action or let go and choose inaction. You either decide to take charge or learn to do something differently. Sometimes, if you do the same old thing, expecting different results and shun change, it works. At other times, doing so keeps dysfunction alive and growth is impossible. It has been said that, "the definition of insanity is doing the same thing over and over again, expecting the same results." That is a choice you make as the mature adult running your home. The question is, is it more of a sanctuary, an insane asylum, or something in between?

Brace yourself for your child's changing needs. As a parent, it is a given that you will continually be required to make further adjustments in understanding your child, adapt to change, and choose your parenting decisions accordingly. Take care of yourself so that you can take care of another. Learn to breathe with it, release the fight to be right, stubborn, stoic, inflexible, or fixed in place so you accept, adapt, and move with the continual change. Continual change is a real part of life and parenting; understanding and accepting that fact makes it easier to go with the flow of it. Your child changes, so do you. This process of change and adaptation will continue, whether you want it to or not.

Hold onto your sense of humor. It will help to keep you grounded during the rapid changes and unpredictable moments that occur during parenthood. I can remember a couple of times going on a family hike and getting stuck on the top of the mountain or miles way down the walking path of park trails

. . . you are
inspired to learn
and grow in
your personal
development . . .
you both learn
and grow from
the experience.

during a sudden thunderstorm or severe rainstorm. We had
to fight the urge to panic and focus on getting back to our car
safely. We made a game of it, doing running races and taking
breaks—huffing and puffing, dripping with rain while the skies
opened up. We talked about the beauty of the weather as we
got wetter and muddier by the moment, laughing, running,
drenched and sweating. By the time we got to the car, we were
happily giggling, soaked in rain and sweat and had a great
adventure. What could have been an experience of panic shifted
into a joyful family adventure, simply because of a conscious
change in perspective.

It became one of many more shared positive memories.
Treasure the times you can lighten the load on your travels, even
when you get rained on or stuck in the mud.

Communicate with your child, and then also communicate
with other parents. Take comfort in the knowledge that even
though your child may be putting your patience to the test,
someone else's child is playing Russian roulette with their
parents' sanity, too. Talk with those parents. Laugh and
compare notes. Share only what you are comfortable sharing to
protect appropriate boundaries, as well as your child's dignity.
Pick appropriate people with whom to share personal details.
Exercise, meditate, write, create, or just lie down. Let off some
steam before you explode.

Be steadfast and learn your child's unique developmental,
physical, intellectual, emotional, and spiritual needs. Keep
those needs in your focus. Wear your steady-parenting sea legs
as reliable travel companions; allow your intuition and parental
love to keep you calm, centered, and confident as a parent while
you ride the waves. You have the power to live your life's journey
gracefully and with an open mind, using intention and higher
purpose to light your way. Inevitably, what you do to show your
child that you are open and willing to learn and grow alongside
her maximizes your relationship potential. Your personal growth
reinforces the implicit message you value and teach her about
the importance of a lifetime of love, humility, and lifelong

> Continual
> change is a
> real part of life
> and parenting;
> understanding
> and accepting
> that fact makes
> it easier to go
> with the flow
> of it.

learning. Learn your child, walk beside her as she learns about herself. Offer her a safe place to learn and grow.

Think about how you feel when you enter into a sacred place of worship, meditation, or sanctuary. Get in touch with the feelings and energy that gently wash over your entire being for having been there. Feel your breath change, your heartbeat slow, your thoughts mellow, and your feelings become calm. Recall the sense within your heart when entering this special place. Get in touch with the essence of the spirit within. See how you become harmonious with those around you, all with one cause, one thought, and one heart. Listen with a clear head. Listen with a calm heart.

In order to create a place that feels like home to everyone living in it, it must have an aura of acceptance for uniqueness and individuality. No one is like anyone else. A child cannot be expected to replicate his parents, friends, or siblings. Each child has divine rights and abilities. To foster an environment of acceptance and peace, show openness versus non constructive criticism. Be alert to your child's attitudes, preconceptions, and expectations. Be aware of what drives you to drive him. The place (literally and figuratively) shared between you is a sacred one.

> Be steadfast and learn your child is unique developmental, physical, intellectual, emotional, and spiritual needs. Keep those needs in your focus.

Be careful to choose well, when to confront, and when to back off, and be wise in your choices. Do not whittle away good feelings with measly, petty matters. Keep your priorities straight. Follow the wisdom of your heart, know who your child is, and seek help when necessary. Use the love you felt when bringing your child into your world and keep love's presence known to all, no matter what. Talk things out and have healthy boundaries. Find a way to build upon the peace, not to simply "keep" it.

The physical space that you share matches the energy in it. Open windows to your mind and home to keep home happy, clear and fresh. The environment in which you raise your child needs consistent upkeep, uncluttering, and re-organizing. In order to create a clear picture of your ideal home desires, you must clarify it. It is like anything else, such as getting in shape, getting the right job, creating healthy relationships, and making a difference in the world. Hold a specific and strong imagined outcome and match it with strong desire, associations, and emotional responses for receiving it. It is with that clarity of mind that a safe and nurturing home life is designed and provided for all, with you as the master designer.

To foster an environment of acceptance and peace, show openness versus non constructive criticism . . . The place (literally and figuratively) shared between you is a sacred one.

Homework Assignment 2

Take a Physical, Mental, and Emotional Inventory

Take this time to observe your physical environment and the feelings that you associate with it. Be open to incorporating new ideas into your familiarized way of living. Allow your mind to have all the answers, even if you do not know them just yet. Get out your *Parenting Journal* and begin to add a journal entry. Here is your assignment:

- Begin to think about the qualities of your ideal home.

- Write down adjectives, images, feelings that describe your ideal home environment. Be sure to include both the physical space and the energy you feel within that space. Include your perceptions of everyone living in your shared space.

- Start a new list that incorporates your ideal home needs with your current living environment.

- Take the time to observe if your physical, mental, and emotional spaces feel aligned and balanced or not.

- Empower yourself by taking action to re-create and align your home's "feel" with you and your family needs.

- Let your list grow and know that you can come back to it later with more ideas.

- Make the necessary changes and alterations both in your physical space and with your mental attitudes and emotional associations to what home is.

- Talk to your family about their perceptions and needs for an ideal home life. Share your insights and enjoy the process of creating your home sanctuary.

- Consciously create the kind of environment you want to live in physically, mentally, and emotionally.

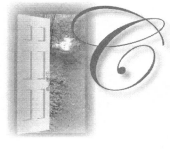larify Your Parenting Style and Parenting Goals

Children need roots and wings. Roots to know where home is, wings to fly away and exercise what's been taught them.

—Dr. Jonas Salk, Physician, Medical Researcher

Who Are You as a Parent?

You know who you are as an individual. Who are you as a parent? What is your job as a parent? What are your roles? What roles and responsibilities do you excel at and what areas do you need tools and support? Listen and look objectively at the messages you send with your words and behaviors in your home. Be especially aware of the consistent messages you send to your child. Are you happy with those messages? Is your child? Ask yourself where you fit in the scheme of predominant parenting styles. The four predominant parenting styles are: authoritarian (dictator/demanding), permissive (passive/ leaderless) authoritative (democratic/nurturing), and uninvolved (absent/deadbeat).

Decide if your current parenting style reflects: 1) who you are and what you feel as a parent, 2) what your parents did, 3) what you want for your child, 4) loosely focused on convenience or other people's advice, or 5) a result of stress and little support. Do you have a clear sense of yourself and your job as parental caregiver? Do you copy the way your parents raised you,

> Listen and look objectively at the messages you send with your words and behaviors in your home.

recycling both what worked for you and what did not work? Do you rebel, completely changing direction in opposition of how your parents treated you? Do you use a combination of styles as a parent? What components of your parenting style are you happy with, proud of, and work between you and your child? What styles in your parental repertoire do not work and do not make you feel proud?

The job of parenting often mirrors how the now-grown parent was parented in their family of origin. That being said, parents make unconscious choices to enjoy, accept, tolerate, or choose to copy what was done to them and taught by example by their parents. In other cases, there is a conscious choice to rebel, spinning in the exact opposite direction and choosing to parent completely differently than the way they were raised. You decide how you want to proceed.

What is your family culture? Are you creating a home in which there is distinct leadership with love and justice for all? Do personal freedoms, respect, and peace exist among your family members? Who is the leader and how are self-worth, a cooperative environment, and life lessons taught and learned in your home? What are the inherent messages that you are sending as a parent? All of these components make up the culture and closeness within your family.

Relax your mind. Ask yourself to open to your higher wisdom and covet the prize of self-knowledge and personal introspection. Think about how you were parented. Consider the style one or both of your parents used with you when you were growing up. Were you parented in a style that fit your individual learning style and personality or that fit your specific personal needs growing up or not? Regarding specific parental caregivers, consider whose care you most preferred and which qualities created this preference. What is your adult relationship with your parent(s) like now? Were there any inconsistencies in the way that your caregivers took care of you, what you needed, and how you parent now? Did you get what you needed? Do you currently parent in a style that is working? Do you parent consciously with

Were you parented in a style that fit your individual learning style and personality or that fit your specific personal needs growing up or not?

specific parenting goals in mind or do you parent unconsciously? Only you can answer these questions, being self-honest as a true student of life—above all else. In the parenting classroom of life, this lesson is a vital one.

What is Your Parenting Style?

There are several kinds of general parenting styles. All have their roots in generational and family styles of parenting. Choices and decisions are made to either continue or cease patterns. Some of this is a conscious choice, some is unconscious. In some cultures and families, it is a sign of respect to continue the family legacy. The unspoken (and sometimes spoken) message is: *"This is how we do it in our family."* There may be a rigid versus flexible attitude toward opening up to healthy change or for them that system may work. But that attitude implies an expectation of silent obedience. Most parents are well-intended even if unaware of a better, different approach. I believe that the best approach is to offer a healthy balance of love, protection, respect, and clear, definable goals set out by the parent leader who listens to the voice of the child. Lead the way by creating the family feel/tone and by setting good examples while guiding the whole family team to victory from start to finish. As your child develops, the goals are with his locus of control and his responsibility for himself as part of the family team. Be prepared to become completely familiar with your own parenting style and what you are responsible for. Be willing to adapt, tweak, and suspend definitions that may not serve life as it is now. Take a good hard look and be honest about what you see.

Take a look at the styles of parenting most referred to: authoritarian (or dictatorial/demanding), permissive (or passive/leaderless), authoritative (or democratic/nurturing), and uninvolved (or absent/deadbeat).

The authoritarian parent takes on the role of "taskmaster," the authoritative parent is the "guide," the permissive parent is the "friend", and the absent parent is "invisible."

Many parents operate using a combination of all styles

> Be prepared to become completely familiar with your own parenting style and what you are responsible for. Be willing to adapt, tweak, and suspend definitions that may not serve life as it is now. Take a good hard look and be honest about what you see.

(within the first three), with a penchant for one style most of the time. Sometimes combinations of two styles exist within one parent. How these styles manifest as parenting behaviors has an impact on a child, for better or for worse. For example, a parent who is authoritarian will create a win-lose scenario, capping real authentic expression or natural learning moments that lead to resolution, mutual respect, and closeness. Instead, the authoritarian (or dictatorial/demanding) parent operates in a dominating, mutually unsatisfying, harsh, and unfair way. The relationship becomes a power struggle and deteriorates closeness and emotional stability. If the parents are too rigid or unreasonable with important matters, the child will be likely to become fearful, angry, secretive, or rebellious. The child will naturally not feel completely safe to be herself.

A very permissive (or passive/leaderless) parent lacks the leadership needed for the child to follow and the roles reverse as to who is in charge. The parent can be unstructured, unskilled, overwhelmed, lack boundaries, or act in ways that are overly indulgent with themselves or their child. Without the structure that keeps a child feeling cared for, safe within the love and limits of parental love, permissive parenting can invite anarchy. Once begun, it takes a lot of work to reinstitute healthy order, trust, reasonable expectations of who cares for whom and how to correct family roles and uninvite the anarchy that was accepted and tolerated.

This can create an essential lose-lose scenario. A permissive parent with no ground rules or consequences helps to reverse the parent-child roles. For example, broken agreements without consequence or with a positive consequence give a child permission to continue to break her agreements. She knows she cannot seek guidance or limits, so to learn from her rule-breaking. If the parent allows an "anything goes" policy, chronic acting-out and anarchy can result at home. Conversely, if the parent is authoritative when it comes to their child's missteps, a more naturally win-win scenario emerges. He or she offers a sense of learned inner control, personal awareness, and accountability and help provide the child with love and

The home of an authoritative-led family is comfortable for all—the child feels safe to be herself, as the motivators and consequences are balanced and logical.

CLARIFY YOUR PARENTING STYLE AND PARENTING GOALS

respect, guidance, and learning opportunities. The home of an authoritative-led family is comfortable for all—the child feels safe to be herself, as the motivators and consequences are balanced and logical. She does not need to repress, rebel or act out like the child who is parented by the first two styles. There is a sense of love and limits that feels good. The parent who is uninvolved misses many of the key functions of the parent role and the child essentially raises herself. The child of an absent parent suffers, has a tendency to act-out, can develop (or inherit) depression, addictions, a tendency toward making bad choices, mental illness, personality disorders, the need for surrogate relationships, and lifelong insecurity or searching. When styles combine or fuse within a parent, it is necessary to uncover the values and motivations for switching gears or adapting the parental repertoire.

Too much vacillation of style, or using a style that does not work, especially regarding matters that are important to the child will eventually backfire. Consistency is the name of the game, even when flexibility is welcome. Too many extreme reactions or parenting styles could cause confusion and emotional strain in a child. If an authoritative or democratic parent offers occasional or negotiable options, acting more permissive when it is safe does not do significant harm. For example, to allow a supervised dip in a pool or a sport enjoyed outside before dinner one summer evening will not harm your child or your relationship. The act of enjoying a spontaneous moment together can bring you closer and can certainly create more memories and flexibility while negotiating your way. By the same token, if a parent evokes fear or is too authoritative and refuses to allow spontaneous joy or safe risks just to protect or over-control a child, the child is maimed emotionally. The moment of experiencing or creating joy is thwarted. There are a few keys that assist each parenting step that you take: balance, consistency, and a conscious long-term vision. It is also key to consciously walk the path with your child at every age and stage, and to have awareness in each moment.

The authoritarian (dictatorial/demanding) parent needs

> Too much vacillation of style, or using a style that does not work, especially regarding matters that are important to the child will eventually backfire.

45

to dominate and control above all else. External controls are presented in the form of authority. The desire for control and power, micro-management and one-sided gain classifies this style. The parent is in charge and the child has no voice. It is an "old school" and often dominant-submissive, fear-based style of parenting. Parents who use this style often overuse punitive consequences and miss out on getting to know their child well. These parents try to harness their child's will, like training a repressed animal. They also miss out on sharing a satisfying lifetime relationship with their child. The dominant parent demands order and discipline over dialogue and mutual respect. There is little room for open communication about many subjects. Above all else, punishment is equated with teaching lessons in the form of harsh or negative consequences. The climate in the home is emotionally and sometimes physically cold, tight, starved for attention, hostile, scary, sneaky, overly structured, superficial, emotionally unsafe, punitive, and centered around parental control. This is style was widely used in the past and is still practiced in parts of the world. Alienation and distance, anger and resentment result using this style of parenting.

Social change in the 1960s offered baby boomers a chance to befriend their children and thus be more lenient and accommodating than generations before. Many modern permissive (passive/leaderless) parents still use this method which leaves the family system loose and disorganized—essentially leaderless, especially in an increasingly chaotic, fast-paced, and impersonal world. Children still need rules, boundaries and governance, along with acceptance, expression and healthy freedoms. There is a middle ground, which keeps a sense of order and structure within a healthy leadership model. In today's world, children and parents connect with fast, high-tech distractions and diversions and a new style of relating needs to emerge. In recent generations, a "friendlier" parent emerged. That led the way to fewer rules and consequences and less authority. The "Me Generation" instilled self-empowerment and self-indulgence, at times, to the detriment of social and

> Children still need rules, boundaries and governance, along with acceptance, expression and healthy freedoms.

family dynamics. In permissive parenting, the child virtually controls the environment, while the parent retreats or remains in a child or teen role. The roles are reversed, even with loving and well-intended parents in this system. The child is permitted to create the household rules, priorities and boundaries based on their wants and needs while the parent allows it. The system is virtually without structure or management from the adult in charge. The child is in charge and it is as though the child has a voice while the parent does not. These children practically raise themselves. While the child is being placed in the position of authority when they are not equipped to do so, the parent remains ineffective. The permissive parent is uninformed of rules and guidelines or chooses not to enforce them, offering little self-control over himself or herself or anyone else. There is a lack of limit-setting and there is an increased need to befriend, rather than lead, guide, and protect the child. A high level of tolerance exists with the permissive parent who accepts an "anything goes" attitude. Communication is open about many subjects, yet the family is ineffectively leaderless and unstructured.

This parenting style promotes role reversals between parent and child. It confuses the child and robs him of healthy boundaries, logical consequences, appropriate role modeling, and protective caretaking. A child needs a healthy balance of love and rules, structure and freedom and feels safe in knowing that the adult will provide it. Rather than growing up as a child bit by bit, he is positioned in the role of decision-maker. This forces the child to essentially be without ample structure and raise himself. There is no parent or leader in charge of keeping the team on course and ensuring complete health and happiness. He misses out on having a strong role model who actively guides him to maturity.

The authoritative (democratic/nurturing) parent is a variation on the dominant and permissive themes. There is structure, leadership, and a place for everyone to exist and be understood, loved, and respected. There is no need to over-control and more balance of power exists between parent and child. Expectations about behavior are clear and

The authoritative (democratic/ nurturing) parent is a variation on the dominant and permissive themes. There is structure, leadership, and a place for everyone to exist and be understood, loved, and respected.

developmentally appropriate. Ground rules, boundaries, and natural consequences are created for safety and privileges are earned and reinforced. Love is easily expressed and both physical and emotional safety are practiced with the utmost consistency. The home climate is open and friendly with loving and firm parenting being expressed unfailingly. Good listening, empathy, and healthy limits on the part of the parent build respect and relationship closeness between parent and child within the group dynamic. Personal accountability is modeled by the parent and the child follows suit.

Open dialogue in the family communication, mutual care, and cooperation are welcomed and encouraged. Individual differences and conflict are tolerated and resolution is promoted. This helps to develop internal order, a strong sense of self, strength of character, and mutual respect derived from a healthy mix of structure and flexibility, while focusing on everyone's needs being met. The authoritative family leader is indeed the authority figure leading the way. The child follows and is sometimes allowed to lead (when appropriate), but the parent does not use his or her power against the child, nor give the child an excess of power. The aura of mutual love and respect with *the parent in charge while the child has a voice* exemplifies a shared responsibility and agreement that conveys a solid, healthy team. To me, this is the preferred way to parent. Loving leadership provides consistent presence, support, encouragement, and guidance on a path toward progress and empowerment for all. This helps the child to feel included, special, and a part of a solid team. Much of *Parenting for Life* is written with this parenting style in mind.

The uninvolved (absent/deadbeat) parent cheats both child and parent of a special human connection. For whatever reason, the uninvolved parent is unable or unwilling to participate in his or her child's life. The relationship is either virtually nonexistent or riddled with pain and heartbreak, unless a surrogate relationship is provided to help replace and help heal the damaged, broken one. This kind of parenting connotes a lose-lose scenario and sometimes the emotional void can remain

> Loving leadership provides consistent presence, support, encouragement, and guidance on a path toward progress and empowerment for all. This helps the child to feel included, special, and a part of a solid team.

forever. If the parent is deceased then the circumstances of how the relationship ended changes. The child needs to fill the gap with a surrogate caregiver and supportive relationships to help compensate for the deficient, neglectful, or absent parent.

So after all that, what kind of parent are you? Did you recognize yourself or your parents? Give it some thought, and then come back to it again later.

Define Your Parenting Purpose

You know what you have to do, but may not realize fully who you are as a parent until you look a little deeper. If you look at the big picture, you can envision an overall teaching that, as a parent drives you to parent well. You parent according to your values, history, and ability to teach, learn, and love unconditionally. You may not have thought about your lifetime parenting purpose before. You live day by day, year by year and go along with the flowing changes of life. Over time, you decipher what is most important, if your love has been received, if your words match your actions, and if your teachings are effective. You may have reconciled your parenting style or may want to re-visit your current approach. You may be focused on creating your best lifetime relationship with your child or you may not. You have goals for yourself, your work, and personal life in addition to being a parent. You have goals for your child, goals around how you want to love, nurture, and help your child grow and be happy and healthy.

> You parent according to your values, history, and ability to teach, learn, and love unconditionally. You may not have thought about your lifetime parenting purpose before.

Break down what you need to know. Get clear about your parenting style and parenting goals stage by stage, issue by issue. Own your history and do your best to resolve your issues away from your child. Take responsibility for what you create in your home and in your relationship with your child. Your history running in the background impacts your attitude, expectations, and behavior. It is without doubt that your parenting style and parenting goals comprise your overall *"parenting purpose."* The style(s) in which you parent and what motivates you as a parent for your child are where your purpose lies.

Explore your intentions with your child. Discover if you understand what makes your child unique and if you have connected on that level with the utmost respect. Stop, look, and listen to your inner wisdom. Take a moment to clarify your job as parent and define your style and bottom-line core parenting goals. What is your purpose as a parent? Start from right now. No matter what has already happened in your parenting experience, you have the power to re-create your goals, vision, and approach now. Not only do you have the opportunity to create your future and influence your child's future, you have the power to redesign present-day life (the parts that you can control) in every moment. All it takes is the desire, tools, and self-discipline to work toward those goals. Explore which goals match up with your child's needs at the time. Discover your unique parenting goals and see how they align with your child's developmental age and stage, temperament, skills, and needs.

> No matter what has already happened in your parenting experience, you have the power to recreate your goals, vision, and approach now.

What have your thoughts been regarding your role as a parent until now? Are you living proof that your actions as a parent match up to your current values, goals, and authentic self? Are you willing to do the work to become your child's advocate and heal yourself, your younger, wounded and vulnerable "inner child" self, if need be? Recognize opportunities and challenges that make you seek help, support, guidance and healing. All along the way, (from the beginning to the end of your time together) notice how your child is responding to you, telling and showing you as their truth—as "feedback from your universe." Learn from the feedback. Notice as your parenting purpose and self- image change as you parent with greater awareness, love, compassion, and understanding. You allow yourself to evolve to who you truly are. Once your goals are refined and clarified, you can re-write the script that has already been written. Your wisdom speaks volumes and it is time to look and listen to new meaning and new words.

Children are very forgiving of their parents, especially in an honest, open, personally responsible, and forgiving environment, no matter what has transpired between them. Children thrive when being raised by and related to by positively motivated, self-aware parents. There is a sense of freedom to be oneself in the environment, a built-in assuredness that anything can be dealt with, worked on or resolved. You cannot be punished for being honest and open or for being yourself. You get "natural consequences" for your behavior, the positive and the negative ones. You can be rewarded for your courage and then find solutions. How do you want your child to view you and feel about you? What kind of relationship are you building with your child? Trust your inner wisdom to help define who you are and who you seek to become as a parent.

When you are a parent who can learn to alter your attitudes and responses to adopt more appropriate responses, your child sees flexibility and growth in you, the role model. Keep in mind that growth is a fluid thing; the oceanic powers of transformation and healing are contagious, ongoing, and life-giving. As you approach the path of lifelong learning and personal growth, you continue down the road of continual self-awareness for all the days that lie ahead. You become responsible for all that you know, all that you do not know, and all that you seek to know. Know where you are going and who you are leading along the path of life alongside you.

Know your original, heartfelt parenting ideals. Think back to when you were a child or young person who knew, dreamed, and wished that someday you would become a parent. If you are thinking about becoming a parent currently, then ask these questions now. Identify when you first saw yourself as a future parent. What did/do you fantasize your role, relationship, and influence as a parent to be? Who did/do you *want* to emulate as a positive parenting role model? Who did/do you *not want* to be anything like? Did/do you have mixed feelings about how to lead and guide because of the way you were parented? Was/is there any ambivalence about your future job as a parent? Who influenced you most that helped you define your parenting style? Who was/is your greatest role model as a parent? Who is your least favorite role model as a parent? Take your time to quietly reflect.

> How do you want your child to view you and feel about you? What kind of relationship are you building with your child?

Question Authority:
You Know Your Child Best

When it comes to seeking the advice of specialists, whether medical, educational, religious/spiritual, or psychological, remain open while trusting your knowledge of your child. Famous American poet, Walt Whitman, wrote:

His own parents,
He that had father'd him, and she that had conceiv'd him in her womb, and birth'd him,
They gave this child more of themselves than that;
They gave him afterward every day—they became part of him.[9]

Trust your own parenting instincts. Listen to your child's words and observe your child's behaviors.

Question authority and feel free to ask any and all questions because you know your child best. Trust your own parenting instincts. Listen to your child's words and observe your child's behaviors. Young children do not have the words to tell you how they feel or what they want or need, so all they can do is show you. Older children, teens, and grown children have verbal skills and still benefit from parents who help them to connect the dots between actions and words; someone who helps keep the child accountable, happy and doing well. Trust what you know and how you know it. When in doubt, by all means, ask for help.

When parenting children, consider the active role that outsiders have in influencing the family dynamic. If the issue is a medical one or involves the safety, health, education, or your child's well-being then absolutely seek expert support or intervention. Be an active participant in your child's care as an important person on her support team. However, if you know what is going on with your child or exactly who or what she needs, do not relinquish all expertise to the professionals. Take each situation as a separate event. Listen with your ears and take action with your head and heart. After all, you know your child best and must take into consideration what makes the best sense for her growth and development. Work on yourself, trust your instincts, and be aware of your tendencies alongside your child, young or grown.

Be discerning as you sift out information you must continually process as a parent. There is a fine line between taking 100% advice from a professional or a book and taking information under advisement, sifting through what works and does not work for your family. The same is true for advice from relatives, friends, and strangers when it comes to raising your child, relating at every age and stage of life. These individuals may not be authority figures per se, but may come across as authoritative and convincing. They may be your friends, relatives, or strangers on the street. See the difference and keep your wits about you just the same. Thank them for their input and take feedback into consideration. Be aware of where the feedback is coming from and see it as a possible key to a solution while confidently practicing (sometimes experimenting with) what works for you, your child, and your family. When it comes to receiving advice (especially when unsolicited), know who it is coming from, see if there is truth and relevance in it, and follow the mantra "take the best and leave the rest."

When it comes to receiving advice (especially when unsolicited), know who it is coming from, see if there is truth and relevance in it, and follow the mantra "take the best and leave the rest."

Homework Assignment 3

Parental Style Checklist

For this chapter, identify your parenting styles and personal parenting goals that make up your *"Parenting Purpose"* in your "real life" parenting. Honestly assess how you most commonly parent in each area of life, according to the various parenting styles listed below, naming your predominant style and goals around that issue. After that, you can begin to construct your unique *parenting purpose* as a whole.

Use your *Parenting Journal* and make a list like the one below of a variety of parenting topics. Check off what most consistently applies to your style as parent. If you vacillate between more than one parenting style write them down, placing your predominant style first. If you notice a gap, that your usual style of parenting differs in any areas, write about that in your parenting journal.

See where your tendencies reside with your child in the following areas:

Authoritarian (Dictatorial/Demanding) "Taskmaster," Permissive (Passive/Leaderless) "Friend," Authoritative (Democratic/Nurturing) "Guide," Uninvolved (Absent/Deadbeat) "Invisible," and then see where you want to be:

- Food, eating, nutritional, health and fitness needs

- Personal grooming habits/skills, physical self-expression

- Affection (physical and verbal)

- Safety (physical and emotional)

- Homework, project completion, and quality of work

- Doing chores at home, jobs outside of the home, making and spending money

- Making friends and choosing a circle of friends (including dating)

- Family communication
- Dependence, independence and autonomy
- Discussing feelings
- Conflict resolution
- Personal responsibility and accountability
- Teaching values and morality (including personal, social, religious and spiritual)
- Physical and emotional boundaries, limit setting
- Sibling relationships, handling successes, rivalry and conflicts
- Discussing difficult or challenging social, personal or family subjects

- Leading your family team
- Setting limits
- Letting go
- Instituting consequences (positive and negative) for behavior
- Social causes, discussion and expectations
- Spiritual awareness and religious or spiritual practices
- Expressing unconditional love, acceptance and support

CHAPTER FOUR

Once a Parent, Always a Parent

*When you have children yourself, you begin to understand
what you owe your parents.*

—Japanese Proverb

A Permanent Truth

Your job as a parent never ends; it only changes. Once you welcome your child into your home, your parent-child relationship transcends time and becomes a permanent reality. You signed up for the job, one way or another. You learn the rules as you go and you must be willing to adapt your roles and responsibilities as your job description reflects the passage of time. You remain true to your parenting purpose while adapting your style when life calls for it.

You witness slow, progressive evolution and sometimes rapid growth of your child day by day and year after year. You may sometimes live your life at rapid speed, forgetting to notice subtle changes and positive learned behaviors as they occur in your child. You have to be observant, honest, receptive, loving, and intuitive. Some progress is subtle, like a whisper spoken during an act of a dramatic play. You have to pay attention and acknowledge the quiet, yet powerful reality shifts of each character and each scene. When fully present, you can grow right beside your child in emotional, psychological, behavioral, and spiritual ways. This fact is another permanent truth, a unique opportunity you are given time and again, and one that

> Your job as a parent never ends; it only changes. Once you welcome your child into your home, your parent-child relationship transcends time and becomes a permanent reality.

you can look forward to when you consciously and intentionally parent for life.

When it is your turn to become a parent, recognize all the advantages and opportunities that present themselves over time. Behold the gift that parenthood and practicing Parenting for Life will bring. You have the single most important job and role in your child's life. Your influence is felt across someone else's lifetime. You lead by example, love your best, teach what you know, and learn what you do not know. That is all you can do until you become more self-aware and more motivated to learn new skills. As your child grows, you always have the chance to strengthen, enlighten, support, and inspire your relationship with him. Your love and compassion are at your disposal and are always present all the days and years of your relationship. Know that it is never too late to improve your parent-child relationship. You always have the opportunity to seize the day, learn more, self-correct, and improve your skills to connect, heal and create a better way in the many parenting moments you are given in the days to come.

Your child needs love, respect, empathy and closeness. Give her this and she feels acknowledged, encouraged, safe and understood by you. You heal her and heal yourself simply by understanding that your love for her is forever, as is her love for you. The greatest truth exists in the heart's need to connect. It is an endless human desire that needs to be satisfied. Keep that in mind and know that it is never too late to connect with the one you love.

Set the Stage for All Future Relationships

Relationships with family members, particularly parents (both same and opposite-sexed parents) significantly foreshadow your child's future. These significant relationships are role-models and become the barometer for all future relationships. The relationship with mother and father, grandparent, foster or adoptive parent, or other primary caregivers, sets the stage for all future interactions with significant partners. The early and emotionally significant associations and relationship patterns

Know that it is never too late to improve your parent-child relationship. You always have the opportunity to seize the day, learn more, self-correct, and improve your skills to connect, heal and create a better way in the many parenting moments you are given in the days to come.

provide blueprints for future relationships. The same is true for how parental caregivers relate to each other. Your child memorizes how parents or caregivers relate to them and to one another.

"Parents who take good care of the marriage (or the relationship they share)—who listen and respond to each other's needs—provide their kids with great role models for healthy relationships."

John and Julie Gottman go on to say, "Our research has shown that growing up in a strife-filled environment can have a strong negative impact on children's attitudes and achievements." [10]

The early and emotionally significant associations and relationship patterns provide blueprints for future relationships.

The relationship dynamics that exist and persist in your home become the genesis for re-creating familiarity of feelings and relationship choices your child makes later on in adulthood. How you relate with each other becomes reinforced over time. When repeated enough and paired with emotions and memory, strong psychological associations are formed. Expectations result and similar relationships are sought out to re-create and/or resolve that original relationship and original feelings. Familiarity becomes the norm unless your grown child questions, rebels, and chooses a different path to walk later. Relationship dynamics learned at home become the standard in relationships unless the original model no longer serves your adult child later.

Imagine your family as players in a play or a movie. The roles may change depending on your personal history, family dynamics, and events. When you see each person as a character with a distinct part, not necessarily with assigned rigid roles, it can become more fun, more freeing to observe and learn from family scenarios. As a parent, it is important to know when to take action and when to "detach with love." You can filter out when it is appropriate to emotionally or physically remove yourself and simply observe what roles are being played out. Notice assigned parts for each family member, played out on auto-pilot. Rigid roles are not always constructive for the individual or the whole family team system. As hard as it is, like

doing complex yoga postures early in the morning after a late
night, flexibility is absolutely a valuable tool. Act your part and
watch how your child acts his.

Use your powers of observation while detaching
emotionally and notice what happens. See if you can identify the
roles, labels, and feelings you experienced as a child growing up
in your family of origin. Next, check in with the roles assigned
and played out in your current nuclear family today. Is labeling,
whether negative or positive, obvious or subtle, a common
dynamic at home?

Examine the feelings these dynamics elicit in your child
and yourself. Do you clearly understand the messages sent
between the players or are they mixed and confusing? How
would you recast the people involved and how could they be
better served with updated character roles, lines, or scripts? Is
the dialog working between you or are there more monologues
not being fully heard? What are the messages in the nonverbal
communication between you? Are the individuals happy,
learning and evolving? How could you better support your
growing lifetime relationship? Who is the hero, the controller,
the leader, the sidekick, the bully, the enabler, the drama-seeker,
the victim or martyr, the scapegoat, the identified patient, the
invisible, voiceless one, or the peacemaker? No need to react, just
notice.

How could
you better
support your
growing lifetime
relationship?

Now pretend that you are the director of this play or movie.
How best would you direct the character playing the part of the
parent who is expressing unconditional love, respect, and support
toward their child in each scene? Identify the roles played out by
the parent whose messages sent are clearly received by the child?
How would you inspire a healthy relationship between the two?
Do you see and feel what the child does, almost through her
lens? When does this parenting relationship truly end? In reality,
it never does, so what can you do to perpetuate the best possible
relationship with your child?

Be aware of the casting and underlying storyline. Maybe
the teenage boy is wolf man because he can change into a

crazed monster at will because of sporadic teenage hormones? Maybe the dad is the absent-minded professor because he means well but cannot get his act together and is overwhelmed with too much stress from work? Maybe the four-year-old is the hulk because she runs amok and smashes things when she is overtired or has eaten too much sugar? Maybe the mom is like Hermione Granger and needs to cast spells to keep the house running smoothly? Who is showing up in your family story? How would any parent direct that crew? Bear in mind that it is not wise to publicize these funny insights, label, ridicule, or mock anyone; simply use whatever fuel you can find to keep your sense of humor and understanding alive.

Family members can try on new roles as they feel most safe; providing that "parents are in charge and children have a voice."

Unlike a movie, life's realities have real consequences and more depth and ramifications to consider. Undeniably, a grown man or a woman will often re-create the relationship communication styles, habits, and behavioral patterns that were reinforced at home with his or her parents. Much of that is initially unconscious, which explains why people consistently repeat relationships patterns until they learn to relate consciously. Even when a person opposes that which has come before, there will be some elements that reenter that person's life later. Your job as a parent is never-ending and your child's early imprinting lasts forever. However, it is never too late to communicate better, love and accept more fully, and begin to heal emotional wounds. If wounds resulted from mistakes made in the past, the present holds a precious opportunity for a healthier, safer, and closer future relationship between you and your child. Either way, you both benefit when you are open to deal with shared wounds and learn to heal. In real life, you always have the chance to heal what ails you, stretch, release, and renegotiate with the one you love so that better days lie ahead as your walk the path of your unique lifetime relationship.

Like a yoga master, allow for some flexibility and opportunity for family members to try on new roles and behavioral postures at different times. Encourage some breathing room. Family members can try on new roles as they feel most safe; providing that "parents are in charge and children have a voice." Roles that hurt others, micromanage, overcontrol, demean, or assassinate characters stunt your child and your growth. Rigidity and recycled negativity from your childhood or current life must be rejected because they are toxic and destructive for your relationships. Being negative and rigid, instead of being positive and open, sends your child the wrong message. As a skilled caregiver while you parent for life, you nurture life in each moment, allow for trial and error, and invite a happy future. You just have to open your eyes and ears and let growth happen. Welcome love, peace, healthy flexibility, and inspiration for you and your child always. Bend with each breath and flow with each new movement.

People living together in a family must have the freedom to be seen for the people they are, not seen as extensions of a parent's unfulfilled potential or extensions of anyone else. Individuals need to be seen for their uniqueness and deserve respect and care beyond any issues, past mistakes, or behaviors. High-pressured expectations, unreasonable demands, and negative or rigid labels promote shame and stagnation in a family, stunt your child's emotional growth, and stunt your relationship closeness. With awareness, understanding of your child and yourself, proactive solutions appear and the stage is set to produce a happy and abundant future.

> With awareness, understanding of your child and yourself, proactive solutions appear and the stage is set to produce a happy and abundant future.

Constant Opportunities for Mutual Growth and Healing, at Every Age

Parent in ways that make you feel proud and make your child feel proud of you. Keep this concept in the front of your mind and heart every day. Talk with and teach your child by example to "do what makes you feel proud." Find ways to positively reinforce this important message, planting the seeds for potential success in all areas of life. It is one of many simple but powerful mottos that work wonders as you learn how to reinforce what is most important. Allow your self-esteem as a parent, as well as your parental devotion, to motivate you. Focus on your positive intentions as ideal targets when you are blown off-course or while fine tuning your parental bullseye. By showing your child (throughout your life together) that you are capable of learning your own lessons and put someone else's needs before your own, you teach him the willingness and courage to learn to do the same.

Give your child your protection, care, and trust and she will learn that she is safe, loved, and lovable and will learn about emotional safety. Show your child respect and she will show you greater respect in return. Since life is about learning and loving, know that the constant opportunities to grow and heal are timeless, so growth is never-ending.

Since life is about learning and loving, know that the constant opportunities to grow and heal are timeless, so growth is never-ending.

No matter what anyone tells you, there is no "best" age or stage of your child's life, only ones that make adapting, learning, and relating easier. Each developmental stage matters and each time brings with it joys and revelations that make life between you awesome. There are always positive attributes to enjoy as your child grows, stumbles, and matures. You will find that family, friends, even strangers offer their unsolicited advice or commentary. Hold steady and enjoy the moment, whatever age and stage your child is at. Do not believe other people's stories and opinions when it comes to appreciating the joy of each time, each age, and stage you get to be with your child. We all have a neighbor or friend of a friend who says, "What, the baby is walking already?! Oh well. It is all over for you now." Or "Your child is hitting the teen years, good luck! Your days of rest and sanity, being in charge of your life and your time are numbered." Necessary benchmarks are designed to help your child as he passes through to the next level of personal mastery. As a parent, you can choose to ignore the incredible chances to be grateful at each age and stage or be closed-off with a negative or punitive attitude. Take a stand against negative expectations and reactions; rather relate to your child with consciousness, mindful compassion and joyful appreciation. Keep him safe in both the seen and unseen ways that a good parent knows.

Opportunities for growth and learning exist for both of you, at all stages of life. You both grow into the beautiful masterpieces that you are intended to become. You remain the parent, while your child remains the child throughout all your advancing shared time together. Eventually, you will relate adult-to-adult, no matter how your journey started out. Even after your child grows up and leaves your home, he will come back to you, continuing your shared journey in another way. You may relate to each other differently. You may relate in the in same way, but you remain parent and child. This permanent truth lasts a lifetime.

Together, as parent and child, you receive the gift of a shared life, with a beginning, middle, and end. It is with this perspective that you parent best. Keep in mind and heart the longevity of your relationship when interacting with your young one. Do your best to hold a present consciousness to be fully available to your child as best as you can now, and a future consciousness to build upon later. This awareness will cement trust, communicate deeper values, and create a stronger bond. This is solid and unbreakable between you and your child throughout your entire life's journey.

One phenomenal aspect of humanity is the mind and heart's accessibility for constant growth and knowledge. Since knowledge is a form of power, by knowing or learning new skills and by showing empathy and understanding, your relationship will deepen and soften. You will advance, your child will advance, and you will create a harmonious, workable relationship while you utilize the power of love and learning your lessons. Know that there are constant opportunities for mutual growth and healing at every age. The truth is, like in all relationships, one person can make positive changes while the other does not. In that case, the permanence of that relationship may or may not stay constant while the growing individual rises above the old behavioral status quo. When one person changes in attitude or behavior, the other changes even if only indirectly or, depending on the bond, the relationship is altered or let go. One person cannot change without the other person or dynamic changing with it. When one person changes, it forces changes that, on some level, must be dealt with between them. In a growing relationship, both people seek to be understood

> Together, as parent and child, you receive the gift of a shared life, with a beginning, middle, and end. It is with this perspective that you parent best.

and known, find meaning, satisfaction, mutual acceptance, and harmony—above all else. Being happy is more highly valued than being right. In those cases, both individuals set the stage for improved communication and can work and relate better, no matter what situations do arise, and believe me, they will. Be open to growth and dialogue to keep your hearts open.

When your child is young, sustaining your child's overall well-being and protecting her are the main priorities. Slowly, the goals expand to include guidance and teaching elements beyond the basic need to protect (and be protected). You establish authority over your child's life and your child needs you to do so. It is during this phase of a person's early childhood that the caregiver cements the role of primary model and moral compass for the child to emulate. Once your child begins to speak out and express her own needs, feelings, and differences from your agenda you have to pull out another set of tools from your parental tool belt. The parent-child relationship changes while the balance of power is being tested. By that point, you can let your child wear her pajamas all day and not worry about it. When she is older and wants to do that on a regular basis, and maybe sleeps the day away or refuses to chip in at home, then that is another story to be concerned about.

In a child's adolescent years, both early and later on toward the teen years, things change again. You may as well try and create a time machine; it might be easier to figure out than your growing child. Keep in mind that he feels exactly the same way about you. As a parent, understand the importance of your child's need to question, mimic, be confused, act out emotionally, be detached, or rebel. This helps him to push against the given authority figures, the existing status quo, if you will. Your emerging child needs to find himself. He may try on roles as an athlete, participant in student government, be a creative artist type or expressive musician, motivated scholar, social butterfly, social isolate, unidentified individual, or a combination of those. Remain in the adult role as mature, dependable, and steadily supportive rather than being judgmental, reactive or pushing back as he finds himself. Take care of yourself and get plenty of

> When one person changes, it forces change that on some level must be dealt with between them. In a growing relationship, both people seek to be understood and known, find meaning, satisfaction, mutual acceptance, and harmony— above all else.

hugs and support so you can keep up. Go with the flow of your changing child and be there for him as best as you can be.

Children need limits and boundaries as well as personal freedom, a balance between structure and reasonable flexibility. They also need interactions and relationships that feed them in a myriad of ways.

As Urie Bronfenbrenner noted, "Development, it turns out, occurs through this process of progressively more complex exchange between a child and somebody else especially somebody who's crazy about that child."[11] This is where interactions, interpersonal experiences and family meetings with clear expectations and negotiations begin to create a balance of both (see Chapter 10 for more on this). A key element is to build upon and maintain mutual respect and trust. Respect, when at the heart of any relationship, will ease the transitions, help to resolve conflicts, and help propel the overall relationship along to new and enhanced levels of relating. Ultimately, treating others (in this case your child), with respect will instill empathy and empower each person to begin to bloom at his or her own rate. Trust is the proof that someone is who they say they are and can be counted on, no matter what.

A child is not fully formed as soon as she becomes a teenager. A teen is not fully an adult the moment she moves on to middle school, high school, or college life. It takes years of additional life experience to complete adult development. Teen brains are not fully rational or sensible often until the mid-twenties: personal choices and judgment can reflect that. A parent's mantra during these years can often be, "What were you thinking?" Frankly, the teenager and young adult may not know. The frontal lobes that govern judgment are slow to connect, unlike a fully mature brain. Time, maturation, experience, and natural consequences help define the emerging young adult. Just because a child is practically or fully grown does not mean that she no longer needs you or your parenting. The specific parenting needs change and evolve as your younger and older adult child does. This is another example of how you as parent

> Respect, when at the heart of any relationship, will ease the transitions, help to resolve conflicts, and help propel the overall relationship along to new and enhanced levels of relating. . . . Trust is the proof that someone is who they say they are and can be counted on, no matter what.

must grow with your child. You will both reap the rewards of seeds planted early on, parenting in the now with an eye on creating a happy, healthy future. The garden of your relationship becomes fertile with closeness, healing, and personal revelation at every stage. While your child continues to develop and evolve, make good choices, and learn from experience, your relationship will reflect the same.

If relationship patterns and issues remain unresolved in childhood, the same issues will be repeated throughout adulthood. Keep in mind that unresolved pain, resentments, disappointments, and life-altering arguments are bound to resurface. They will either be dealt with by your child alone or between you together. You may not always be ready to deal with whatever issue or drama emerges; just be ready to love, listen, and understand at every turn. When you as the parent help your child to deal with difficulties as they arise, including difficulties between you, he is free to learn better ways of relating and resolving conflict. How to relate to others well and how to address and negotiate conflict are essential skills. We have all had that parent-child conflict moment when the door slams between you and your child utters, "Meanie" (or worse), and as the parent you mumble, "Brat!" (or worse), and you both stalk off in a huff. When you parent for life with awareness, the door swings open again and you fix things before it slams again, preventing the "or worse" situation of it closing forever.

When you as the parent help your child to deal with difficulties as they arise, including difficulties between you, he is free to learn better ways of relating and resolving conflict.

Homework Assignment 4

Expand Your Vision

This exercise will help bring your focus into view regarding your attitude and expectations about your child and you. What you sustain in your thoughts and beliefs creates patterns and results in your reality. Open your vision to see what exists now and what is possible later.

- To practice expanding your vision, choose something that you notice, observe, and revere in nature. It can be an animal, an insect, a plant, a sound, a fragrance, an event, a season, a metamorphosis, or a physical place. In your *Parenting Journal* write down any and all of the details that come to mind when describing this natural entity or event. You are emotionally neutral, simply recording what you observe. Notice and appreciate the beauty, details, strengths, joys, and challenges and vast potentials in the outer world. Appreciate the universe's natural, simple gifts with continued appreciation for the joy, beauty, and potential that you just described.

- When done completing the description, turn your awareness toward your child. In a similar fashion, observe without emotion or intensity. Keep it simple and focus your writing on the positives about your child, what you like, love, and admire about him or her. Write about the relationship between you and your child as it is now, what works between you in a few words or sentences. Incorporate the simple truths of what makes this relationship special, sacred, and uniquely beautiful to you. Add thoughts that expand your current bond, envisioning your ideal future relationship and write them down. Be sure to take full responsibility for your part as parent in support of your child moving forward.

- Re-read the key elements of what you have chosen to focus on and be sure to honor them. Commemorate your increased awareness as a parental visionary by writing down three to six action steps to move your current relationship forward. Make your action steps clear and realistic. Set a reasonable time frame and put these into action immediately. Be proud to be a parent who takes a heartfelt interest and is responsible for your part in developing the best relationship possible between you and your child.

- Take a few moments each day to check in and observe yourself. Ask yourself what your underlying intention is with your child or children in that moment or for that day. Notice if your attitudes, words and behaviors reflect your intention. Be willing to change your game plan to line-up with the family team goals and with your parenting purpose. Do your best and acknowledge when you parent well.

- Look ahead with an open mind and loving heart as you continue to create your lifetime relationship with your child.

CHAPTER FIVE

Family: The Ultimate Chance for Belonging

The family is the nucleus of civilization.

—Will Durant, Writer, Philosopher, Historian

A Basic Human Need: From Birth to Death and All the Stages In Between

People are not meant to be isolated creatures. Everyone needs a place to call home and a place to come home to, whether physically, emotionally, in memory, or some combination, depending on the time of life. Emotional and social connection, affection, and deep meaning are for the taking in every family. That connection translates outward to all other relationships over time. The need for belonging captures the heart of what family is. The strong sense of belonging can exist in traditional and non-traditional family systems with one or two parents, straight or gay/lesbian parents, extended family, adoptive or foster caregivers.

> In today's world, there is no longer a typical or standard family unit or one-size-fits-all parent or family.

In today's world, there is no longer a typical or standard family unit or one-size-fits-all parent or family. Variety in preferences, styles, and choices determine the vast landscape of what makes up today's culture and shifting family scene. All children must be advocated for. All parents and families deserve to be honored and given the same opportunities to create a sense of family in whatever way they see fit. Where there is love, respect, and trust, combined with a system of shared responsibility and goals in place, family exists. Belonging to a family offers shelter from the storms of life and also shines a beacon on those storms when they are happening inside your home. Family offers the perfect fusion of deep connection with other people who are both similar and different from each other, and offers unconditional support, acceptance, and shared group identity. That being said, family also provides a safety net for individual expression and risk-taking. This experimental breeding ground allows for the flow of individual identity within the group identity. When one belongs, he can be himself.

Renowned psychologist Abraham Maslow[12] suggested that the need for belonging must be present. Virginia Satir, considered "the mother of family therapy" wrote, "We need four hugs a day for survival. We need eight hugs a day for maintenance. We need twelve hugs a day for growth."[13] The human need for connection, specifically touch, is so profoundly vital that if humans receive too little, they can fail to thrive. A baby can literally die if there is not enough physical contact and healthy touch. Adults and adolescents can feel as if this is also happening to them, especially with lack of touch of from the ones we love.

> All of these human needs matter and must be met as well as possible for a lifetime of healthy development and personal evolution. The constant search for satisfaction and mastery on all levels stay with us for life.

Maslow's pyramid of basic human needs has at its base the physical needs (food, shelter, physical protection), followed by the emotional need to belong (family support, a sense of group connection and association, a safe place to call home and derive identity). Next are educational needs (learning new information to advance self and promote practical and intellectual capacities, promoting a knowledge base from which to spring) and societal needs (to reach out to a social group and sense of social consciousness, going beyond the family to worldly issues, connection, and service). The top tier of the pyramid comprises spiritual needs (seeking understanding of a higher purpose, awareness of greater forces beyond the ordinary, earthly world influences, pursuing meaning, connection to a divine power and the universe). All of these human needs matter and must be met as well as possible for a lifetime of healthy development and personal evolution. The constant search for satisfaction and mastery on all levels stay with us for life.

As Maslow pointed out, all varying basic human needs and points of development span a lifetime. Beyond the basics, there is no real beginning or end to some of those needs. Instead, individual needs change and personal development advances across a lifetime. Depending on maturity levels and needs being met or unmet, a person's growth toward the next level of personal mastery is either promoted or thwarted. In adulthood, the basic needs level out as social and spiritual needs and mastery begins to take on greater importance. The relevance and presence of the higher, spiritual needs speaks to each person's personal timing, motivation, awareness and own life conditions. Personality, family and individual priorities impact the meaning and significance of achieving the higher rungs of mastery. Moving up the developmental ladder calls for mastering each stage, one at a time, before exploration and mastery are possible for the next level to be attained. Personal needs and life lessons present themselves throughout a lifetime. All you have to do is pay attention and follow your guiding star.

The basic human need for a sense of belonging is a powerful one that persists from birth to death and all of the stages in between. Family, no matter what constitutes its members or its relative size, supplies the first place to belong. The notion that "no man is an island" is exquisitely relevant because a person who is raised with physical and/ or emotional disconnection or social isolation or who self-isolates for long periods of time is more likely to regress and wither psychologically and emotionally than one who enjoys meaningful human connection and is motivated to reflect. The built-in support system and emotional connection to family is irreplaceable, particularly in the early years, but still holds its power throughout life. The human need for belonging, affection, and feeling connected to others are paramount to physical health. There are physical maladies and many psychological disorders linked to being or feeling interpersonally disconnected, rejected, or isolated. Anxiety, aggression, and memory impairment have been linked to isolation. This includes self-imposed isolation, which is becoming more of a reality in our

> The built-in support system and emotional connection to family is irreplaceable, particularly in the early years, but still holds its power throughout life.

racing plugged-in, socially networked, and digitalized world. It is time to reclaim the importance of human connection, starting at the beginning of it all, with the family.[15-17]

All families experience their unique troubles and problems at some stage or another. In all fairness, these events usually pass. We all know this. Life in this millennium is not designed to be a straight line without hitches and bumpy rides now and again. However, when problems reoccur frequently in the home, parents need to be aware of them and pay attention to their remedy if they are to avoid permanently dysfunctional relationships within the family.

Symptoms that may be the cause or effect of a dysfunctional family may include one or more of these consistent behaviors:[18]

> However, when problems reoccur frequently in the home, parents need to be aware of them and pay attention to their remedy if they are to avoid permanently dysfunctional relationships within the family.

- Difficult parents without adequate flexibility and insight

- Absent parenting style (there, but not there)

- Ridicule or belittling, or over-criticizing

- Prejudice towards one or more family members

- Mixed feelings of love and hate

- Faulty communication

- Lack of attentiveness to issues of importance (brush off, downplay or avoidance)

- Lack of care or concern for the needs of another (absent care or denial)

- Lacking in the ability to empathize with children, siblings or parents

- Dual values and double standards, or lack of clear boundaries

- Diminished ability to make decisions

- Over-interest or micromanagement of one member or the entire family

- Insensitivity towards other family member(s)

- Emotional intolerance

- Emotional outbursts

- Emotional insecurities

- Depression, deep rooted anxiety and feelings of gloom and despair

- Childish behaviors in adults

- Poor self-image and worth, or lack of sufficient self-identity

- Controlled/contrived speech or stifled speech

- Verbal abuse which others must tolerate

- Sexual or physical abuse that other members must accommodate

- Overworked family environment lacking any family fun (workaholic—no recreation)

- Perfectionist behaviors, over demanding parents or children

- Disowning behaviors of parents or children

- Isolation or inadequate socializing with others

- Narcissistic parents or children

- Rule-by-fear parenting

- Bullying (to regain the upper hand)

- Growing up too fast because of advanced roles

- Reduction of roles and responsibilities caused by over protectiveness

Studies show that the damage done from failed group interaction within a family has irrevocably detrimental effects, sometimes causing personality disorders, dysfunctional family relationships, anti-social behavior and failed relationships in adulthood. Feeling connected to other people helps to establish both an important sense of group connection and defines individual identity within current and future group structures. Once a strong inner sense of security is established and your child knows that isolation or abandonment does not pose a real threat, she has the confidence to take healthy risks in her world.

The child knows who she is, where she is going, and knows that she can always go home.

Individual and Group Identity Starts Here

The bond between parent and child permits both togetherness and separate selves. This dichotomy is healthy, especially as time moves on. As you and your child develop, new friendships, relationships, classes, work, colleagues, participation in seminars, groups, and social causes all provide necessary additional outer connectivity. This works well in combination with an intact family unit, a healthy support network and positive interpersonal work dynamics. Safe, positive social environments with personal meaning and connection, especially when consistent, cement both self and group identity. If needed, professional help or support groups can serve as good substitutes during times of family crisis and when needs arise. Sensing that there is safety and trust in a group is mandatory in order to be your authentic self, engage with others, take healthy risks, and gain the full benefits of any joined assemblage. Your bond, born of some degree of comfort and trust, is necessary for shared togetherness and healthy separateness.

All groups have their own mentality, feel, purpose, and basic modus operandi. That is true both within and outside of the family system. Role assignments naturally align with individual personality and group dynamics. In group scenarios, members unconsciously fall into comfortable roles or have been assigned to roles by the perceptions and needs of other group members, sometimes by its leader. It takes a good leader with good observational skills to keep this tendency in check. Being a part of something greater than oneself helps individuals to appreciate differing perspectives and their role in the dynamic and can facilitate growth. Working in a group simulates family life and the potential to rediscover and reinvent roles, find one's voice, and foster self-awareness.

The simple act of belonging to a family and other groups helps assimilate a sense of community, validation, purpose, security, self-esteem, social skills, and social conscience. It

Feeling connected to other people helps to establish both an important sense of group connection and defines individual identity within current and future group structures.

permits the "larger than myself" mentality, which is important to the development of personal, relational, social, leadership, and career growth. It takes you outside of yourself to a place of "group identity." The most ideal scenario is one in which all members make room for the unique qualities and strengths of each other. The group's purpose, when consciously crafted or agreed upon, becomes more about the whole first, contributed by the sum of its parts secondarily. Each person has a voice and someone takes the lead, similar to your parenting skills when running an ideal authoritative household. Being part of a group provides a place to learn, stretch, and to be both free and attached at the same time.

When there is room for everyone to be seen, heard, understood and respected in any group, then belonging to that group is an empowering experience. If there is some fluidity in role assignments, participants try on new roles and perspectives and it is a healing, transforming experience. In a family, as long as you stay within your parental role, as described earlier, you remain the *parent (adult) in charge and your child has a voice.* This is another wonderful mantra to repeat to yourself and say out loud when you or your child need reminding. The roles can switch within reason, particularly the ones that liberate and empower. Families can openly discuss roles being played and each person's place and gift within the family team. Avoid labeling, especially if is consistent, negative or ego-deflating, or overly accommodating, as both (especially when repeated and perceived over time) are destructive and ultimately disempowering. It is best to accept all members as they are and reserve judgment. Family and group participants can agree to disagree or opt out of role assignments completely. That form of democracy works well, as everyone feels empowered to be exactly who they are, rather than who the group expects them to be.

The sense of belonging promotes a secure psychological safety net while young people emerge as themselves. In a setting where your child feels that he truly belongs, then he can be who he truly is. He can try on new ways of thinking, new ways

Being a part of something greater than oneself helps individuals to appreciate differing perspectives and their role in the dynamic and can facilitate growth.

The sense
of belonging
promotes
a secure
psychological
safety net while
young people
emerge as
themselves.

Your job is to
offer shelter
from the storm,
sanity from life's
challenging,
tumultuous,
insane influences,
and love her, the
best you can for
a lifetime.

of being, and new ways of communicating his needs. He can question, intelligently challenge others, and express himself. He knows that he will be accepted, because he belongs to this solid group that always accepts and welcomes him. He is in it for life. He is a lifetime member. There is no threat to his good standing and therefore he becomes free to explore and express who he is. That degree of emotional security is essential for your family relationships to grow and strengthen over time. This level of acceptance promotes a freedom that transcends all lifetime events. Your child, throughout his life, will know that he has a safe haven. Better yet, he knows where his safe haven is.

Emotional Health for a Lifetime

"Having somewhere to go is home, having someone to love is family, having both is a blessing."[14] Feeling emotionally secure and valued is everyone's birthright and promotes emotional health for a lifetime. Whether raised in a two-parent or one-parent home, traditional or nontraditional, modern or old-fashioned home, a child needs to feel safe and loved. This sense of belonging transfers across time and distance as is one of the strongest needs that human beings share. There is no shame in making mistakes as long as learning from them is as important as making them. Once your child recognizes that her family remains a steady force and offers her a place where love and forgiveness are practiced well always while keeping a place open for her to return and be herself, she is free to spread her wings. Your job is to offer shelter from the storm, sanity from life's challenging, tumultuous, insane influences, and love her, the best you can for a lifetime.

Once your child reaches adulthood, the family unit is changed, yet many of the deeply held beliefs and feelings you share remain the same. The foundation has been set and your grown child knows from whence he came. Real trust and acceptance rival social trials and tribulations giving way to a strong sounding board of love and reason. Communication remains open while mutual verbal and nonverbal agreements persist as they were when your family group was first established.

Negotiation and renegotiation skills are incorporated into the group's working system. Trust and acceptance transmitted between you and your child are established strongly enough in childhood for optimal inner security later. If trust, respect, and acceptance lacked in childhood, then your grown child must self-parent, get professional support, and create nurturing relationships and groups to compensate the lost sense of family (self and group identity) and support. In many instances, a grown child must learn to self-parent himself in order to gain mastery of self-care and relationship life skills to move ahead in adulthood more effectively.

The importance of group affiliation and association, a "greater than one's self" mentality, mixed with respect for the individual matter most here. The correlation between emotional wellbeing, personal self-esteem, and healthy group identity offers the freedom to safely risk, challenge, and explore varying groups and styles of relating within them. All group interactions stem from family connection, the sense of belonging or not belonging to the group, and how the individual rises or falls within the group. You teach your child about reaching out to others while reaching inside of her all at the same time, and it is all good.

> All group interactions stem from family connection, the sense of belonging or not belonging to the group, and how the individual rises or falls within the group.

Homework Assignment 5

Reach Out to Family Branches

In your *Parenting Journal*, write down all of the things that connect you to your parents, child, and all your family members, past and present.

Include both positive and negative aspects and consider that all have helped shape your personal lifetime development in some way. Write down key lessons about yourself, family, parenting, and life that you have learned or continue to learn from each person you listed.

You can choose to learn and grow from all of your relationships and circumstances. You may invite surrogate mothers, fathers, extended family and siblings to help you work out your unmet family needs and feelings. This can help create happier, healthier relationships moving forward.

Acknowledge the gifts you have received from these special family connections in your life. Acknowledge the love, loyalty, innocence, wisdom, resolved conflict, and opportunities disguised as challenges and choose to be grateful for them. Write them down.

Thank everyone in your family tree for who they are, what you have learned from them, and how they make you a better person. This can be done in person, in a letter or in your heart if someone is no longer here as they once were.

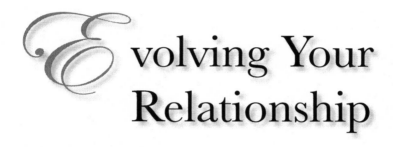

Evolving Your Relationship

CHAPTER SIX

Let Everyone Evolve: Learn Life Lessons

We are not human beings on a spiritual journey.
We are spiritual beings on a human journey.

—Steven Covey, Author

Be a Student of Life

When you go to school, you have some clear expectations. There will be teachers, desks, supplies, other students, information to learn, and knowledge to be tested. You learn quickly what you know and instantly recognize what you do not know. The more you learn, the more you realize you do not know it all and the cycle continues. It is easy to recognize your strengths and areas in need of improvement almost immediately. At varying points, your goals evolve and priorities become clarified. You participate in an external learning environment. Your personal learning curve is characterized by your learning style, the literal or symbolic school, teachers, and other students in your environment, as well as your own expectations, habits, aptitudes, and skills. You internalize what you learn, perceive, and understand through your experience, style and what impacts you.

Similar to starting school, when you become a parent, you may find yourself starting out with little or no experience with new tasks, in this case the care of another human being, especially someone who is so much smaller and completely

> You learn quickly what you know and instantly recognize what you do not know. The more you learn, the more you realize you do not know it all and the cycle continues.

dependent upon you. You learn what you can by reading and talking to other parents. You parent by instinct and by heart, or you copy or rebel against the way you were parented. You learn as you go. Eventually, hopefully, you know your unique and lovable child well enough to support his learning curve. You help build his confidence, by loving him unconditionally and believing in him. You build trust, respect and affection in a safe environment and are prepared to learn as you go.

Your accumulated life experiences actually help prepare you for this one grand event. You bring all your former experiences with you into this relationship. The past is with you, holding hands with the present, and must be acknowledged to help you on your path moving forward. The future is ahead of you and needs to be blessed with positive attitudes and actions that support the eventual reality of what is to be.

Your job as a student of life continues when you are a parent. You teach and you learn. Know who you are while you discover parts of your nature and relationship aptitudes as you relate to your child. Keep your heart, eyes, and ears open and your feet firmly planted on the ground. Do not dodge difficulty, but move through it with an open mind and your head held high. If you lose your way, find your way back home to yourself and your life. Your child will thank you for providing your love and stability when she is grown. This personal clarity and generosity of spirit can create a family legacy that you pass down to your child and which she will pass down to hers in return.

You had a life before your child; you had a personal history of life experiences, attitudes, roles, and values in place. As some say, "what goes around comes around." Your personal karma, so to speak, as you evolve and learn from life experiences is more of what you bring to your lifetime job as parent. The lessons unlearned will continue to present themselves. Also, what you did, thought, felt, and chose yesterday created what is in your life today. What you do, think, feel and choose today is what creates your tomorrow. You and your child belong together, for many

Do not dodge difficulty, but move through it with an open mind and your head held high. If you lose your way, find your way back home to yourself and your life.

Perhaps each soul needs the complementary soul of the other to work through karmic lessons. Learn how to make peace with yourself and your child for life!

reasons and are a permanent part of each other's lives. Perhaps children and parents choose each other? Perhaps each soul needs the complementary soul of the other to work through karmic lessons. We do not know this information; we can only surmise that something is going on and use the match to everyone's advantage.

Learn how to make peace with yourself—and your child—for life!

Some relationships flow more easily than others. Some relationships are difficult for a multitude of reasons. In your family, see how compatible or challenging the matches are in order for everyone to relate well, progress and self-develop. Be a conscious student as a parent. Learn from your child's words and behavior; find a place to meet and share. Learn from your heart and parental wisdom. Learn from your mistakes and the mistakes your own parents made. Make your relationship with your child worthy of study and attention. Take the lessons you learned when you were a child, use your love and knowledge to do what is right, and apply them now. Drop your defenses and excuses or need to blame anyone else. Develop your relationship with personal responsibility and put it as a high priority on your to-do list. Study your life, see what is in front of you now and act accordingly.

> Be receptive to lifelong learning, no matter what you think you already know. There is an endless supply of teachable moments for you and your child on your shared life's journey.

Dare to define yourself as a work in progress. Accept who you are and learn who your child is at the same time. Be a teachable person. Be receptive to lifelong learning, no matter what you think you already know. There is an endless supply of teachable moments for you and your child on your shared life's journey. Each moment, lesson, love, and loss has helped define who you are at this point in time. You have been preparing for this job of caregiver (whether you know it or not) and are the perfect person for the job. Use what you know and learn further how to be a better parent than you ever realized you could be. While improving yourself as a person, you become a better parent. Your other relationship skills will also improve. Teach relationship principles by example to ensure a lifetime of closeness. Your child sees you as the one who knows it all, the one with the implied maturity and wisdom. Be wise enough to know what you know and what you do not know and keep parenting real.

Being a parent is an awesome lifetime responsibility, not a momentary stage of life. This daunting task includes a large emotional investment as well as ensuring the total physical, mental, and social welfare of another human being. Allow for personal error. Mistakes are bound to happen on both your parts. As self-help guru, author and publisher Louise Hay says, "It is okay to make mistakes while learning." [19] Be thankful for your imperfections, humanity, and ability to learn and grow. When you can accept and tolerate your own imperfections, you can, in turn, accept and tolerate your child's imperfections. You acknowledge your points of development and welcome insight that brings changed behavior. You have faith in each other as people; your humanity and ability to learn and grow humbles and elevates you. By practicing this, you set both of yourselves free.

> Be thankful for your imperfections, humanity, and ability to learn and grow. When you can accept and tolerate your own imperfections, you can, in turn, accept and tolerate your child's imperfections.

Have an open mind and be a "student of life." This open, positive attitude is one that carries both weight and lightness. Adopting an attitude of positives, awareness and willingness will help carry you and your child through during the tough times. Having clarity of mind sets your purpose and keeps your heart open and receptive. Feeling the energy of positive thinking boosts your attitudes. Your positive attitudes will inform your actions and more favorably perceive the actions of others. Positive, proactive steps will further your purpose, parenting, and overall life experience. In Rhonda Byrne's book, *The Secret*,[20] this shift in self-awareness has within it the keys to unlock principles that change lives. The reader becomes the student, in a deeper and more conscious way than before. Life feels like a mystical adventure. Dreams can become real, as long as the student is open to doing what works to manifest them.

The weight of the responsibility of raising a family is lifted with positive thinking, clear vision, and reasonable expectations. A healthy life attitude offers a solid perspective on varying parenting experiences, both easy and challenging. Attitude is one thing that you can count on to either elevate or bury you. The open, loving lightness of your attitude frees old-standing conventions of how to think, respond, process information, prepare for the future, and how to let go and implement new skills. What may have been done before by previous generations may not work now. What may have worked for you or your child in the past may not work currently. What may have caused you pain, suffering, confusion, and defensiveness before can be changed into greater peace, healing, courage, understanding, and hope for what can be.

Become an apprentice of life in your day-to-day living.

Become an apprentice of life in your day-to-day living. You are on this earth for a reason, even if you do not know what that reason is. You have two choices: let life happen to you or design your life the way you want it to be. You were born, you are here, and you are parenting so you may as well be open and willing to "learn and grow." Be open to the process while contemplating the final outcomes you are trying to achieve. You may already expect this enthusiastic and self-confident attitude for your child. You may expect him to have faith and learn well in school and at home and continue to learn as he matures. Why not expect the same from yourself? Remember that actions speak louder than words, and your child learns volumes by what you say and do. This is an excellent way to teach about the endless opportunities there are for self-introspection and the invaluable learning potential that is possible throughout your mutual lives.

The wisdom of your love for both of you creates miraculous moments, a saga worth repeating for generations to come.

See how the wisdom and beauty of personal growth heal and transform relationships. There is nothing more joyful than a happy ending or beautiful beginning that mends broken hearts and resolves unhappy issues. While perfection is nearly impossible, perpetuate healing interpersonal wounds so that you can enjoy harmonious, healthy relating. This sincere effort to make peace is very possible and worth striving for. The wisdom of your love for both of you creates miraculous moments, a saga worth repeating for generations to come.

How Personal Growth Heals Relationships

Life is a balancing act. Take good care of yourself and your child with conscious and purposeful actions that provide balance. Living in balance includes physical, mental, emotional, social, spiritual and environmental needs. This balanced living is a worthwhile approach that all family members deserve to achieve. To strike a healthy balance, take good care of yourself while taking care of your child. Take charge of your physical, mental, emotional, and spiritual, social and environmental well-being. Do what it takes to ensure that your basic needs are met. Be kind to yourself. Be kind to others. Be kind to your child. The reason why the airlines encourage you to put on your own oxygen mask first during an emergency before helping your child or children is simple. If you as a parent are not well, who is there to take care of your child?

Factor in Regular Self-Care

Prioritize sleep, good nutrition, and exercise. Take reflective time and socialize with friends and family in addition to your work and parenting responsibilities. As you begin to heal yourself and your life, learn that you must order your time and energy. Your life depletes or energizes you: some days it may do both. There is an endless supply available for greater happiness, peace, clarity, and learning. This is as long as you believe, are motivated, and led by what creates intrinsic joy and does not hurt you or someone else. In that way, you are experiencing heightened awareness, personal growth, maturity, and personal satisfaction. When you are receptive to doing what it takes to learn and grow as a person, your choices reflect that wisdom and your ability to give increases. You can only give from fullness, not from scarcity or depletion. Once you take care of yourself, you can take care of another. Factor in regular self-care and see how much more you have to give.

> To strike a healthy balance, take good care of yourself while taking care of your child.

Satisfy your basic needs and give yourself healthy treats and rewards for jobs well done. Nurture yourself with healthy outlets for your body, mind, and spirit. Take time out for yourself and your reflections. Make room for contemplative moments to go within, think and feel. Enjoy your life as a whole. Find time to do that which gives you joy and personal pride. Find what fuels you, energizes, empowers, and comforts you as long as you are not sabotaging yourself or another. Keep a daily "gratitude journal" to remind you of all that you have, all that you dream, all that is working, progressing, and healing in your life and all that is possible. Be honest about your mistakes, your triumphs, and your attitudes. Then when you give to your child, your love, care, support, and guidance, you do so from a place of honesty, wisdom and humility.

Enjoy being pampered (by yourself or someone else) and giving to yourself. Teach your child by example the loving discipline and importance of self-care. Recommending self-care is not meant as a preachy platitude. It is not intended to invalidate anyone's morality or life situation. Everyone may have different access to sources of self-care. The concept of self-care and management of one's time, environment, work, finances, and emotional, physical, intellectual, and spiritual lives requires desire, personal significance and practice. Taking care of your overall health and wellness is your right, just like parenting your child is your privilege. The goal is to ensure a high quality of life for both of you.

Balance out your time, arrange for support, and schedule what you need to keep you happy, calm, and fulfilled as best as possible. Balance out what you give to your child. Rekindle the flame of care and devotion for your child after you refuel the burned out candle of your being.

> Taking care of your health and wellness is your right, just like parenting your child is your privilege. The goal is to ensure a high quality of life for both of you.

Allow Yourself and Your Child to Evolve

Allow yourself and your child to "evolve." The *Oxford English Dictionary* defines the word "evolve" as "to develop gradually, especially from a simple to a more complex form."

Synonyms for the word evolve are progress, develop, advance, emerge, grow, and elaborate. When you break down the sum of its parts to understand the whole, like Gestalt therapy does, all things work better. Insight and resolution come more quickly, as conditions and resolutions are better understood. It is a simple fact that age and experience coupled with insight result in wisdom. Aldous Huxley wrote in *Texts & Pretexts, An Anthology with Commentaries,* "Experience is not what happens to a man. It is what a man does with what happens to him." [21] You will notice that sometimes, often times your child is wise beyond his years. While age helps to grow wisdom, it is not a prerequisite. Aging itself does nothing other than reveal a life lived, or perhaps, a life unlived. Adding accumulated insight to the process makes aging a worthwhile journey filled not only with stories, but wise morals and necessary insights worth passing on to future generations. As you welcome personal advancement to unfold, live and age with grace and insight so you can continually expand and evolve, and then reveal a life *well-lived*.

When raising a child from infancy through adulthood, the underlying love you feel must be expressed consistently. This love defines everything beneath and beyond the "terrible twos," tantrums, power struggles, moral dilemmas, mistakes, rebellious adolescent and teen behaviors to eventually help guide you in letting go. Elizabeth Crary refers to the consistent practice of a parent, no matter what, to "Let the message of love shine through." [22] Her message is geared toward young children and the parents who love them. She also suggests her basic tenant of using, "two yesses for every no" as a tried and true strategy that works wonders when providing structure, positive reinforcement and teaching natural consequences to children up to age eight years. These two principles apply to all ages, while simple and easily attainable as they sound, they are not always so easy to implement. When engaging with your child, adolescent, teen, or adult child, you can feel worn out and exasperated. Even when frustrated or downtrodden, you hold in your heart the basic human need to connect, feel, express, and share love. Even when

> When raising a child from infancy through adulthood, the underlying love you feel must be expressed consistently.

you are exasperated, your child needs you to love her with your whole heart and never give up.

Keep your heart open for your lifetime of love. Love flows easily back and forth between you. Remain a student of life and know that your job requires you to teach and to learn. Be willing to continually learn about and accept your child and yourself, warts and all, at every turn. Enjoy the process, and watch your child and yourself evolve, even if you do not understand exactly when it is happening.

Feeling and sharing love takes awareness and willingness. There is an endless supply of love to be tapped into when the heart is willing. Knowing this, as you advance side-by-side, you invite inspiring moments, healing places once vacant or hurt, with the wisdom of true love.

Even when you are exasperated, your child needs you to love her with your whole heart and never give up.

*H*omework Assignment 6

Evolve Your Love

Here is a good exercise to help fine-tune your focus and bring your attention back to the love you feel for your child.

- Carve out 10-20 minutes for yourself. Find a comfortable place to be still, calm, and quiet.

- Take a moment, relax, and take several deep cleansing breaths. Like the breathing techniques used in yoga, slowly inhale in through your nose and exhale out through your mouth. Do this five times for the count of five with each in breath and each out breath.

- Allow for present circumstances or emotional stress to temporarily melt away. Gently remind yourself to let go if thoughts or feelings emerge. Clear your mind of any and all chatter, tension or distraction. Be willing to release your current focus until you have reached this point of inner neutrality, where you know your thoughts and feelings exist yet they are not running you. Rather than a motor constantly running, moving and rushing about, you become a vehicle that is still with noises turned off and parked in peace.

- In this moment, go within; listen to your heart of hearts. Be silent and patient, discover what comes to you. Ask yourself how you feel deep down about your child. Ask what you most desire to share in this life with him or her. Be open to what feelings and messages arise and listen to and trust the wisdom of your heart.

- Take this renewed insight and reconnect with your child, whether personally (if your child is near you) or symbolically (if you child is not present at the time). Walk through your day keeping your loving heart open. Be sure to express the underlying love you feel when dealing with your child. Allow your love to permeate every interaction and conversation in some way.

- Make sure that you find ways to convey your love and give your child the feeling that he or she is indeed loved by you, no matter what. Express your love in a consistent way so that your child learns he or she is lovable and worthwhile just for whom they are.

- Write down any important insights and proactive ideas in your *Parenting Journal.*

CHAPTER SEVEN

Recognize and Nurture Your Child's Gifts

*Promise me you'll always remember: you're braver than you believe,
and stronger than you seem, and smarter than you think.*

—Christopher Robin to Pooh by A.A. Milne

Meet Your Child Where He or She Is

*E*very child is special. See your child as a gift whose
life is a blank canvas. Your child has the potential to
be blessed with a happy and healthy life. One filled with love,
positive life experience, good coping skills, and self-actualization.
Every child is born with rights and deserves a chance from the
start, at the middle, and at the end to feel loved, safe and worthy.
Every person is born with a distinctly unique purpose, gifts, and
reasons for being alive.

You and your child must learn to acknowledge and value
the gifts with which you each have been given. Accept and know
that your child is entitled to be unique and to find and fulfill his
life's purpose, just as you are. You both need acceptance for who
you are and who you are becoming. People, in general (especially
parents and children) do the best they can with the skills and
information they have at the time. Accepting who and where
you both are on your journey is liberating. It frees you from the
emotional roller-coaster that accompanies negative responses,
creating a space for more honesty and understanding between
you. Give your child the assurance that his specialness is real

Give your
child the
assurance that
his specialness
is real and
enough. He will
learn to value
himself while
he continues to
discover why
you believed in
him in the first
place.

and enough. He will learn to value himself while he continues to discover why you believed in him in the first place.

A Singular Voice

The task in today's world is to find one's singular voice that honors oneself within a huge, complex, loud, and chaotic place filled with a myriad of things and billions of people. Your child's voice belongs squarely to her. Listen and share yours (without over-sharing) in return. She came into this world as an open slate, a soul in search, a mind and heart ready for love and learning. Since your child, at every age, from little to grown is always your child, choose to love, respect, and accept her as she is right now with all of her gifts, talents, struggles, challenges, growing pains, and imperfections. You cannot give your child back, and since she is living under your roof anyway, enjoy her, even the parts you think should be different or those which you just do not understand. After all, being accepted for who you are drives a lifetime of self-esteem and mutual respect. Recognition and validation are what you both want and need, no matter how the gift is packaged. Honor and respect your child's individuality so she can, in turn, share who she is with the world. While you are at it, do the exact same thing for yourself. You will both stand taller and feel your right to walk with courage, speak with honesty, and elevate your lives with deserved personal power. As Ellen DeGeneres so powerfully said, "Find out who you are and be that person. That is what your soul was put on this Earth to be. Find that truth, live that truth and everything else will come."[23] That is good advice for anyone who wants to build personal self-esteem, help empower others, and lead a personally meaningful life in a big, impersonal world.

> Listen to your child's individuality so that she can, in turn, share who she is with the world. While you are at it, do the exact same thing for yourself.

Your child's place in your family, his unique contributions, feelings, and the way he expresses himself as a spoke in your family wheel makes you think and moves your heart. He can lighten your life and strike many deep chords. His DNA blueprint reveals health, innate talents and interests, genetic and temperamental tendencies, true individuality, and raw potential. Each person has great potential for doing, being, choosing, expressing, and creating a great deal and has the freedom to do so once it is recognized. Every child is a gift from heaven, worthy in his or her own right. Just as your child "honors his mother and father," so too must you "honor your child" for being here and for who he is. Cradle your child's individuality every step and stage as he travels down life's path. Treasure his contributions, feelings, thoughts, and ideas (even if you cannot relate or do not appreciate his perspective) as he expresses himself, revealing a specialness he shares and honors you with while he is just being himself.

Learn Well

When you observe, interact, and get to know your child well, you see who she is. Pay particular attention to her positive traits, actions, beliefs, intentions and progress. Take the time to acknowledge all of your child's gifts, talents, preferences, tendencies and interests no matter how small or how great. Make it a sort of human treasure hunt when you interact. Observe and let her know that you appreciate what she loves, is good at, struggles with, or is successfully improving upon. Your child is worthy of attention, so pay attention. Notice her own perceptions, interpretations and style, and what it means for her to genuinely "be herself."

When you honor who she is as she keeps learning and maturing, you teach her to honor and respect herself while moving and progressing through life.

Remove your blinders, take your ear plugs out, cast your expectations aside, and be still. Receive and reflect on what your child shows and tells you. Be aware that your child's personality, perception, motivation, aptitude, passion, and personal self-expression are his alone. You do not have the power to change him or the right to overly control and micro-manage him, only to encourage and inspire him to stay safe, happy, and healthy and to keep being himself as he develops over time.

There is no exact formula for being a human being. Everyone is born with something special. When it comes to parenting your child, remember to keep your mind and heart

> Cradle your child's individuality every step and stage as he travels down life's path.

open and be observant without being judgmental. Make it a practice to stop, look, and listen to your child, and notice who she is and who she is becoming. Teach your child to stop, look, and listen at home and in life too. Observe how your child behaves to get a clue into what she is feeling. Children often "show" in actions what they cannot often "tell" in words. This non verbal process of expressing with behavior can also be true for teens and adults, particularly for those who are less verbal, less articulate, or less emotionally skilled. Notice tendencies, likes, dislikes, reactions, abilities, talents, sensitivities, strengths, and areas that need greater mastery, understanding, and healing. Your child, like you, is only human after all.

Listen to what your child tells you, both about his world (inner and outer) and his feedback about you as a parent. Believe that what he says is true for him. If it is true for him, then it is important enough to be important to you. Choose to listen to feedback from your universe, both out in the world and at home. Listen to feedback about how you parent. The minute you sense you are going to hear something about yourself, you do not need to grab your running shoes and bolt out the door. You can sit (or stand) and listen. Only when you see yourself and how your behaviors affect others can you truly learn to empathize, adapt, be your best, and learn to change. Change implies growth which improves situations, at home and at work, in large and small ways, and helps you to evolve yourself and your relationship. It pays to listen to your child. He wants you to know who he is and will let you know in whatever ways he can. He may know something about you that could enlighten and transform you or mirror back to you something you need to see.

Release Comparison

Commit to a clear, singular view of your child and do not compare her to anyone else. If you have more than one child, be sure not to compare or contrast your children behind their backs and especially not to their faces. Each child needs to be cared for, experienced, and respected for their own individual identity and their own special worth. Be sure to always help your

> There is no exact formula for being a human being. Everyone is born with something special.

child maintain her personal dignity. The mere act of comparison eventually diminishes your child's sense of self, self-expression, and feeling safe, supported, and completely honored for who she is. Even if you intend to motivate your child, comparison is unfair. Like laying heavy bricks on top of a fragile foundation, comparing injures dignity, insults, and breaks the spirit. Nothing is solved or built if you parent by condemning, belittling, disempowering, or comparing. Those actions only weigh a child down with guilt, shame, and doubt or built up hurt, anger, and resentment toward you or their sibling. Your child should stand alone in her own spotlight.

When you either subtly or actively compare your child to a sibling or someone else, or pin-point differences between you and your child, you create emotional distance and disconnection. Emotional distance can last and make your child feel invisible, insignificant, resentful, and lonely. Be aware to take action and send messages that cement the closeness, safety, communication, trust, and respect between you.

Let's face it—as a parent, you are only human. If there are similarities between you and your child, or between your child and someone else, you will absolutely notice it. You may see how your child talks like or has the same penchant for being strong willed or stubborn like your mother, father, a sibling, or maybe even yourself. Would you ground yourself for the same behaviors? It is often best to simply observe differences and keep this information to yourself unless it is positive and flattering in nature. Even if the similarities are positive, allow for your child to be his own person and have his own style within the similarity. The ideal way to raise a confident, happy child in a loving and mutually respectful relationship is for you to respect and enjoy him as his own unique person. The same respect you deserve, your child deserves in return. Later, your grown child will see you as your own person, not just mom or dad, worthy of a different, more mature level of respect.

Walk the journey of life with your eyes and ears open and be receptive to all around you, especially when you are parenting

> Even if you intend to motivate your child, comparison is unfair. Like laying heavy bricks on top of a fragile foundation, comparing injures dignity, insults, and breaks the spirit.

for life. Take stock of what you see and hear and how you interpret, react, and respond. When you recognize the present moment, feelings, observations, and realities, it is easy to allow acceptance. Allow the same steps to exist when you choose to meet your child where you are compared to where she is. Walk the path side-by-side.

Keep the channels of perception and awareness open. If they are closed, it will render you ineffective and helpless to promote healthy understanding, acceptance, and change. One of the simplest ways to achieve a consistently loving relationship with your child is to see him as a unique and constant gift in your life. You become the student as well as the teacher every day and learn deep, profound life lessons. In your child's eventual self-mastery and growing self-awareness, you will witness the transformation from one developmental stage to another and see gradual progress. When your child is not compared to anyone else, he will feel free to grow at his own rate and truly be himself. When your child makes mistakes, behaves experimentally, tests limits, or tries something that clearly does not work for him, turn those moments into teaching opportunities. Rather than taking a punitive approach, instill and promote a lifelong love of learning about himself, making good choices, and how he can be his best. Be a perceptive and aware "lifelong learner" as you role model a desire for lifelong learning and see the magic that happens in your relationship.

> When your child is not compared to anyone else, he will feel free to grow at his own rate and truly be himself.

Support your Child's Right to Blossom

Find ways to encourage your child's natural curiosity, tendencies and expression. She will find a way to grow, mature, and fly on her own eventually, so help give her wings. She is trying to be herself and first needs to find herself at home, then in a loud, busy, crowded, ever-changing and chaotic world. She has a right to be who she needs to become, wherever her curiosity, tendencies, and self-expression take her.

Your goals, timing, expectations, and priorities will not match those of your child. Your role is to support whatever natural growth occurs, sometimes with your encouragement and at other times without it. E.E. Cummings expressed it best by saying, "To be nobody but yourself in a world which is doing its best, night and day to make you everybody else, means to fight the hardest battle which any human being can fight; and never stop fighting." [24]

Negative tactics dishonor your child and make him your opponent in a power struggle. Remember to align with your child on the side of compassion and justice while you can also butt heads. Negative tactics dishonor your child and make him your opponent. Negative tactics can also start or fuel a power struggle.

Once started, it is easier to stop a moving freight train than to completely stop a parent-child tug-of-war, the worst struggle of wills. Sometimes it is easier to take a break, set a time-out, or go somewhere fun just to break up the power-struggle pattern. Do your best to let your child be and let him explore, express, and learn on his own. It is better for you to take a moment to calm down, maintain empathy, self-control, and perspective; do not initiate or respond to a power struggle in the first place. Let go of your side in the tug-of-war. It takes a lot of energy, and in the end someone must fall in order for the other person to stand. If you find yourself engaged in a psychological or behavioral battle, it zaps positive energy and is powerful like the tides. Overused negative tactics between parent and child often backfire. Instead, try and stay calm as the adult in charge. Practice consistent displays of unconditional love and acceptance and healthy limit and rational consequence setting. Catch your child doing things right, being a good person, and trying his best. Acknowledge your role as his model. Constant streams of negative interaction cement the battle stance between you and your child. Consistent negativity brings everyone down and then your relationship suffers. Love him well, strive to minimize negative interactions, and get back to the love and respect you share. He will never forget it.

When you provide a healthy balance of consistent love and appropriate (firm) boundaries for your child, you then

> Find ways to encourage your child's natural curiosity, tendencies and expression. She will find a way to grow, mature, and fly on her own eventually, so help give her wings.

define yourself as an effective, nurturing parent. Welcome better strategies to connect, understand, reach compromise or resolution, and create harmony. Be open to opportunities for you both to heal and learn important life lessons.

Use specific rather than generalized praise by first noticing, and then positively reinforcing (verbally and nonverbally) positive behavior as it is happening in the moment. Notice and comment on times that your child is "doing positives." This form of positive feedback is a system that works over time, building a specific growing repertoire for your child to build her sense of who she is becoming and what is expected of her in relation to others. This system also encourages you to really experience your child in a heartfelt and present way. The closeness and trust between you grow naturally. The behaviors or qualities that you consciously praise can best reflect her talents and abilities, progress, morality, ethics, manners, social skills, hard work, unique nature, and feelings of being lovable. Specific praise gives her what she needs most of all—a place to feel noticed, acknowledged, and special for who she is, not for who you want her to be.

> Welcome better strategies to connect, understand, reach compromise or resolution, and create harmony. Be open to opportunities for you both to heal and learn important life lessons.

> Be a "Behavior Detective" Take the time to expand your awareness, limited thinking and perception as you parent.

Homework Assignment 7

Be a "Behavior Detective"

Take the time to expand your awareness, limited thinking, and perception as you parent. Be willing to notice who your child is at every point in time.

- Listen twice as much as you talk.

- Pay close attention to what your child is telling and showing you.

- Notice what your child is naturally good at, interested in, passionate about, motivated by and sensitive to. Notice what is not easy or natural and what upsets or distresses him or her.

- Ask for and notice feedback that your child gives you, whether verbal or nonverbal.

- Remain receptive to what your teen, young adult, and adult child needs from you.

- Believe in your child and tell and also show him or her that you do.

- See your child as separate from yourself or any other family member.

- Notice and verbally reinforce proof of your child's talents, interests, gifts and individuality.

- Reinforce your child's happiness and learning who he or she is.

- See, hear and experience your child as a living being for you to cherish and empower. After all, what your child needs and deserves most of all is your care and unconditional love, respect, and support.

- Record any insights or revelations about yourself as a parent in your *Parenting Journal*.

earn to Re-Parent Yourself

*Inner Bonding is a process of connecting our Adult
thoughts with our instinctual gut feelings, the feelings
of our "Inner Child," so that we can live
free of conflict within ourselves.*

—Margaret Paul, Therapist, Author

Get to Know Yourself Better

You deserve
to get to know
yourself, who
you are now
and who you
are becoming,
right alongside
your child. You
deserve to be
happy and
get what you
need to be
empowered
in life.

You have lived your life in your own way, in your own
time, and with learned skills and experiments. You
have experienced some great successes and other times your
experiments have not gone according to plan. You are the same
person, yet you have changed as you have grown, matured and
evolved. Ultimately, you still live with yourself and experience
life as you go. You deserve to get to know yourself, who you are
now and who you are becoming, right alongside your child. You
deserve to be happy and get what you need to be empowered in
life.

Once you become an adult, you have learned about
yourself and the time for self-deception or living in blissful denial
are hopefully habits of the past. You may still need to become
more self-honest. You pull together all the self-honesty you can
about your life and your path as self-awareness is paired with
maturity. When you parent for life, you must be as fully present
as you can be. Seek clarity, wisdom, and joy in the truth of life,
even with its waves of difficulty and pain. You see what may not
always be pretty, and what you hear may stab you in the heart.

You could feel betrayed, hurt, angry, and maybe regretful but what you have been awakened to is far greater than the pain you have endured. Your chance to own your life is upon you. Be honest about the environment and honest with yourself. Walk the path of truth and do it with your head held high, shoulders back, and chest out. Walk strong.

Your self-honesty keeps you real and keeps the story you tell yourself undiluted. The truth (and your perception of it) helps you keep growing your self-love for your authentic self, unraveling the story of your life. You become stronger in who you are and clearer in where you are going. In order to be honest with someone else, you must first be honest with yourself. Find a way to get to know yourself better with a satisfying mixture of self-love, self-awareness, personal accountability, and self-discipline. Getting to know yourself, just like getting to know anyone else, can be painfully awkward, intriguing, or surprisingly pleasant at times. How you love yourself, how you awaken your awareness, how accountable you are, and how self-disciplined you become will determine how well you parent yourself. The parent in you is called upon to take care of your inner child. Listen to the call and do what any good parent would do: respond with care and attention.

You have reached your developmental milestones, survived the test of time, and had many and varied relationships. Your experiences and your feelings and perceptions about your experiences are keys to unlocking deeper levels of who you are becoming. Accept yourself as you are and your history as it has been and continue to learn and grow into your future. Just because you age does not necessarily mean you mature. People learn and grow when they are ready, motivated, and willing to do the work, change, or let go. You have the chance to develop yourself. The moment you choose to do so, you begin to put aside your history, old programming, fear, anger, hurt, sadness, excuses, defense mechanisms, and self-sabotage. It is up to you if you want to take the leap of faith into safe risk-taking to resolve your past and envision your future. Walk through the door of

The parent in you is called upon to take care of your inner child. Listen to the call and do what any good parent would do: respond with care and attention.

self-awareness so that you can move forward with intention and inspiration.

Listen to your inner "self-talk," observe your own behaviors, interactions and patterns with others, and examine your thought and feeling patterns. Discover what you require to feel happy, peaceful, and proud of yourself every day.

As a parent, being self-aware is a gift that keeps on giving to both you and your child. As a conscious lifetime parent, examine what you value because what you value will be taught and modeled directly or indirectly to your child nearly all the time. Teach by example what it means be fully human and evolving. Teach that you learn and grow along with your child but in different ways. This is because adults and children are at such vastly different developmental places and the tasks and responsibilities are quite dissimilar.

> As a conscious lifetime parent, examine what you value because what you value will be taught and modeled directly or indirectly to your child nearly all the time.

It would not be appropriate to consistently share what you are working on in your life unless your child is older or it directly relates to improving your relationship. If you do tend to overshare, work on your awareness and self-discipline and find someone more appropriate to talk to. Some of the lessons however could be similar, as you become more aware, unresolved issues could come up and you need a safe place to unleash as you re-parent yourself. Pay close attention to your beliefs, words, and actions and what they consistently express; they are extensions of your own perception and focus. Your thoughts, feelings, and beliefs are gatekeepers of your bliss, depending on which direction you follow. Your child learns who he is based on how you treat him, what your attitudes are, and how you command yourself. Your child interprets how you feel about him, as your child and as a person, by all that you say and do. Teach your child how to love himself and how to give and receive love with others in return. Re-examine your "inner tapes, negative self-talk or programs" to release messages, negative associations, or memories linked to the past. Be in the moment now and release the pain of the past. It is that simple.

Live with integrity. Live within your core values. Aspire to elevate your vision and knowledge to that of a monk, watching and listening with loving detachment to the sound of your own soul's rhythm, separate yet intertwined with all of life. Be kind when you talk to yourself, reveal your feelings of happiness and joy as you discover greater peace and confidence that come from living with open-heartedness and integrity. Treasure the positive habits that you are passing down to your child while he learns by osmosis more about a higher form of self-love.

By paying close attention to your inner world and the outer expression of it, your child absorbs and understands who she is as a direct reflection of you: her parent, a primary person to either mimic or reject. By being aware of what you received as a child, what you did not receive, and what you need now, you will be ahead of the game.

Become more intimate with yourself than you have been in a while. Ask what you stand for and how you feel about what you value most. What patterns, beliefs, and underlying messages do you repeat or promote in your family and in your own personal story? Who in your personal story has brought you to where you are today? Give yourself a hug, a pat on the back, or a serious talking to, whatever applies to your personal journey as a parent so far. Acknowledge your accomplishments and deficits, fears and triumphs. Congratulate yourself for successfully making it to this point in your own personal development despite or because of your parents and family relationships. Be willing to lift the veil of masked illusion and go for what is deep and real. That is your best bet for finding your authentic self. An authentic person lives in alignment with their core values, beliefs, words, goals, behavior, stature, and public image. He thinks, speaks, and lives true to his integrity. He is who he says he is and does not change his status for anyone. There is no false, public or ego-driven state or expression or endless desire to take; only a life lived and felt with integration, alignment, and congruence for the authentic individual who wants to give. An inauthentic person

> Give yourself a hug, a pat on the back, or a serious talking to, whatever applies to your personal journey as a parent so far. Acknowledge your accomplishments and deficits, fears and triumphs.

is misaligned and separates what he says and does, thereby self-deluding and compromising his integrity and full potential. The authentic person is upright. Self-respect becomes more important than popularity. The possibilities of that potential are endless.

Be Honest with Yourself: Pay Attention to What You Truly Need

Once you lift the veil of self-deceit, you more easily identify what you need. While learning to meet your personal and inter-personal requirements and take care of yourself, ask for what you need and set limits with the people in your life. By doing this, you empower yourself by taking control of the one person you have the power to change—you. Set this example for your child. Learn where others end and where you begin. Teach others how to treat you because what you allow, you condone. Since you love yourself, do not tolerate mistreatment or neglect from someone else or from yourself. Take space to do what calms you, empowers you, and regenerates your mind, body, and spirit. Be willing to give yourself what you need in your self-care, personal, educational, and work life.

Because you have more love for your inner child, you have more love to give to the child you are raising and are relating to now . . . Finding enough time and space to call your own is difficult for many busy parents today but it is your right and a necessity.

Choose to surround yourself with the people and things that nurture you. You are entitled to protect your sense of inner balance, harmony, and physical and emotional safety. It is your right. By doing this, you teach your child about practicing and developing healthy self-love. Acknowledge your "inner child" (the once small child who still resides in you and needs your care), you may need to re-parent that part of yourself with tender, loving attention. Because you have more love for your inner child, you have more love to give to the child you are raising and are relating to now. Make your world your sanctuary; remind yourself and get back to it as a daily and lifetime goal. Feed the garden of your life with all that makes you shine and glow.

Finding enough time and space to call your own is difficult for many busy parents today but it is your right and a necessity.

Family, friends, education, work, career, and social needs often claim precedence. Modern life has become a major balancing act. Technological, political, economic, and rapidly advancing social trends keep everyone on their toes. Add parenting and you will need a rope to help you hang on while you are climbing up the mountain of your life, not a rope to hang yourself. Learn how to detach emotionally; take care of yourself and meet your basic needs. When you are replenished, you have more to give. Do you as best as you can. Be your authentic self and recharge your personal batteries. Do what is right for you and align to your core values; live with true integrity. This is the best path to making your life your own and to finding peace.

Manage your emotional comfort level by realizing that you choose your personal boundaries. When you set limits with people around you, especially with difficult people or circumstances, you prevent major regression and unnecessary upsets or outbursts. You can keep a close relationship feeling comfortable and safe for both people to negotiate when the time is right. You can remain loving, interested, and involved while protecting yourself from absorbing another person's negativity, drama, hostility, or extreme self-involvement. Do this with clarity, respect, consistency, and strength. You have the power to dial up or down your own comfort control. You can monitor what you accept and reject. You can become aware of your emotional and interpersonal reactions as a result of giving away your power or letting unhealthy people or patterns into your life. You can be in charge of what you need and how you meet those needs or not.

Know that your relationships require your emotion, intention, intellect, time, and energy. The demands of learning new skills and technologies in our everyday lives and for our careers make it difficult to have enough time to relax and connect more personally sometimes. We may miss a lot of important details along the way, especially those necessary to maintain healthy relationships. If you are not paying close attention, personal relationships may suffer. Your lifetime relationship with your child and all of your significant

> Your lifetime relationship with your child and all of your significant relationships, no matter how stressful life can be, are worth contributing to on a regular basis, like an endless bank account with high dividends.

relationships, no matter how stressful life can be, are worth contributing to on a regular basis, like an endless bank account with high dividends. When all is said and done, what is more important that your most personal relationships, especially the ones you have for life?

In this fast-paced, hyper, technology-focused, crowded, stressed and impersonal world, you can lose yourself and your immediate and intimate connections. People need connection with other people, plain and simple. We have begun to lose that connection as technology, and the growing dependency on it, eliminates some essential human interaction.

Families, in particular, do not always find ways to regularly connect with each other either. Nowadays, it is common to see couples, parents, and children sitting around tables at restaurants and cafes, plugged into their hand-held electronic devices, looking down in unison, and eating in silence. They are more plugged in to their electronic gadgets than their relationships or the people sitting across from them. Real-time conversations are being replaced by digitized texts and electronically supported visuals, removing the personal component more and more. Dr. Sherry Turkle, in her book, *Alone Together: Why We Expect More from Technology and Less from Each Other*,[25] discusses this phenomenon of human disconnection. A big part of life is feeling connected to other people, sharing, feeling, getting feedback, and being naturally responsive. We are losing the innate drive to connect to each other, by trading the connections with our device-driven world.

> Put down the device and make eye contact. Reflect and respond as humans are programmed to do. Be present. Make eye contact. Smile. Listen to the person sitting across from you.

The focus on relating without constant interruption is another seemingly lost art. Put down the device and make eye contact. Reflect and respond as humans are programmed to do. Be present. Make eye contact. Smile. Listen to the person sitting across from you. Set limits on how you spend your time, the people with whom you spend your time, and what you need to maintain healthy connections. Choose to connect and teach your child to connect with what is important, including positive and close relationships, relaxation, and quiet time to reflect and recharge the human battery.

Be aware of the people and things that trigger you. If you know from experience that with certain issues, people, or topics of conversation, the interaction may go south, plan accordingly. Make time with certain people and topics of conversation time-limited or off-limits if they cause you stress or may not be productive at the time. Being emotionally and sometimes physically detached from those who trigger negative emotions in you allows you to calm your mind, body, and spirit. Be willing to observe the silent (and sometimes not-so-silent) triggers that have the potential to run you or run your life in ways that do not serve you well.

Many people experience dysfunctional family relationships in which violations and manipulations of personal rights run rampant. In those families, respect or trust may be broken and the needs of another often trump your own. Examine how you have learned to interact with other people and look at how you have learned how to give and receive love. Look at how you approach commitment and group cohesion. Reflecting on how these skills originated can help you find a jumping off point for new ideas for healthy, happy, balanced living. You are free to rewrite the script for a happier, more functional and personally connected way of life.

We live in a world filled with narcissists and competitors who have difficulty connecting for its own sake rather than for mutual gain. The need for attention and material success has become an important necessity to survive, often leaving the inner world behind. The goal is to find balance between your needs and the needs of those in your life. When you learn that you are a priority in your own life and that you teach others how to treat you, you are truly free. The attitudes and actions of those around you become less important motivators for you. You learn how to trust yourself and connect in real and authentic ways. Congratulations to you and keep it up.

> You are free to rewrite the script for a happier, more functional and personally connected way of life.

Allow Your Inner Parent to Take Care of Your Inner Child

Think about the idea of re-parenting yourself. You have the chance to develop yourself in many ways as you learn to love yourself even more. What feelings and images does that phrase conjure up for you? Regardless, the ability to heal yourself through positive re-parenting techniques can be learned at any time. You can parent your physical child and your inner child simultaneously. When you parent for life, each day you grow a little bit more on the inside while your child grows on the outside and the inside. You take good care of those you love.

Learning to re-parent yourself is an essential skill to becoming a better parent now. It will better prepare you for the ongoing task of truly loving yourself unconditionally and will open your heart to giving your child greater unconditional love, acceptance, and support. Self-parent your inner child; meet your needs now with ease, enthusiasm, and the quest for real health, happiness, and healing. This focus on taking care of the smaller, younger part of yourself is humbling. It will expand your awareness as the adult in charge of your family team, ready to nurture, protect, encourage, and empower your child in the process. You will learn to notice and respond to the once small, helpless part of yourself without having to ask anyone else for anything. You know what you need. As your sensitivities grow, so will your sensitivity toward your child.

Take a moment to quietly imagine the little child inside of you. Recall an easily accessible childhood memory—a time when you felt open, happy, sure of yourself, and loved and accepted for who you are. Think of a time when you perceived yourself as a separate and special unique person. Enjoy the positive feelings from this memory. Notice your approximate age in the memory and be aware of how you felt in the moment. Ask how you defined yourself, what mattered most, and who and what you needed most in life then. Become aware of how you felt at this time, looking back to that phase, and imagine cradling

> When you parent for life, each day you grow a little bit more on the inside while your child grows on the outside and the inside. You take good care of those you love.

your once small self in your big adult arms now. Ask yourself where you are going from this point forward in your life and if it is in the direction of your hopes and dreams.

Next, examine your present life and notice if you are living consciously. Are you willing to learn life lessons and grow from them or are you living out of habit and familiarity? Gently accept that you are at the perfect place for you now with the skills and experience you currently have. When ready, consider what Carl Jung articulated, "I am not what happened to me, I am what I choose to become." [26] By re-focusing on your choices moving forward, you will achieve an important first step in re-parenting yourself. Your focus becomes a mindful, moving meditation in the complex arena of your life.

To be your best parent to yourself, it helps to remember what it was like for you to be a child. Be mindful of the met and unmet needs of your inner child. Remember and identify with the small, wise and vulnerable child inside of you. Be observant, and then acknowledge what you need to meet those needs within yourself now. This skill will result in greater empathy that you can then give to the child you are raising and relating to. Remember you are evolving as a strong adult and vulnerable inner child. See yourself living as an adult, in an adult's world holding your inner child's tender soul—needing attention and nurturance in order to grow. Take your inner child by the hand, placing him or her safely in the back seat when parenting your own child. Notice, respect, and respond to the small voice inside needing care. Take the time to get to know yourself, your feelings, responses, and tendencies as well as possible. Be the mother or father you need.

Personal discovery is a worthwhile process. Over a lifetime, it can be a rewarding and satisfying experience, despite the work and pain it can take to get there. Leap courageously into new terrain with your sights set on exploring brave new territory. Anais Nin explained beautifully in her poem "Risk" from her book *Children of the Albatross*, "… and the day came when the risk

> To be your
> best parent
> to yourself,
> it helps to
> remember
> what it was
> like for you to
> be a child.
> Be mindful
> of the met
> and unmet
> needs of your
> inner child.
> Remember and
> identify with
> the small, wise
> and vulnerable
> child inside of
> you.

to remain tight in a bud was more painful than the risk it took to blossom." [27] You are worth taking that risk, as long as you feel safe while stretching out of your comfort zone into a place of emotional ambiguity forcing fierce introspection. Allow your inner parent and your inner child to discover what suits you best together.

By working on yourself, healing, and creating your best life ever, the quality of your life, work, and relationships will morph into a new personal world view. There is no end, only the beginning of learning more about yourself and all that your life has to offer. Moments of personal introspection can be thought of as special visits with a dear old friend. Your lifetime journey can lead to personal enlightenment and inner peace, generating greater happiness in your relationships and more joy and harmony in your life. The self-discovery process is cyclical, like moving through a revolving door of consciousness in a constantly changing world. Your life will feel better all-around because you are healing from the inside out. Once you do that, sunnier days are ahead.

The door of self-discovery is worth walking through. At different stages of your life you have walked through that door and grown in leaps and bounds. At other times, you were unable to move forward and remained stuck or back-peddling. When you are ready to progress in your self-mastery, begin from your present position. In a changing world, and as you evolve yourself and transmute your reality, remember that the only way out is through. Widen your vision and re-think your perceptions. Challenge long-held beliefs that may no longer serve you in your life today. Keep what works and let go of what is no longer necessary. Keep moving ahead with faith, wisdom, and courage and be sure to take with you all that you have learned so far.

When you develop yourself and seek greater personal understanding, your partner, children, family, and friends become secondary beneficiaries. Notice if your thoughts and actions reflect openness, loving, kindness, forgiveness,

There is no end, only the beginning of learning more about yourself and all that your life has to offer. Moments of personal introspection can be thought of as special visits with a dear old friend.

compassion, respect and optimism or have other motivations behind them. The Dalai Lama said it best: "Love and compassion are necessities, not luxuries. Without them, humanity cannot survive. True compassion is not just an emotional response but a firm commitment founded on reason. I have found that the greatest degree of inner tranquility comes from the development of love and compassion. The more we care for the happiness of others, the greater is our own sense of well-being. Cultivating a close, warm-hearted feeling for others automatically puts the mind at ease. It is the ultimate source of success in life." [28]

By taking care of yourself, living with integrity and your own moral code, you love yourself well. Your inner parent is taking care of your inner child and you are successful. Your self-care success inspires your child's success. Successes teach and motivate your child by example. As you pursue self-mastery, new skills, and personal enlightenment in life's open classroom, you teach your child about the possibilities of life, placing self-love and respect as high priorities in your widening education.

Carl Jung articulated that, "There is no stronger influence on a child than that of his parent's unlived life." He also asserted, "If there is anything that we wish to change in our children, we should first examine it and see whether it is not something that could better be changed in ourselves." [29] This speaks to the importance of resolving one's life as best as possible while offering love, care, influence, and hope to another.

When you strive to fulfill your life's dreams and raw potential, your influence is more greatly felt as a successful role model to your child. Essentially, you parent yourself so well that you win and everyone around you wins because you are coming from a place of satisfaction and resolve. When you live your life fully and grasp all that supports who you are, you teach honestly and abundantly. It is only then that personal mastery and self-actualization is achievable for you and may then be offered as an example to your child.

When you are ready to progress in your self-mastery, begin from your present position. In a changing world, and as you evolve yourself and transmute your reality, remember that the only way out is through.

Sometimes revisiting your past dredges up memories, emotions, and unmet needs and can hold you back from living your best life now. Remember that when you were growing up your parents (probably) raised you the best that they could with the information and skills available to them at that time.

Reflect on yourself as a parent now who can learn and parent compassionately with new information and skills leading the way. Remember, throughout the various stages of your life, some of your needs may have been left unmet. How comfortable were you when asking for what you needed or expressing how you truly felt? How receptive are you when hearing the needs of others, specifically from your child now? What was the underlying message about expressing needs and feelings in your family of origin? What was the typical way your parents responded and related to you while you were growing up? What light can you shine on how you were parented that helps you to face yourself and your parents (or your memory of your parents) now?

Now fast-forward yourself to today, right now. Be honest with yourself and pay attention to what you truly need to live your best life in the present. Be willing to be your own internalized mother or father, capable of the specific nurturing you still need. Be an attentive parent to your inner child. When you distinguish your needs from your wants and remain open to new insights and new growth, you clarify your core priorities and become a better parental example to your child. When you honestly love and respect yourself, giving the best you can, and setting limits when needed, you are on the road to sublime emotional health and wellness for both of you.

Your attitude is contagious. Your sense of satisfaction in life (or lack thereof) is like a skipped stone in a vast lake rippling outward to those around you. Therefore, as family leader, you teach positive and negative lessons about life's journey because of the adventure you have had so far and the life attitude you carry today. Based on your own life experience, your child remains ready to accept and emulate your personal perspective.

> Reflect on yourself as a parent now who can learn and parent compassionately with new information and skills leading the way.

> Be willing to be your own internalized mother or father, capable of the specific nurturing you still need. Be an attentive parent to your inner child.

Like psychologist and parent educator Haim Ginott said, "Children are like wet cement; whatever falls on them makes an impression."[30] These wise words are worthy of serious consideration. Children naturally absorb their environment and influences.

Successful self-nurturing enables you to trust and respect yourself. Trust what you need in order to feel good, loved, happy, peaceful, fulfilled, satisfied, and happy. You give yourself what you need, rather than expect others to give it to you. You accept people's limitations and seek what is right for you. You live by your own standards and see people for who they are. Your consistent self-care allows you to respect, acknowledge, and reinforce your individual rights and self-worth. You are able to define your needs better than anyone else. With that in mind, the task of re-parenting yourself is already in motion. Over time, you will realize that you can always count on yourself, do what is right for you, know when to protect yourself, and know when to let go. Your self-love and moral compass dictate how you live with integrity and make yourself feel happy and proud. That is the crux of good and effective self-parenting.

Self-parenting automatically improves your parenting skills. It makes you a better parent when raising, relating to, loving, and letting go of your child when the time is right. By re-parenting yourself, even in small ways, new habits of self-care emerge improving your ability to love, nurture, and empower yourself and your loved ones. Do it now. You are all worth it!

> Over time, you will realize that you can always count on yourself, do what is right for you, know when to protect yourself, and know when to let go.

Homework Assignment 8

Your "Inner Child" Creative Visualization

Here is an assignment to help you come into contact with your "inner child" using creative visualization. This discovery is important because it relates to how your sensitivity and awareness of the smaller, younger parts of yourself improves your parenting skills with greater awareness, empathy and compassion. When you visualize what makes you feel safe and connected to your core self and what really matters to you, and work on your goal with consistent practice these skills will emerge with greater ease.

- Go to a quiet room, an undisturbed place in your home. Make sure you have privacy, space and comfort, and that you are not needed by anyone at this time.

- Quiet your body in a comfortable chair, bed, or soft surface. Take several deep, cleansing breaths, in through your nose and out through your mouth. Close your eyes and be willing to explore your own inner sanctuary.

- Notice if your inner sanctuary (a special place of your own design that brings you comfort and peace) is indoors or outside and invite your "inner child" to join you there.

- Greet your inner child. How old are you? How tall are you? What do you look like? How do you feel? Notice all the smells, sights, textures, feel and sounds around you. Are you alone or is someone with you? Take the time you need to become reacquainted with your small self while standing, walking, sitting, or playing with your "inner child." Be open to take a walk or sit quietly with this young part of yourself.

- Ask him or her what you need from your adult self now.

- Ask if there are any messages that your young self needs to tell your present self now.

- Open your eyes and return to where you are in the room.

- Record the information you received in your *Parenting Journal.*

- Go back and re-visit this place again and see what you can glean.

Be gentle, kind, and patient—open to what and who appears to you. Hold your inner child's hand or give your inner child a loving hug (symbolically). Assure your inner child that you will always be there to give love, awareness, empathy, and compassion. Assure him or her that you can revisit at any time, keeping your self-awareness and self-love alive. Record your additional impressions, inner messages, inspirations, and insights in your *Parenting Journal.*

Live in the Now with an Eye on the Future

Go confidently in the direction of your dreams!
Live the life you've imagined.

—Henry David Thoreau

Stop, Look, Listen, and Breathe—Focus Your Attention

> Each second is precious, like a newborn baby. Each moment is just a new breath away. It is what you *do with each moment* that counts the most.

Stop, look, listen, and breathe. Focus your attention. You are fortunate to be alive in this moment. Be thankful that you are here. Take a moment to appreciate the value of now. Notice, recognize, and cherish your life and the instants that make it. Every decision you make and perception you have constitute what might happen next and how the rest of your time will follow. Recognize that this moment has never occurred before. The possibilities contained within it are limitless. Each second is precious, like a newborn baby. Each moment is just a new breath away. It is what you *do with each moment* that counts the most. Only by acting with consciousness, integrity, imagination or previous experience you can predict what may come next. Focus on right now, pay attention to what is around you and what is inside of you, and breathe. With that full, open breath, be sure to be mindful and choose wisely.

Take the best path to stay present in the moment, using your learned insights to lead you to a successful future. You welcome the potential for love and healing when you live in the

116

moment. Carry your past along with hopes for your future. Each moment has yet to happen, so expecting history to automatically repeat itself is unproductive and unwise. It is with clear insight and correct action that positive results are possible. Keep an open mind and pay attention to your attitudes, fears, judgments, and preconceptions as you go about your day. Expect the same results from before and you will find them. Expect different results and you will find those, too. Practice this radically observant mentality as you go along your parenting journey with your child. Stay on course, follow its winding ways, and keep on.

Expectations often are a result of past experience, learned coping skills, and personal projections about people and events. If you pre-judge, you put yourself at a disadvantage with knee-jerk reactions to people and events, rather than responding to them. This behavior is unconscious. When you hold preconceived judgments and close yourself off to new insight and potentially positive experience, it becomes difficult to live fully in the moment. Being reactive instead of responsive darkens momentary awareness and suppresses the ability to realize potential peace, joy, and healing. A new, happier experience of the moment is lost. When you are living in the moment, you are not a slave to your past or a victim of your circumstances. You decide how you proceed with clarity and a fresh perspective. You learn to relax, release your expectations, and live expectant instead.

As you know, people, circumstances, choices in life, and priorities change. They are supposed to. Growth occurs over time, so allow life's natural flow to steer you by remaining open to the moment. There is so much you cannot control, but you can control yourself and your interpretations. With that said, you can review your options for taking action. As long as your choices serve you and are not destructive, manipulative or backward moving, welcome each one. Respond differently and see the best version of you emerge. Watch how your relationships change, blossom, deepen, and become clear. Look ahead to the grand "aha" moments and the not so grand ones

When you are living in the moment, you are not a slave to your past or a victim of your circumstances. You decide how you proceed with clarity and a fresh perspective. You learn to relax, release your expectations, and live expectant instead.

with an open, honest, joyful approach. A small "aha" moment is when your young child repeats a "bad" word she heard you say and you can actually laugh about it, so long as it is not in front of your mother-in-law, favorite clergyman, or aged spinster aunt with the heart condition. You may as well laugh because there will be many more times your child will shock and surprise you. A big "aha" moment is when your child uses her voice to tell you how she feels, who she is, and what she needs. Her decisions about education, career choices, sexual orientation, or politics may not thrill you. She wants you to listen to her, so open your ears and hear her voice. Allow for flexibility, growth, and another perspective. Welcome change and go with the flow of life.

Raise your Awareness

> Be open to constant life lessons and patterns that keep re-emerging and present themselves to you. Learn your lessons well so that you can then move on to higher forms of self-knowledge.

Raise your child and raise your awareness at the same time. Learn and do what you can to stay present in the moment. Stay present-day and observe yourself and others. See each moment with fresh eyes, ready for new proof of who you are in the form of intention, introspection, insights, and interactions. When living in the moment, you open your inner telescope with a fresh perspective to preview the moments that lie ahead. In the moment, choose to alter your behavior using inner wisdom as your guide. Empower yourself and know that you alone have the power to manifest the best outcomes for tomorrow. You raise your spirit and your child's all at once.

Since reality is subjective and perception is reality, then reality or the experience of "what is real" varies individually and momentarily. Be open to constant life lessons and patterns that keep re-emerging and present themselves to you. Learn your lessons well so that you can then move on to higher forms of self-knowledge. See your life experience as a giant classroom; take it slowly, learning every day, one lesson at a time. Use this open-minded attitude as a tool that you pass on to your child. Exemplify personal empowerment, faith, and trust in life's lifelong learning process. Take notice of the large and small gifts symbolically and literally unwrapping in your world. Like in school, learning can be joyful, tedious, and sometimes painful, but is always worth the effort. The key is to maintain the highest level of awareness and retention that you can. If you get off course, simply remind yourself to get back into the driver's seat and steer toward clarity.

Be inspired by the quest for healing the past, moving forever forward to a bright future. This process will enable you to release unhealthy learned beliefs, habits, and wounds. It will also allow you to parent in the moment, projecting the essence of being truly courageous in the face of the unknown. Whether you are currently raising a child, have already done so, or will do so in the future, you know that so much of the journey is about standing in your truth, faith, courage, and strength as changes and challenges naturally present themselves. Learn to let go of the past. Learn from it and use this great teaching opportunity as a gift to your child in your words and actions as leader of your family team moving forward.

> Be inspired by the quest for healing the past, moving forever forward to a bright future.

The ability to "self-correct" is a wonderful parenting skill. When speaking negatively or using limited thinking, you hinder yourself and your child. Train yourself to realize the situation at hand and focus on what you are doing. Consider your words, feelings, intonation, and body language. Strive to be proactive and consistent so that your words and actions match and hold positive meaning. If you find yourself having said or done something that you realize is counter to your heart's goals as the family leader, own it. For example, if you lost your job or cannot pay your pile of bills and have over-reacted to your child's music or electronic games being too loud, recognize your need for a quiet place to unwind and regroup. Maybe you need to blow off some steam and get in a good workout or take a brisk walk. Apologize for over-reacting and take responsibility for it. Make sure you convey that it is your responsibility, and not his fault, for your reaction. When it comes to attachment and resolving conflict, apologize from your heart for causing distress and stop the pattern as well as you can. Remember that you are responsible for your part in the dynamic you help to create at home.

When you Mess Up, Fess Up

When you are accountable you take personal responsibility for yourself, your attitudes, and actions and teach your child strength and humility. She learns to give herself permission to do the same.

By revealing your humanity—being imperfect, then self-correcting—your child is taught the same value. Learning from mistakes and taking responsibility for your part trumps the need to be right or make others wrong. Humility and self-honesty become part of an ever-evolving process, something revered and valued in your family. "When you mess up, fess up" works wonders for all family members. This willingness to be accountable serves as a cushion that comforts the family team while you navigate bumps in the road, safely permitting self-acceptance, honesty, personal accountability, and forgiveness. You become free to be fully human. Elizabeth Lesser describes, "May you listen to the voice within the beat even when you are tired. When you feel yourself breaking down, may you break open instead. May every experience in life be a door that opens your heart, expands your understanding, and leads you to freedom." [31]

Because many learned responses become habitual and once set are hard to undo, positive or negative habits may as well be turned around to produce true family blessings rather than crushing momentary mishaps that are difficult to erase. When you take responsibility for your mistakes, a sincere and heartfelt apology is in order. Be sure that you work on changing negative or destructive habits as you go. Simply notice, stop, and change behavior in the moment as best as you can, even when you are stressed out and in a tense or sensitive and reactive mode. Doing so takes awareness and self-discipline and does not preclude additional incidents from occurring. With practice, like in mindful meditation, you can learn to slow the urge to react and respond too quickly. Learn the habit of observing without emotion or judgment, breathing with ease, and simply being

> Humility and self-honesty become part of an ever-evolving process, something revered and valued in your family. "When you mess up, fess up" works wonders for all family members.

120

without effort to gain insight and awareness. Like many things in life, you are a work in progress that requires conscious refining to be your best. Learn to respond without habit and let the joy and healing unfold.

Be Open and Aware in the Moment

Because parenting is the constant practice of being present amidst a great deal of change, it is wise to be consistent with what matters. Be open and aware, *"loving and firm, firm and loving,"* no matter what. Be firm with the non-negotiable issues around safety and essential priorities that are reasonable for your child's age and abilities. For example, behaviors that jeopardize your younger child's physical safety are off-limits such as running across a busy street to grab a ball or climbing up on the roof for fun. Older children need to know that they are not allowed to regularly pull all-nighters before the next school day or eat sugary foods exclusively. Teens need to know that they must drive responsibly and get home safely in time for curfew. When you parent for life, you live in the moments. You learn to combine love and limits and let both messages come shining through.

Even with the necessary limits to keep your child safe, love your child above all else, guide him and maintain some flexibility. Help ensure that your child lives and grows a happy life. If the situation is not particularly dangerous and will be a fun and a good learning experience for your child, you can be more relaxed. Keep the dialog open between you and create a workable agreement to ensure that your child is safe in his freedom. You can go with the flow and not be worried about the sleepover, party, or play date/hangout with kids you may not know well. Have faith in your child's or teen's competence and ability to learn from his experience. If he has not learned from his experience yet, then more opportunities will surely present themselves over and over again for your child to realize his lesson. All you can do is guide him, set reasonable rules, and hope and pray for his safety.

When you parent for life, you live in the moments. You learn to combine love and limits and let both messages come shining through.

What you will find is that over time, as your lifetime relationship blooms, momentary interactions are the sprouting seeds of the blossoming bond between you. When you realize that you teach by example with love and respect and welcome learning garnered from mistakes, your child will appreciate your supportive attitude. The future growth in your parent-child relationship depends on the seeds of a shared past. By then, hopefully, you will have been reaping the rewards all along.

Your job is to identify and then release unhealthy relationship tendencies in yourself as you build your lifetime relationship with your child. Notice your defensive defaults when you feel ill, overwhelmed, stressed, concerned, and afraid, disrespected, or unpleasantly surprised…or if you feel many of these at once. Be aware of how you move away from the current moment into a past feeling or memory, or a negative definition and label of that experience. You may return to the roots of your feeling like a victim, loner, scapegoat, bully, hero, the invisible one, the sick or troubled one, the enabler, or worse. Consciously return to the moment so that you are clear in what you say and do. Your personal awareness and accountability frees you to become the best parent you can be from this moment onward. Reveal your relationship demons courageously and then set them free.

Move beyond assigning blame, shame, judgment, threats, and negative labels. Do not let power struggles stay alive. Stop them as soon as they start. Better yet, prevent them from happening in the first place. Once they start, it is easy to fall back into their pattern. Choose to acknowledge, encourage, and grow with your child rather than stay stuck in the mud. An interesting experiment is to daydream about your child's future. Imagine her as an adult when you are with her and then again later when you are alone. Try this often over time as a way to envision how the present moment might help define future outcomes. Be willing to expand your perspective of your child as she is now. Include your child's emerging physical, emotional, intellectual, educational, social, career, and spiritual wholeness. Include

> Your job is to identify and then release unhealthy relationship tendencies in yourself as you build your lifetime relationship with your child.

projecting thoughts, images, and feelings for your lifetime relationship. Notice if the defensive or unproductive ways you needed or used in the past or in other relationships have served you before. If so, that is fine, and if your old coping devices no longer work, or are detrimental to your child's well-being and your precious relationship, then it is time to let them go. Every day is a new day to let every question, struggle or challenge inspire love and respect to be the answers.

When interacting with your child, see him both as he is now and as he may become later. Know that your influence is shaping his future. Have faith in all your teachings. Have faith in your child and his capacity to absorb vital teachings from you, himself, and other significant people in his life. Have faith in possibility. Savor your child's stage of development now; enjoy your vision of him later. Imagine that in every interaction, the seeds of your future relationship are planted while he slowly grows into the man he will become.

Allow for the awareness of the passage of time as your child develops. Your child is influenced by peers, teachers, home environment, life experiences, other relationships, and the unique relationship you share. Envision what the future might bring with the reality of life today. Keep in mind that the future comes when you least expect it. Enjoy every age and stage of your child's journey. After all, life is the sum of lived or unlived moments strung together over time. It is with this realization kept in your present awareness that your precious lifetime relationship with your child will unfold.

> When interacting with your child, see him both as he is now and as he may become later. Know that your influence is shaping his future.

Wisdom from Other Places

While your parental influence is monumental and a unique force like no other, recognize outside influences as valid. Other significant adults, children, life experiences, friends, and members of your family team play a part in this lifetime development. Relatives, teachers, coaches, helping professionals, and friends supply alternate feedback, teaching, influence, and experience for your child. Varying feedback helps your child know who she is in the world and helps identify her social and world skills. Through external feedback, your child learns how others perceive her and about different kinds of relationships. Sometimes immediately, and often with trial and error, she learns what her opinions are and has to decide if she is to believe herself or the other person. Once she decides, her own wisdom will develop.

> Through external feedback, your child learns how others perceive her and about different kinds of relationships.

While external wisdom is valid, remember that you know your child best (and he knows himself best). Teach him to honor, and thus know himself. Outside feedback is helpful because it can open a window of truth about an aspect, a grander scheme or a worldly, social, or educational aspect that you are not aware of. Some feedback is accurate, thought-provoking, instrumental, transformational, and educational. Other feedback may not be on track, supportive, or appropriate. In that case, be diligent in your limit setting. Smile, say "thank you," and be on your way. This is especially true with uninformed, unsolicited feedback or opinions regarding your child or family system. When you parent for life, you learn to filter out what is not useful and fine-tune what makes sense to you as a parent. Sometimes you know your child as well as he knows himself. Other times you have not got a clue and wonder if you have taken in a boarder or accepted a foreign exchange student and signed the papers in your sleep. That is alright, who your child is now and who he becomes is still a life in progress.

As you progress on your lifetime parenting journey, you find pieces of the puzzle of how to parent "right" for your child and for you as a parent. When you rely upon your wisdom, heart, gut feelings, intelligence, and leadership, the pieces of the puzzle become clear. Remain committed to your ongoing love for your child and your relationship. New puzzles, brain teasers, and mysteries will arise, so be ready for the challenge. Follow the positive example of how you were parented in the ways that worked for you, and then customize what works well for your child along the way. It might be necessary to parent in a completely different direction or try some new combination of tools rather than the way you were parented. That is okay because that was a different time and you are different people. Listen to your heart and pay attention to your child. You will know what to do. Listen to other parents, read helpful books, and get professional or social support to bolster your knowledge and self-trust. As much as knowledge and experience will guide you, so will your ability to let go and start anew. Be willing to walk through the door of uncertainty and arrive joyfully on the other side, ready to meet your child wherever she is.

Welcome the Future

Know that in no uncertain terms do you have complete control over your child or the future. Individual choice, life events and experiences, and responses to events and unforeseen elements all factor in. Be realistic. You cannot micro manage anyone effectively, except maybe yourself. You do, however, have control over the thoughts, beliefs, and actions that help the future be better matched to your vision of it.

Listen to your heart and pay attention to your child. You will know what to do.

If you are an optimist, you will expect a bright future and all that you say and do will reflect that. You appreciate all the good that exists and teach that sense of gratitude. If you are a pessimist, you reverse positive expectations and life today may lack hope, faith, and enjoyment. The good news is that you have a choice. Your life attitude helps you to see where your child gets his. Welcome the future, support your positive imaginings, hopes, dreams, and wishes. Awaken to a greater sense of peace and joy by dealing with your past and the negative influences that caused your pessimism in the first place. Once reconciled with where you have been, you will naturally expect a better place ahead for where you are going. Optimism is only a thought away.

Try and see yourself as an eternal student. This applies to you as an individual and as a parent. Learn to enjoy self-discovery. Take pride in what you know; accept what you do not know. Ride the waves of life's transitions and difficult, challenging, stressful negative distractions. No matter the challenge, struggle, or opportunity, be true to your north star;

have faith in yourself and in learning to see the silver lining
or life lesson inherent in everything. No matter the pain or
discomfort, learn anyway. Enjoy when all (or most) is working
and well in your life. Find creative solutions for what ails you.
Become the optimist who eagerly awakens each day, excited for
what will be.

No matter
the challenge,
struggle, or
opportunity,
be true to your
north star; have
faith in yourself
and in learning
to see the silver
lining or life
lesson inherent
in everything.

*H*omework Assignment *9*

"The Doorway" Creative Visualization

This exercise is a way for you to discover more about your perceptions about your life and time.

- Start by providing a safe and comfortable, quiet place in which to relax. Take five deep breaths, slowly inhaling, holding each breath for five seconds then gradually exhaling for five seconds. Breathe in through your nose and out through your mouth.

- Clear your mind, allowing all thoughts, ideas, worries, concerns, and current feelings to be put on an imaginary shelf in your mind's eye. Envision the shelf, what it looks like. How large and sturdy it must be to hold all of your preoccupations. Allow all mental energy to sit atop your shelf until you need to deal with the specific issues later.

- You can also imagine a balloon, its color, shape and size. Put everything on your mind inside of the balloon, open a window, and watch it float away. You can retrieve your balloon later when you need to by simply pulling the imaginary string that controls it.

- Once your mind is sufficiently clear, you have all the space leftover to work your imaginary magic. Allow your mind to see yourself standing in an unknown space. Make sure that there is solid ground beneath you and that you feel strong, sturdy, supported, and open. Be open to the space you are in as it reveals itself to you, whether it is known, unknown, magical, realistic, indoors, or outdoors.

- See yourself standing there, feeling safe and strong, before a doorway. Look at the door and notice its size, how it looks, and how you feel facing it. This is your doorway. Look at it, touch it, and feel its unique beauty. See what the door is made of, its color, material, size, shape, feel and location. What kind of handle(s) does it have on it? Feel what you feel in your emotions and body while standing there.

- Know that where you stand now is your current life's reality. Feel yourself opening this door while being in touch with your feelings while standing before it. Do you feel hesitant, excited, energized, frightened, confident, curious, anxious, ready, unsure or calm?

- Now look at the door again. Reach for the handle and open the door and walk through it. Notice what you see, hear, think, feel, and imagine as you cross over the threshold into the unknown space beyond. Stay in that place for a moment and be still. Feel the powerful potential that is present without your having to do anything. Only your presence is required as you keenly observe.

- Move through the door and reach the other side. You have just symbolically moved from your present into your future. Your awareness of the process and your openness to what lies ahead based on choices made in the moment are key. Both allow you to take responsibility and accept where you are in the now and keep you receptive to your awesome future. Notice how you feel: happy, sad, enthused, worried, empowered, confused, ready, anxious, scared or peaceful? Do nothing but notice. No self-judgment is allowed or required.

- Come back to your present state of your body in the room, become aware of your breath while you are sitting in the chair or the sofa or bed, wherever you currently are. Breathe that reality in while you again notice, this time what you experienced. Take the information of your own personal doorway to help you move forward with clarity and intention when the time comes. This awareness will help you to envision the future with your child, wherever you are in your current stage of your unique and precious lifetime relationship.

- Write down anything you want to in your *Parenting Journal* about this experience. If need be, come back to it later when you are ready for more clarity about the direction you need to take.

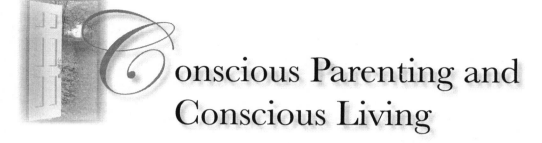

CHAPTER TEN

Conscious Parenting and Conscious Living

With every rising of the sun, think of your life as just begun.

—Unknown

Your Choice: Be Awake or Asleep

When you parent for life, you take responsibility for
what you create and co-create in your life and with your
child. You are conscious and devoted to your job of creating
your best lifetime relationship with your child. You choose how
you move through life. You live with awareness about your day
and care about the people closest to you, your responsibilities,
and what is most important in your consciousness. What you pay
attention to matters and you can choose what to focus on and
how you feel in your life. You can focus on the positives or the
negatives, blame and shame yourself or others, or engage in old
or new patterns. There are many things you pay attention to.
There are also many things you choose not to pay attention to.
You may ignore or reject these events, life lessons, and people.
Only you can focus your mind, heart and intention to live fully,
aware of the outward and underlying messages all around you.
Your energy and focus on what and who you pay attention to
are your own as you live each day. You choose to see your life's
events and relationships as helping you evolve or deflect and
deny that idea. If you are motivated to live more deeply, with
more honesty, curiosity and courage, you can face life head-on.

> When you
> parent for life,
> you take
> responsibility
> for what you
> create and
> co-create in
> your life and
> with your child.
> You are
> conscious and
> devoted to your
> job of creating
> your best lifetime
> relationship with
> your child.

You can change the way you go about each day, if you choose to live with conscious purpose.

How much you know about your beliefs, core values, attitudes, and choices dictates how much you can continue to learn. To parent well, you must be conscious. To live well, you must be conscious and ask yourself the difficult questions. Once you are truly mindful, the answers will come easily.

A few examples of questions are: What is your life's purpose, your life plan, and specific "parenting purpose"? Do you live your mission? It is okay if you do not know what it is. What matters is that you strive to remain open and aware while discovering who you are capable of becoming and why you are here. Whether you know it or not, you have a distinct reason for existing. Your child does, too, and it is your job to help him realize it. Like in business, one lives and dies by a personal mission statement. A good idea is to incorporate a "parenting purpose" or a "family mission statement" into your everyday life. This moral directive will lead you well and keep you on course for what you are trying to accomplish in your relationship with your child. By choosing to be awake rather than sleepwalk through life, you choose how to live and teach your child how to live openly and honestly, too.

> The choice to live consciously or unconsciously is entirely yours. You are the master of your own fate, in a real sense.

The choice to live consciously or unconsciously is entirely yours. You are the master of your own fate, in a real sense. When you are living a quasi-alert life, you operate on auto-pilot. You automatically respond and may live in denial or self-deceit so then much is predictable and little is questioned. When you are living fully awake, with a deeper sense of awareness and purpose, you notice much more detail in everything, and the deeper meaning that life has to offer. The ordinary becomes extraordinary. The extraordinary becomes sublime. Your life's lens opens and you see, feel, and respond with more sensitivity. When your awareness widens, you develop more of an appreciation for creative options and other perspectives. You become more honest with yourself. Your relationships deepen and become more honest. The possibilities of life broaden and your life becomes richer. Because you are willing to grow and expand your awareness, your child's emotional bank account grows, too. Stephen R. Covey powerfully expands on this idea in *The 7 Habits of Highly Effective People: Powerful Lessons in Personal Change*,[32] about creating paradigm shifts, abundance mentality, and the emotional deposits and withdrawals made in relationships, impacting the feeling of trust and safety felt with another human being. What you do is up to you. When you parent for life, what you choose will either enrich or deplete your reciprocal life's experience.

A wonderful by product of increased perception is the deepened sensitivity to both your own experience and to the experience of others. Increased consciousness raises your ability to feel compassion and propels your mental comprehension. Your third eye of wisdom, a gateway of higher consciousness, opens inward and outward. You become an advocate for yourself and those around you. Consciousness and truth breed understanding. Understanding paves the way for empathy and forgiveness. All the channels of communication open and the path is made clear. The path may not always be an easy one, but the journey is worth it. The path to enlightenment is filled with the benefits that result from hard work, struggle, and a quest for freedom. You choose to live with your eyes wide open or tightly closed. Choose to sensitize rather than desensitize yourself to what is happening. Emerge from darkness into light as you continue to relate to others.

Transform your life from ordinary to extraordinary by how you choose to live, love, learn, work, create, and parent. Keep a sense of curiosity, of not knowing and let that be okay with you. Your desire to learn, grow, and be your best, helping you to personally evolve is what motivates you. Your original sense of wonder and innocence is reborn with an open mind, heart, and ear. Either way, you pass on these personal principles toward living. Rachel Carlson said in her beautiful book, *The Sense of Wonder*, "If I had influence with the good fairy... I would ask that her gift to each child be a sense of wonder so indestructible

> A wonderful by product of increased perception is the deepened sensitivity to both your own experience and to the experience of others.

that it would last throughout life…If a child is to keep alive his inborn sense of wonder without any such gift from the fairies, he needs the companionship of at least one adult who can share it, rediscovering with him the joy, excitement and mystery of the world we live in."[33] A life well lived stands as a testament to your attitude toward living. Treat this attitude like an heirloom to be passed down to your child and future grandchildren. All that is required is a shift in focus; first acknowledge your own emotional and historical truths, then seek the extraordinary as a student of life on your journey. Remember, as Auntie Mame said in Dennis, Patrick's *Auntie Mame: An Irreverent Escapade,* "Life is a banquet and most poor suckers are starving to death."[34] Do not accept crumbs or anything less than spectacular in whatever ways you need or imagine that feeds your soul. Make sure your child is also nourished the same way as you parent for life.

Once you recognize your own needs, style, focus, and personal process with honesty and courage, you can move on to someone else. Once you are clear within yourself, you may then give compassion and empathy to your child; you will see her perspective more clearly. After that, listen to the message of your child's behavior. Hear her words rise above your own emotions and respond with the wisdom of your heart. With practice, this process can be cycled through in a day or two, hours, or even minutes. The practice of "getting real" with yourself rids denial, defensiveness, and resistance. Be self-honest: being true to yourself keeps you truthful as a role-model, protector, teacher, and guide. Your child will thank you for your humility by following in your footsteps.

Your openness and self-honesty free up your ability to self-correct, share unconditional love and support and work through any stuck places felt between you and your child. By "getting real" with yourself first, you will discover an invaluable tool for your lifetime relationship. Just think of how many arguments, misinterpretations, and hurt feelings will be averted simply by choosing to live with greater awareness. You can wear blinders, but you will accomplish a lot more by seeing what is really there:

Your openness and self-honesty free up your ability to self-correct, share unconditional love and support and work through any stuck places felt between you and your child.

the whole truth. With each wave of awareness and insight come larger circles of understanding, creating a ripple effect. Because of your widened perspective, expanded blessings continue to grow in the garden of your lifetime relationship with your precious flower.

Free Yourself and Commit to Parent with Awareness

Free yourself from antiquated ways, ineffective parenting styles and strategies or knee-jerk reactions by committing to parent with awareness. By making a conscious commitment to living with an open mind and heart, you free yourself from old habitual patterns, belief systems, and unconscious, inappropriate, or defensive responses. Try an expanded view and version of the old or ineffective style and strategies. Learn to do what works and release what does not. With awareness, you build acceptance and strength to deal with your child and his needs, both now and for the future. Sometimes, that is much easier said than done. Let illusions of reality, outmoded ways of thinking, responding, and living that do not support you or your family go.

Resistance is not just a good workout session at the gym and "Denial ain't just a river in Egypt!" People resist and deny as natural coping mechanisms to avoid taking responsibility or introducing real change. Be willing to receive information that boosts your self-knowledge, your life, and your world. Accept that your child is also a work in progress and as your awareness grows; your love for him will deepen and your appreciation for his process will be cultivated.

Accept yourself, be willing to accept and receive feedback, and practice forgiveness for reasonable sins. By being accountable for your expectations and how you process information, you are taking responsibility for that which is yours. Being more responsible in turn makes you a more effective and responsible parent. As you and your child age, you will find that deeper and more open communication will develop between you as you become less rigid and more approachable and receptive.

> Free yourself from antiquated ways, ineffective parenting styles and strategies or knee-jerk reactions by committing to parent with awareness.

Accept your humanity and take feedback as a sign that you are just as human as everyone else.

Awaken to Endless Opportunities to Learn Life Lessons and Heal

Even when it is painful, often because it is painful, awaken to opportunities for life lessons and healing. Awaken to your true potential as a human being, to move past struggle into insight and positive action. Awaken your potential as an exceptional parent. Be self-assured in your journey because only you know what kind of parent you are and how you have moved from point A to point B before. You may not know how you will move from point B to Point C as your child's needs grow and change and (hopefully) you grow and change. Be ready to embrace a deeper awareness that allows you to question your intention, purpose, level of understanding, and next strategy. Listen to the music of life; it is loud and it is clear only if you are willing to hear it. It is not one instrument or one melody. The sounds resonate with time and the lyrics are written by your interactions and your heart. The song is heard by the child in your life, and she watches how you move to it. Give her a chance to write her own melodies, too. Every moment is a gift. Every blessing and challenge is an opportunity for renewed gratitude and perspective. Be thankful for all of the opportunities, whether positive or negative. They both signify life's call to your soul.

The simple truth is that you are the master of your own reality and until you say so, your attitudinal ship has not fully sailed. Opportunities like this are often referred to as "teachable moments" and "learning opportunities" (further explained in Chapter 13) and must be expanded to include both children and adults. Learning is not just for those who are in school. In the "school of life," learning and growth are goals for all who wish to benefit. There will be bumps in the road, but perhaps the key is to let go rather than to hold on. The choice you make will impact the life of your child. Choose wisely: the eventual outcome of your choices will pave the way for the child you

Even when it is painful, often because it is painful, awaken to opportunities for life lessons and healing … Awaken your potential as an exceptional parent.

are designed to lead (and sometimes follow). Try to steer your way toward happy winds in your sails so that when storms do arise you will be better prepared to both lead and follow with a joyful attitude. The wonderful Marianne Williamson in *A Return to Love* wrote, "Our greatest fear—it is our light not our darkness that most frightens us. Our deepest fear is not that we are inadequate. Our deepest fear is that we are powerful beyond measure. It is our light not our darkness that most frightens us. We ask ourselves, who am I to be brilliant, gorgeous, talented and fabulous? Actually, who are you not to be? You are a child of God. Your playing small does not serve the world. There is nothing enlightened about shrinking so that other people will not feel insecure around you. We were born to make manifest the glory of God that is within us. It is not just in some of us; it is in everyone. And as we let our own light shine, we unconsciously give other people permission to do the same. As we are liberated from our own fear, our presence automatically liberates others."[35]

Enjoy Your Time Together

Open yourself to living in a conscious and deliberate way. That includes enjoying the time you and your child spend together, whether you have moments or hours at a time to do so. When you live and parent consciously and really just enjoy your child, any time you spend together becomes priceless. You could be engaged in an activity away from home, driving somewhere important, special, or mundane. You may be having dinner together, talking on the phone, texting or emailing each other. The key is to enjoy the contact and to keep the dialogue and positive interactions open. You might be playing a board game or a sport, cooking together (age-appropriately), creating art or music, sitting close to each other watching a movie, or just sharing quiet time together in the same room at home. This is when you must increase your awareness that the time to enjoy spending with your child is now. When your heart remains open, your child feels it. When you take care to find joy in being in the company of someone special, you are both enriched.

> Open yourself to living in a conscious and deliberate way. That includes enjoying the time you and your child spend together, whether you have moments or hours at a time to do so.

Your beliefs, expectations and behaviors focus on creating win-win outcomes for all. You become a partner to the process of life's experience. You are a witness and a guide to help empower yourself, and your child, help him to be happy, and help him to evolve. When you remove old illusions, delusions, and defenses you are free to live in the now, love in the now, and respond in the now. As a parent, you are more fully present and open for your child. You accept the differences that exist between you and your child and you try and create positive solutions to avoid conflict and ensure both of your happiness. Your creative problem-solving skills expand and your perceptions widen to make room for everyone's truth, not only your own.

With expanded awareness your world begins to open up. You discover more love and understanding unavailable to you before. Validate your own experience and, once done, see the truth of other's intentions underneath their behavior. The habits of emotional over-reactivity soften while empathetic neutrality enters the room. Life, including your family life, becomes happier, more peaceful, and harmonious, preparing the way for a healthy, happy future. Keep your mind and heart open. Separate out your emotional reactions so that you can be proactive and kind. Do this to enrich your lives and transform your shared life experience. This will help you and everyone around you grow.

When given the choice, how would you prefer to experience life? What do you remember as a child? What do you want your child to remember? How would you prefer your child to feel while moving through life? Ask yourself, how does your child feel while being himself? What are your child's dreams, passions, gifts, fears, and struggles? Do you talk and listen to your child about his interests, feelings, unique gifts, triumphs, struggles, and life's purpose? Are you role modeling how to live your values, live with positive attitudes, and how to find joy? Where do your attitudes about life come from? How have your parents lived their lives? What messages did your parents send to you about your life and how to live it? Ask the right questions and the right answers always emerge.

> When your heart remains open, your child feels it. When you take care to find joy in being in the company of someone special, you are both enriched.

> What do you remember as a child? What do you want your child to remember?

Which takes priority in your life: the quest for self-knowledge and growth or the emphasis to stay stuck or maintain the status quo? The million dollar question is: "What are your daily intentions and awareness focused on?" Are you more concerned with relationships that serve everyone well or that cloak and hide truthful relating? How comfortable are you to get outside your comfort zone and risk new perspectives and new priorities in your life? How proud are you of the life attitude you pass on to your child? Do you stand by your words and values or have a different set of standards for yourself than you do for everyone else? Do you tend to look for opportunities for growth and learning or do you hesitate and avoid change in order to stay in your self-imposed, shrunken comfort zone? The alarm clock is ringing. Wake up and move into living in the light while you are still here. Decide to know yourself and, at all costs, be willing to learn, grow, and change. Even if it hurts a little (as most growing does) it is for your own good and the good of your lifetime relationship with your child. Start now.

Even if it hurts a little (as most growing does) it is for your own good and the good of your lifetime relationship with your child. Start now.

Homework Assignment 10

Meeting and Befriending Your "Inner Guide" Creative Visualization

This exercise provides you with the opportunity to get in touch with the wisest part of yourself. Be willing to ask the right questions and the right answers will appear.

- Practice intentional yoga breathing with five breaths in through your nose and five breaths out through your mouth, each done slowly to the count of five.

- With each breath, become more relaxed and sink into whatever you are sitting or reclining on as your body becomes weightless and your mind and heart lighter.

- When you feel that your body is relaxed and comfortable in a quiet setting, you can begin. Check in with yourself that you are ready to go inward, connecting to a place of wisdom and courage deep within you.

- With your eyes closed, tell yourself that whatever shows up in this exercise is for your highest good and comes from your *higher self*. Trust your intuitive inner wisdom to guide you well.

- Be still and listen carefully while staying present and grounded in your body.

- Breathe softly, deeply and methodically while observing your breath and do nothing else. Incorporate this gentle form of meditation into your awareness, being present to the moment while letting go of passing thoughts, dreams, worries or distractions that trickle in to your mind.

- Continue to be present when asking to meet your *inner guide*. This *higher self* may present itself to you as an image, a thought, an older or younger part of yourself, a human or animal entity, or a vision and can remind you of something from the past or present. It could also represent the future.

- Begin to ask simple questions directed to your *inner guide* or *higher self*. First ask, "What is it you are here to tell or show me?" Then ask, "What do I need to know right now?" If you do not have a clear picture of your *inner guide* or *higher self*, ask, "Can you please show yourself to me to help me see or accept you?" Once you feel that you have connected to this part of your higher consciousness, say "thank you" and begin to return to your state of being, sitting or reclining in your quiet, comfortable place. Remember that the wisdom you receive is designed for you and will contribute to your waking life, and can be returned to when you next sit to meditate. Once you return to the here and now, then write your experience and any information you received in your *Parenting Journal*. Remain contemplative and welcome new insights that you can also record and remember.

The Best Deal: Parents in Charge; Children Have a Voice

I just think that giving a child a chance and sharing what you have with a child is one of the greatest gifts you can give yourself, as well as a child.

—Hillary Rodham Clinton, Former Secretary of State, Senator, First Lady

The Need for Structure, Leadership, and Democracy at Home

The basic operational success for any business, political, societal, or family system stems from its organizational structure and a fair and pleasant environment. In order for a group to thrive, there must be a leader and each participant, in this case, family member, must be recognized and acknowledged for his or her contribution. The leader is in charge and everyone else has a voice. Everything is intended to support "the greater good" and the group's goal or function.

Although similar dynamics exist, a family is different from a business. Individual comfort and safety and a secure permanence hold greater meaning in families. Important rules that reflect the system's goals and values are kept in place. Other aspects are subject to change, such as when members of the group contribute their feelings and ideas. Individuals are respected, no matter what their role is in the family. Family systems today vary across a diverse range of married, divorced, single, straight,

> In order for a group to thrive, there must be a leader and each participant, in this case, family member, must be recognized and acknowledged for his or her contribution.

gay/lesbian, intergenerational, adoptive, and foster parents raising children. Regardless of the family construct, adults need to be in charge while the children have a voice in the family system. In a single-parent household, the parent is in charge and the children have a voice, although sometimes roles are reversed and the mother or father need to bring the correct balance back into view. In a two-parent family, the leadership role is shared, whether the co-parents live in the same household or not. Leaders who lead well are firm and fair decision-makers. Being a good leader includes a healthy balance of effective and reasonable management balanced with received input and feedback from the team.

The purpose of leadership is to move a group in a particular direction, to accomplish a goal, reach a consensus, achieve cohesion, or develop a task force or open forum. Good leadership teaches, guides, role models, delegates, empowers and organizes. Good leadership knows when to hold on, when to make an issue, when to step back, and when to let go. "Effective parental leadership" exhibits firmness when necessary and shows love and respect consistently, instead of displaying passivity, ambiguity, or force. Leading well respects and honors the rights and voices of those who are learning. As a parent, your child follows you as a loving, kind, firm, strong, and fair leader. Since children of all ages need structure and guidance, use your position wisely and proactively. Allow the wisdom of your experience to teach and guide your child and yourself with love, respect, and empowerment. Both your needs matter, so use the wisdom you have gleaned to lead you. Capture each moment as a chance for potentially transcendent ones—real and healing times that seal your special lifetime parent-child relationship forever.

This level of leadership can take some time and practice, depending on how you have been managing your home up until this point. It is never too late to improve, institute change, communicate more deeply, enjoy greater harmony, have more fun together, heal wounds, learn, and grow. Increase healthy interactions from infancy into adulthood. You are the captain,

> Capture each moment as a chance for potentially transcendent ones—real and healing times that seal your special lifetime parent-child relationship forever.

the one steering the ship to success. Think about the kind of leader you want to become. Think about the kind of leader you already are today. What were your parents like as your family team leaders when growing up? Did their leadership style work for you? What did you wish was different? Did you feel you "had a voice" in your family? Did you feel recognized, acknowledged, encouraged, empowered, valued, and validated? Were you seen, heard and understood? Did you feel supported in who you are and who you needed to become? Were you asked for your opinion? If so, were your opinions valued about your experience with your parents, within your family or in general? If not, how does that make you feel?

In a democratic leadership model, as a *"parent leader"* you lead the way while remaining open to your child and family's feedback. Set goals while encouraging independent thought, ideas, opinions, and feelings. Each person's contribution is directed toward improving personal needs, which enhances the group's greater goals. Cradling the needs of all requires a generous, steady hand—a balancing act worth practicing.

Hold Family Meetings

When leading your family team to victory, encourage family members to be whole individuals on the team. The "greater good" should be clear to all, whether your family speaks of it specifically or not. Share family conversations about how you want to treat each other and how you all want to feel. Be aware of how you speak to your child and how you speak about your child even when he is not listening. Realize your parenting goals and parenting purpose and stylize your intentions and interactions around them. A good way to encourage and reinforce a regular open forum for safe discussions, structure, leadership, and democracy at home is to hold regular family meetings. They can be formal or more informal and creative. It is best to start when young, and is easier to maintain when it becomes a part of family tradition. Set aside a time that is good for everyone. Explain that the meeting is an opportunity for everyone to share and be heard. It is also a time to assign and

You are the captain, the one steering the ship to success. Think about the kind of leader you want to become.

negotiate chores, air grievances, share positive feedback, and discuss goals and desired rewards. Keep your child's "highest good" in mind during the whole meeting. Respond with respect, unconditional acceptance and unconditional love. Create ground rules for your meetings that include safety and mutual respect. During a family meeting, family members can vote on a name for the team and create a family slogan and team vision board. For example, a team name could be "Jones: Team Awesome" and their slogan might be "Total awesomeness since 1999." "The slogan for team "Harmony 3" might be, "We strike a healthy balance for everyone." "The Creative Minds" could live by the motto, "We rock at life." "The Brave Brainiacs" could brag, "We're smart and cool." A family vision board (also called a treasure map) could be on cardboard or cork board pinned with magazine clippings, photos, drawings, and words. An ongoing book of poems, short stories, images, and happy or significant memories can accompany it, if the family team chooses.

Depending on the age of your younger family members, the length of time and attention span will vary. It is best to tailor the meeting to your child's stage of development. Family meetings can be a combination of discussion and play and then progress to mostly conversation as your child (or children) matures. The key is to welcome conscious interaction, build honest dialogue and to communicate without blame or shame as you deal with issues and plan for fun. Over time, the consensus of your team will determine its personal style. Take votes and take turns leading each meeting. Make family meetings time-limited, forward-moving, proactive, solution-oriented, and positive. Deal with the reality of what is happening and what needs to happen in your family. Take one or two subjects per meeting and keep the content manageable. It is not a time for character assassination or ganging up on one person. A family meeting is designed to provide a structure for group interaction, support, and an impartial sounding board that welcomes individual expression, needs and issues that affect the individuals of the team.

> The key is to welcome conscious interaction, build honest dialogue and to communicate without blame or shame as you deal with issues and plan for fun.

Some individual issues may need to be kept private (especially if they are between a child and parent(s) in a household with multiple children). If the issues are generalized to parents and multiple children, then this time works well if the message is delivered with love, clarity, and specificity. Be clear about the limit you are setting and the message you want to send. Be reasonable with your child, and listen with your heart. Be open to compromise and creating positive consequences to reinforce positive change. Make sure individual needs are addressed, individual boundaries are kept, and private discussions remain private. Know that privacy and secrecy differ, the difference being that privacy does not hurt anyone and secrets can. Keep the team focus on what is best for "the greater good" and what is best for your sacred family team.

A win-win scenario encapsulates everyone in the picture. If you have family or relationship issues that need to be discussed, be clear, concise, and solution-focused. Take responsibility for your part. Ask your child for her input, opinions, and ideas for positive or negative consequences. Welcome your child's feedback about you or something you have said or done. Your child can occasionally give you consequences, too. Use this time to listen and introduce and practice good habits and skills. Always offer, suggest, and invite rewards. Make sure that you offer special family time or one-on-one time together as a regular reward and have your child choose the activity most of the time. You can introduce family meetings at any time. If an issue that requires group discussion appears or reappears, anyone at any time can ask for a family meeting to be scheduled, even if it works spontaneously. It is your family's surefire safe place to air dirty laundry, grievances, announcements, and more. It is always best to start this, like any a new habit, early rather than later in life. However, there is always room for growth, innovation, and communication at any time. A family meeting is a good start to getting your house in order, room by room, (symbolically) starting with the family room first.

> Be clear about the limit you are setting and the message you want to send. Be reasonable with your child, and listen with your heart. Be open to compromise and creating positive consequences to reinforce positive change.

Promote Healthy Communication

Healthy communication at home starts with you. Since you are in charge, you are responsible for what you say, how you say it, what you show, and what you stand for. Your job is to speak with love, respect, honesty, and positive intention toward your child. Communicate with consistency and integrity. What you say and do conveys who you are as a person and as your child's advocate and role model. This is especially true for a same-sexed child. You are the prototype of woman or man. This is also true for an opposite-sexed child when seeking a mate later (in any case, whoever your child chooses to love). Again, you are the prototypical woman or man. What you communicate with and around your child reveals what you think is important and what is not. To your child, at least initially, what you value is who you are and what your child begins to later identify with, stand for, or rebel against. What you consistently express with words, or demonstrate in actions is what your child learns is of value and what you prioritize, thus expect.

Your child wants your approval, even if he does not know how to get it. He will make mistakes or show you more negative than positive behavior sometimes. Your child wants your attention and desires to be understood, loved unconditionally, and accepted. Look beneath and beyond your child's words and behavior to his feeling and motivation. Notice your child's abilities, character, and rights as a human being, learning as he grows. Run a household where everyone speaks openly, directly, honestly, and respectfully and learns from his or her mistakes. Make home a safe place to communicate, create, connect, and safely disconnect. Communicate by listening twice as much as you speak. Be sure to be respectful and make no excuses for anything less. Teach by example and behave responsibly while also enjoying your life. Learn effective communication; allow it to grow with you and your child as you develop your parenting toolbox skill set. Acquiring skills to listen better, be responsive, teach or guide well, and aptly role model take time to learn and develop. Be patient with the organics of growth and the process

> Healthy communication at home starts with you. Since you are in charge, you are responsible for what you say, how you say it, what you show, and what you stand for.

of personal evolution over time. Be willing to acknowledge your mistakes and learn from them. You learn as you go. As long as you are alive, you can learn. Observe your child and what inspires him and take him for who he is as he is learning too.

The way you communicate with your child teaches a world of interpersonal skills. Your communication instills lessons about love, trust, respect, ethics, and justice: significant life attitudes about life itself. You teach about optimism, pessimism, or something in between. You demonstrate what you know, mostly what you were taught and have experienced. You teach what you live, discover, and decide for yourself. You teach the language you know and learn the language of your child. Whatever your native tongue, blending your styles of communication will enrich you both. When you prize communication as a key on your relationship journey, you will both travel far.

Learn effective communication; allow it to grow with you and your child as you develop your parenting toolbox skill set.

You expand your repertoire when you pay attention to what works and what does not work, starting with you. Blame-shifting, guilt-trips, and lame excuses disappear when you understand the importance of communicating well. You realize that you and your child both deserve to be heard, seen, and respected. Find the right people to talk to about details of your personal and work life. You measure your needs and spare your child the tendency to over-share as best you can. Keep yourself in check and share what is appropriate with the person to whom you are speaking. Your job is to take care of your child, and not the other way around. All individual needs of each family member matter within the constraints and definitions of who you are to each other. This is especially important as you invite new, incorporated styles of effective communication into the mix. Your repertoire for speaking and listening well, even staying calm when someone else does not, grows. You begin to master clear and appropriate expression, promote better listening, accept differences, open up verbal dialogue, and uncover new strategies to convey and receive messages.

Identify your core statement, feeling, need, or goal before you verbalize a difficult conversation or respond to one. Say what is most important to you without blame, guilt, or excuses in your tone, affect, or meaning. Use "I" statements as much as you can. Speak from your heart with a clear head. Think before you speak. Be mindful and protect your child and healthy boundaries for each of you, depending on the topic, child's age, and the situation discussed. Your child will appreciate your calm demeanor and tone. Take personal space and blow off steam before the conversation, if necessary, to project and maintain calmness.

Healthy communication between you and your child ensures an emotionally safe place in your lifetime relationship. It is the moral equivalent of you giving her a home forever. You remain in the position of authority as you begin to share knowledge, wisdom, ideas, and experiences as your child emerges into adulthood and discovers her own authority. You are still the teacher, guide, and protector in memory and on a deeply emotional level. That has been your job and will continue in the hearts of you and your grown child. What has persisted and resolved over time will remain a part of your relationship forever. Jane Isay, in her book, *Walking on Eggshells: Navigating the Delicate Relationship Between Adult Children and Parents*,[37] discusses this point beautifully. It is your job to teach the value of healthy relationships, built of love, respect, and healthy communication, starting with your own.

Find a Balance Between Limits and Compromise

Parents who teach, guide, and role model in responsible and appropriate ways create healthy growing environments resulting in healthy, happy, and well-rounded children. Most importantly, what you learn about what you can and cannot do, where you can go and where you cannot is first learned at home. The ability to create and enjoy healthy interpersonal relationships is formed within your family. Ultimately, conscious and responsible parenting creates more conscious and responsible children. There must be guidance or a "voice from the top."

> Healthy communication between you and your child ensures an emotionally safe place in your lifetime relationship. It is the moral equivalent of you giving her a home forever.

Parental expectations about moral and ethical standards point your child to their right place. Prizing your child's autonomy helps you lead and helps your child develop a strong sense of self. When you parent for life in a truly conscious way, you learn the fine balance between when to set limits and when to invite compromise. A structure that holds a fair balance between boundaries and freedoms help set positive outcomes, current and future relationships germinated from good parental leadership.

Your child, at every age, needs to feel that his feelings, opinions, ideas, and individual "voice" matter. As your child gets older, take his "voice" into consideration when negotiating, meeting his needs, and helping him interact with others in responsible ways. Be ready and willing to compromise and "meet in the middle" with your child when there is flexibility in limit setting. Sometimes the best way to avoid an unnecessary struggle, especially about a negotiable subject, is to come to a reasonable compromise. Limits are necessary when issues of safety, trust or respect are concerned and less important at other times. Knowing when to hold firm and when to invite compromise illustrates true wisdom and paves the way for peace.

Younger children, especially those who do not have developed language skills yet, will "show rather than tell" you what they are feeling. Remember that behavior is the tangible, visible, proof of what someone is feeling, wanting, or needing. When an older child or adult child does not have the words, confidence, or comfort level to express her feelings to you in plain language, she will show you what is true in her actions, as well. This is just a different, more sophisticated version of earlier "childhood acting out." Behavior tells the story better than words, you can learn to read the person's body language, like watching a political debate and turning the volume down. For example, when a young child feels sad, disappointed, angry, frustrated, or helpless, she may withdraw, cry, or throw a tantrum. When an older child, teen, or grown child feels those same feelings, she may take matters into her own hands and choose to explore and experiment. She may use wild hair dye,

> When you parent for life in a truly conscious way, you learn the fine balance between when to set limits and when to invite compromise.

> When your behavior and language as a parent are inconsistent, the underlying message is weakened, muddled, and incongruous.

sneak a tattoo or piercing or two, experiment with drugs and alcohol, or find friends or boyfriends with interests different than her own. It can be awful to see a child acting out like this, even amusing to see someone with blue hair and black-only clothes or dressed like they proudly scoured your grandmother's closet and consider it hipster fashion. It can be sad, shocking, and even intriguing if it is someone else's kid, but this kind of acting out that rejects your approval is not so palatable when it is your own child.

When your behavior and language as a parent are inconsistent, the underlying message is weakened, muddled, and incongruous. You lost your audience and will need to give a repeat performance to deliver the whole story. Let your actions match your words; your choices reflect your core values.

The goal is to reduce power struggles and poor or ineffective communication to create an appropriate balance of power in which your family can live harmoniously. When that balance is achieved, you and your child feel better about yourselves and are more productive in your lives. The ultimate best outcome is that your relationship begins to flourish. This relationship transformation evolves over time and is forever supported by the healthy bonds you forge early on, as early as possible. Start from there. Make the best of where you are because that is where you are.

As a consciously loving and firm lifetime parent, be willing to hear your child and take his needs into consideration. When your child feels recognized, acknowledged, seen, and heard, he will be more motivated to behave well and stretch to achieve reasonable expectations and goals. When your child of any age feels these things on a consistent basis, he feels acknowledged and honored. He softens his armor and his heart opens up. Rumi wrote, "In your light I learn how to love. In your beauty, how to make poems. You dance inside my chest where no-one sees you, but sometimes I do, and that sight becomes this art."[36] When he feels denied, ignored, belittled or put down he is on his own to try and meet his basic emotional needs. Positive reinforcement

> When your child feels recognized, acknowledged, encouraged, empowered, valued, seen, and heard he will be more motivated to behave well and stretch to achieve reasonable expectations and goals.

for healthy behaviors, skills, and qualities improves your child's sense of self-worth. Honoring who he is—especially his positive qualities and recognizing he does well—increases your child's personal pride. A sense of pride increases motivation to perform well, cooperate, and work better as a team member. Children need structure and goals. They want to please their parents, behave for attention, and have a chance to be their best, even in their uniqueness.

An effective way to modify your child's behavior is to find ways to notice and build upon positive behavior, to use positive reinforcement, and a natural "reward system." It helps your child feel successful, creative, and actively understand the consequences of his actions. At the same time, you are working together to create the most positive outcomes and learning environment possible. In the spirit of "two yeses for every no," think in terms of setting up "reward systems" rather than "punishment systems." Respond to mistakes or infractions with logical and sensible consequences. This may include a reasonable time out (best rule is the time out matches the child's age), losing privileges, or being unpopular with your child for a time. Avoid unrelated, extreme consequences that are used as a last resort or as a form of punishment. Be fair and reasonable, and be sure to keep your emotions calm before you set a consequence. Your job is to instill or inspire the lesson (or a life lesson) you want your child to learn.

Always keep your child's dignity and self-esteem intact. The key is to utilize affirming and creative ways to teach and guide. Let your child's self-esteem and relating patterns with you improve. Since you are in charge, make sure you let the "punishment fit the crime" so to speak. You will do this best by thinking through, brainstorming, and if you are too emotionally reactive to do so in the moment, take your own "time out." You can return to your child clear-headed, and with your older child or teen, you can calmly collaborate the best learning consequence. Your child will appreciate your love, thoughtfulness, imagination, and respect, and still learn a valuable lesson. In fact, you both will.

> Actively listen during family meetings and daily interchanges . . . put your interpretations or distractions aside and really focus in on your child's message when she is speaking to you.

Take responsibility as the parent to promote a lifetime of healthy communication between you and your child. As the team leader of your "family team," lead the way for the verbal and non-verbal dynamics. You lead by example, thus role modeling behavior to be followed or rebelled against. What you communicate is integrated into your child's experience, sense of self, and sense of other people, and the world.

Imagine, design, and reinforce healthy home ground rules with clear and reasonable expectations. The goal is to meet everyone's needs as much as you can as leader of a cooperative household. Be open to new ideas for everything except for the non-negotiable safety and boundary ground rules. Actively listen during family meetings and daily interchanges. That is to say, put your interpretations or distractions aside and really focus in on your child's message when she is speaking to you. Repeat back what you have heard to make sure that you got it right. Respond to your child and her verbal and nonverbal self-expression, respecting her individuality and emerging autonomy. Good communication is promoted in an environment where self-expression, compassion, and understanding are held in high regard.

Healthy communication involves an ongoing willingness to learn and relearn, an awakening of new ways to absorb and express information, for yourself and the ones you love.

All of these factors contribute to an overall feeling of safety and that home is a pretty good place to be. Paradoxically, varying styles of communication born from past experience or patterns used in times of conflict can re-emerge when you least expect it. Take responsibility for yourself in the same way you want your child to do. Just like there are times to talk and times to listen, there are varying ways to set limits, resolve conflicts, argue a point, or disagree. Cultivating respect and empathy for different perspectives is an invaluable skill and first learned in the family. When your child becomes an adult and engages in adult relationships (including the one with you), he will be ahead of the game with this winning communication insight. When the need to resolve conflict arises, learn to respond by first listening calmly, trying to understand the situation before reacting. That is when communication can improve.

Ideally, all family members should feel equally heard and respected and that their needs (not necessarily wants) are met completely. Since family life is rarely ideal, reach for acceptance and tolerance and find proactive solutions to problems. Modes of effective communication vary according to how open and willing family team leaders are to listen, accept, and promote healthy change. As families often operate within parameters of individual and group growth, constant equanimity is unrealistic. Specific tools and strategies must be learned.

Healthy communication involves an ongoing willingness to learn and relearn, an awakening of new ways to absorb and express information, for yourself and the ones you love. Relationships of all kinds require this kind of commitment in order to thrive. People can survive in relationships that lack continuity, stability, and healthy give-and-take, but it feels better to live with the lifelong benefits of mutual love and respect.

Be a parent who is aware and invested in your relationship with your child across time. Be open and willing to take the risk of being completely self-honest. Keep your agreements and only make agreements you can keep. If you need to re-negotiate, be clear, immediate, and forthcoming. Take risks and learn new skills as a parent and as a person. Your job is to cooperate and balance your own needs with those of your child. Cooperation wins over competition. Rebellion and power struggles will subside as your commitment to your child is (at least) as strong as your investment in yourself.

Consistently maintain interest in what your child is telling and showing you. Explore the following communication patterns and where your tendencies lie: passive, aggressive, passive-aggressive, assertive, open, closed, overt, covert, dialogue, monologue, blame, shame, tolerance, acceptance, ridicule, guilt, silence, yelling, and active listening. Create a safe space. Be the adult in charge and honor your child's small, but ever growing voice.

Homework Assignment 11

Family Meeting Practice Run

If you already hold family meetings, be sure to keep the rules of the process clear and satisfying for everyone participating. If this is new to you, then here is the basic art of how to run a successful family meeting while getting all family members involved and on-board for future meetings.

- Choose a time, perhaps during dinner or at a time when everyone is present, relaxed and open to a suggestion, new idea, or experiment.

- Make sure that your family meeting is a pleasant, regular occurrence. Keep it short in duration. Include everyone in the family and revolve it around acknowledging or improving family life.

- Focus on giving positive feedback, airing issues or grievances without blame, shame, scapegoating, or finger-pointing. Create a built-in reward system for family closeness.

- Practice active listening and positive, creative problem solving. Open the floor to individual self-expression, suggestions, creative ideas, and fun activities. Make a list of suggestions and ideas that promote enthusiasm, respect for differences, and group cohesion. Be sure to explore each element suggested by family members at future times.

- Feel free to change the location of the family meetings unless there is a particularly comfortable spot that usually attracts family members as a group to enjoy relaxing in.

- Most importantly, find a way to give everyone in the family a voice while in the family meeting.

- Remember that anyone can call or run a family meeting at any time, not only the parent in charge. This is a wonderful example of how to practice the being a parent in charge while your child has a voice in real, tangible, and recordable ways.

- Thank your child for his or her feedback and ideas and for airing sincere grievances and opinions.

- Thank yourself for encouraging healthy communication for a winning team!

- Record the important aspects of your family meeting in your *Parenting Journal*.

Begin to schedule a regular "family night" each week or a regularly scheduled "family day" when your family enjoys or explores ideas and suggestions brought up during family meetings. Make family time and special one-on-one time part of the family meeting reward system, too. This kind of open communication and natural reward system promote healthy habit patterns that will endure while creating your lifetime relationship with your child. You reinforce open communication and creative problem solving as a team effort at home, and as time moves on you foster open dialogue and discussion about subjects that you and your adult child choose wherever you are. Enjoy your role as moderator and sounding board for ongoing conversations between you.

CHAPTER TWELVE

Question Your Role Models (History/Her Story)

Each person must live their life as a role model for others.

—Rosa Parks

Where Did Your Parents Come From?

You learn and grow based on a number of key factors during your lifetime. Your experiences, identity, perception, learning style, and ability to cope and survive in the home you grew up in all play a significant part in who you are now. You cannot escape family resemblance, even if you wish you did not look like your father or sound like your mother. You may not like how your parents were raised or wish that you were raised differently. Your parents raised you the way they knew how, based on their experience of being parented and what they knew at the time. Like you, they probably learned a little bit along the way. Once you realize your own history and the history of your predecessors, you can understand how you were raised and make peace with it. You are then free to choose—based on wisdom and knowledge—the life you lead and the legacy that you leave behind.

Over time, the collective experiences, family wounds, and long-told stories are remembered and passed down.

Family relationship patterns, parenting styles, and personal defense mechanisms that helped you and everyone before you cope with life are a part of your family history. The legacy (both spoken and unspoken) of your parents, grandparents, and great grandparents and beyond are forever a part of you.

Over time, the collective experiences, family wounds, and long-told stories are remembered and passed down. They stay with generations to come as a part of a shared collective unconscious. Some elements of family life, traditions, rituals, or parenting practices are designed to stay within the family code and are healthy to pass on if it is good for everyone and helps them move forward. However, because of stressful, changing times, there is a need for increased personal awareness and wellness. In wounded or broken, dysfunctional family relationships, the practice of parenting for life inspires healing. With parenting purpose and clear intention, you can begin to realize that some family traditions need to stay in the past and new ones need to be welcomed into your life now.

If the attitude toward learning through life experience is cultivated in a family, then generational patterns can be worked on consciously, resulting in the integration of a more positive approach to family behavior and family relationships. The millions of interactions with your parents and siblings (if you have any) or even those with close extended family members forecast future family relationships, learned patterns, and relationship skills. Family culture introduces you to social skills and helps you to define them before you test your own personal relating style with friends and colleagues.

Insight Moments and Lifetime Insights

Albert Einstein said, "Wisdom is not a product of schooling but the lifelong attempt to acquire it."[38] You choose to be a lifelong learner or not. A healthy risk-taker knows how and when to learn an old or new lesson. The willingness, opportunity and decision to be open and learn are there. In that moment, you discover a special and profoundly true and personal realization: what it means to experience an insight moment. Insight moments are the opportunities that present themselves, to teach, guide and enlighten when the time is right and the person is ready. Insight moments teach and invite great clarity and meaning, for you or your child. They present themselves

. . . They stay with generations to come as a part of a shared collective unconscious.

Insight moments are the opportunities that present themselves, to teach, guide and enlighten when the time is right and the person is ready.

every day. Insight moments, when consistently welcomed and appreciated, are the building blocks for your lifetime insights. Lifetime insights are clear messages accumulated over time. They are born of awareness, introspection, and personal responsibility, and as you continue to learn, they help you to evolve. Do you practice living consciously and know what your life and insights mean on a deeper level? Observe yourself as you engage in the work necessary for success in the relationships at home, at work, and all around you. Your parents and your child, in their own time, must do the same. Your family background, including your parents' life attitude and parenting practices and your absorption or rejection of them makes a difference worth noticing. Meditate and write about your insights and see what they tell you.

You cannot choose your family, so you must deal with who and what they are. Your parents had the parents they had and now your child has you. Nothing will change the past, but you can look at the history of your family's inter-generational relationship patterns. The more you understand about how your parents were raised, maybe also how their parents were raised, the more will be revealed about how you choose your lifetime relationship with your child. You may discover understanding and empathy or something less desirable. What may have repelled you in horror and judgment before may now seem like a quirky family trait or simply something you totally want to avoid repeating. Acknowledge the experience of the past with awareness, self-honesty, and courage and walk the path of truth, knowing what was then and what is now. Hold the vision of who you are and who you want to be for your child to pave the best way for you both moving forward. After all, now that you are running the show, you can help your child find and be true to who he is and who he wants to be.

Ask yourself a series of questions and be open to all of the answers that occur to you. How were your parent(s) raised and what style(s) of parenting were your parents raised with? How were your parents' relationships with their parents during

> Lifetime insights are clear messages accumulated over time. They are born of awareness, introspection, and personal responsibility, and as you continue to learn, they help you to evolve.

their lifetime relationships? How would you characterize those relationships? What messages did your parents learn about themselves, their role models, or how to parent well? How important was developing individual self-esteem, awareness, achievement and a good lifetime relationship in your parents upbringing? Were your parents raised with similar or dissimilar values and styles when growing up? How does the way your parent(s) were parented affect the way you raise or relate to your child now? Is it the same, different, or a combination? Is it working? Are you proud of yourself as a parent? Are you proud of the relationship you are forging with your child? Are you living your parenting purpose? Do you need to institute more effective parenting skills to achieve your parenting goals with your child? Ask yourself how willing you are to adapt and introduce new and improved ways of parenting from this moment forward. Ask and then listen.

What parenting attitudes and roles have you kept alive?

Some broader questions include what kinds of communication styles were practiced in your parents' family of origin. What kind of themes and issues were passed down to you? What parenting attitudes and roles have you kept alive? Are you happy with the relationship climate and traditions you have perpetuated or not and why? What key messages did you receive from your parents? What path are you following and what messages have supported your lifetime of health and relating well? Which messages have stunted your growth?

When reading and reviewing these questions, notice your emotional and physical reactions and observe the memories that emerge. Allow your thoughts to trigger your emotions and vice versa. Learn from insights, memories, life experience, and feelings. Whatever you discover are personal treasures for you and your child and will benefit both of you. Your personal discoveries bolster self-awareness, clarity, and strength of purpose. Keep steady despite or because of your heritage, memories, and family history. Know that this time around, you are the parent and you have choices. You can stay on your current path or redirect yourself at any time you choose. The choice is up to you. Observe the impact your parenting has upon your child from day-to-day and year-to-year. You have constant opportunities to listen, receive feedback, self-correct, and deepen healthy closeness in your relationship. This time, participate actively in the daily practice of lifetime parenting, consciously nurturing your relationship for life. Use your child's feedback about you as a way to learn more about who he is and who you are as a unique and powerful force around him.

How Did You Benefit and Struggle with Your Role Models?

What were the benefits and drawbacks of your childhood role models? Do you still struggle with these drawbacks? No parent-child bond or any relationship for that matter, whether it is a lifetime one or not, is completely free of struggle or conflict. Discomfort or getting outside of one's comfort zone in any relationship can be jarring, yet has the potential to spur insight, growth and a new approach. One hopes that the mutually beneficial, close, and joyful moments outweigh the tough ones. Sometimes it is the negative experiences that determine your method to be different and more positive. It is the combination of the struggles and the joys that define you and guide you to think, feel, and act. The conflicts and joys of your significant childhood (and young adult) relationships directly affect how you behave with your child now. Consider what parts of your childhood struggles with your role models influence or thwart you as a parent today. Think about which positive aspects of your relationship with your parents have impacted you most, influence the way you parent now, and make you feel proud. Ponder the ways you parent well because of, or despite, the way you were parented. Either way, stand up tall inside yourself, do your very best and be proud.

Take a moment to recall the greatest examples your parents set for you that you continue now as a parent. If you feel there

> Ponder what parts of your childhood struggles with your role models influence or thwart you as a parent today.

are less than great or glowing examples, simply acknowledge whatever positive attitudes or experiences you can. Get in touch with the style of communication predominately used in your home when you were growing up and the ways which needs and personal expression were acknowledged or ignored. What stands out in your memory of the single most important life lesson or series of lessons that your parents taught you by example? Were your parents personally accountable for their mistakes or did they use avoidance, denial, blame, guilt, or shame to deal with family issues and conflict resolution? How about you? Is it easy or difficult for you to admit fallibility or wrongdoing to your child? Are you parenting with appropriate boundaries and healthy limits on yourself and for your child to keep her emotionally and physically safe? Can you relax and move beyond struggles or do you get stuck and defensive when there is family or parent-child conflict? In which areas do you feel you need to grow as a parent? Which areas of your parenting are successful? Think about which areas you are working on now to improve your relationship dynamics with your child. Ask and see what is revealed.

> Think about the core messages you send every day in what you say and what you do. If asked, would your child agree with your own self-assessments?

What kind of feedback do you get from strangers, your friends and family, and most importantly, your child? Even if you do not ask for it, do you take feedback as valid, invalid, or do you judge it on a case-by-case basis? How do you take care of yourself while taking care of your child? Do you take the time to practice self-care in order to balance out the care you give to your child? What messages are you sending to your child by your attitudes and actions? Think about the core messages you send every day in what you say and what you do. If asked, would your child agree with your own self-assessments? Be willing to honestly reflect and return to these questions when ready to develop your own personal parenting toolbox. Feedback from your universe can help sharpen your tools.

Rewrite the Script: Take the Best and Leave the Rest

Use what has worked for you in the past and do not feel obligated to hold onto what does not out of a misguided sense of tradition or loyalty. As a parent, use the gifts and positive experiences given to you. Use even the negative experiences from your own childhood to your benefit now. They will give you the best perspective moving forward. Take the best of what you have seen, felt, and lived, and let the rest go as soon as you are ready.

Human behavior is shaped by a combination of genetics, learned environmental responses, chosen (conscious or unconscious) defense mechanisms, and patterned habits (often formed early). You naturally cultivate your personality, learned behaviors and develop personal defense mechanisms to cope with life situations and facilitate immediate relief for specific conditions, traumas, and life events all at appropriate times. Inborn "fight or flight" responses allow you to protect yourself, whereas while individualized tendencies for relating emerge as you develop. Some defense mechanisms work at one particular time and then outlive their efficiency later. Others, especially the ones that historically have worked for you before, will continue throughout your life. According to George Eman Vaillant,[39] defense mechanisms exist along a continuum of levels, ranging from pathological (psychotic denial and delusion), immature (fantasy, passive aggression, acting out), neurotic (intellectualization, reaction formation, dissociation, displacement, repression), and mature (humor, sublimation, suppression, altruism, anticipation). However, a person defends himself to make sense of his environment, cope with it, or defend against it. This is a complex and necessary phenomenon. Sometimes the fight-or-flight urge is inappropriate and is triggered by the past and will not serve you or your relationship now. Still, parenting specifically, and modern life in general, can sometimes feel like a battlefield and protecting yourself as you see fit is your right.

> Use what has worked for you in the past and do not feel obligated to hold onto what does not out of a misguided sense of tradition or loyalty.

When ready to adopt a different perspective or coping strategy, rather than becoming pathological, self-sabotaging, or destructive in one set of defenses, new mechanisms are learned and set into motion. A young child may need to leave the scene of a "crime" that involved spilled orange nail polish on the new suede sofa and say the dog or her younger sibling did it. An older child may have the urge to run after breaking a window with his misguided baseball but will then rely on more developed skills of negotiating a payment plan of raking leaves for the cranky neighbor nearby as a means of retribution and responsibility. We choose the fight or flight response as adults, too. An adult can defend a mistake or negative pattern by denying, rationalizing, or repressing the truth of a white lie or inappropriate, massive indiscretion. Adults may cope with a gaffe or bigger blunder by shifting the blame and denying responsibility by a host of other mechanisms designed to reduce anxiety and conscious pain. The funny thing is that an adult does not think that her child or others notice, but her behavior patterns and psychological machinations are pretty easily observed and most certainly felt.

> People operate much like the hands of a clock, moving along, round and round in relationships and life experiences while the past, present, and future tick on. If not checked regularly, your timing could be off or the rhythm may be inappropriate for the person or situation.

People operate much like the hands of a clock, moving along, round and round in relationships and life experiences while the past, present, and future tick on. If not checked regularly, your timing could be off or the rhythm may be inappropriate for the person or situation. Virginia Satir plainly observed, "Life is not what it's supposed to be. It is what it is. The way you cope with it is what makes the difference."[40] Make sure you stop and become still and silent often enough to ensure that you are living with awareness and wisdom. Simply put, bring your life lessons and lifetime insights with you. Keep your insights in view; do not unwittingly leave them behind.

You have to want to learn. Life is relatively short, so make it count. Like a student who signs up for additional courses to advance his academic career, you will grasp the new information best if your focus and concentration are there. Pay attention to what is important to you. The same desire to learn and grow may or may not be true for the parents who raised you. Doing what is familiar keeps you comfortable. Even if you did not get what you needed from your parents, with awareness and determination, you can grow into the best parent your child needs you to be. On the other hand, you can maintain the status quo, follow suit without examination, and continue the cycle of how you were parented, no questions asked. Hold fast to healthy parenting and release unhealthy patterns. Get off the old, habitual merry-go-round of relating and create a healthier, less dizzying lifetime ride. Even if you need anti-nausea medication now and again, and you may feel your head spinning sometimes, it will be worth the ride and you will both know that at the end.

Evaluate your lifetime task as a parent with courage and wisdom. Ask the right questions. Find whatever it takes to lead a happy, healthy family life. If you come from a family where you enjoyed the way you were parented, respect the style your family used and fine-tune those skills for your child and your relationship now. Do what works for your family. History repeats itself unless a skilled behavioral archaeologist dares to uncover its hidden meaning. Keep the door open for ongoing connection and closeness between you and your child. Gems of parenting wisdom are unearthed when you dig for your own truth in every moment. It is up to you to hold this knowledge up to the light and behold its sparkling beauty.

Eliminate what does not work for you, your child and your lifetime relationship now. Take the best and leave the rest. Start by exploring simple solutions to complex problems. Your history is not abandoned. As an adult now, as with each generation, your task is to be better than the parents who came before you. Your child has the right and the obligation to be better than you. With time comes progress, and with progress comes greater achievement and enlightenment. Learn from your predecessors, both the good and bad. Do your best to teach well by example.

Question authority and enjoy the benefits of clear thinking for yourself. Choose sight over blindness and choose knowledge over ignorance. Question your ancestors as a vital practice of knowing who you are and who you want to be with your child.

You have to *want to learn.* Life is relatively short, so make it count.

As an adult now, as with each generation, your task is to be better than the parents who came before you. Your child has the right and the obligation to be better than you.

Draw a line in your family sand between your father's history, your mother's history, and your history before you became a parent. Imagine adjectives you want your child to use about you and your relationship as you grow, evolve and resolve your relationship. Imagine what inspires pride in you as you develop as a parent.

*H*omework Assignment *12*

History Lesson—A Timeline of Family Adjectives

Chart as far back as you can with this predominantly intellectual exercise.

- Write down in your *Parenting Journal* the names of as many relatives in your family—as far back as you can remember.

- Keep it simple. List only facts. This exercise provides insight related to family patterns and family relationships in your family lineage over time.

- Clearly, behavior in families and individual family dynamics vary and are not hereditary by nature. However, some patterns can be passed down from generation to generation, forming a sort of unspoken family agreement, making family dynamics the norm unless consciously obliterated. For example, start with your great grandparents or perhaps your great, great grandparents. Write down basic traits and attitudes to describe family patterns from stories you have heard or personal observations you have made. Go back as far as you can and jot down all you can remember, key elements in family stories, or what you were told. Come back to it later, if you wish.

- Next, use one-word adjectives to characterize family relationships you know about. Place these descriptive words next to each family member of the same last name. You need not be familiar with every relation in your family tree. Focus on what you know, have seen, felt or heard or what you have been told. You are portraying an inter-generational relationship history in words.

- Continue to write an adjective or two as you think of them.

- Notice any similarities, patterns, or tendencies that you have experienced or can relate to as a child and a parent.

- Now, on a clean page, write down all of the positive traits, attitudes and adjectives you value and envision for your family *now*, as the daily practice of your lifetime relationship with your child unfolds. Underline each word and read your list out loud.

- Make a copy of your list of current family adjectives. Review and post them if you wish, and reinforce yourself each day or week as you parent consciously on your lifetime path.

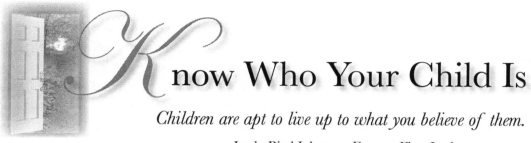

CHAPTER THIRTEEN

Know Who Your Child Is

Children are apt to live up to what you believe of them.

—Lady Bird Johnson, Former First Lady

Accept Your Child Today, Embrace Their Potential for Tomorrow

Take your job as a parent very seriously when it comes to understanding precisely who your child is as an individual. Remember that each person is born with a distinct physiology, individual temperament style, and unique personality. Each person's potential is exclusively theirs. Your child's personality is largely formed approximately by age three years and is solidly established by age five to seven years. It is shaped by both innate and environmental factors (at home and school and through early socialization).

Psychodynamic psychology and the works of Sigmund Freud along with developmental psychology and the works of Erik Erikson and others agree that a child's personality, sexuality and consciousness is formed by the end of early childhood (ages 3-5 years).[41,42] The preschool years seal the deal for the beginning of social development while the distinct patterns of self-expression and self-direction emerge. Once this is done, it can take years to see a shift in your child's unique personality.

Open your window of awareness to your child's core self and growth potential as you both evolve. Consider the simple and complex facts about her. Be curious about hidden aspects and potentials yet to evolve. This balance gives her the emotional support that she needs to be seen, heard, understood, and

> Open your window of awareness to your child's core self and growth potential as you both evolve. You will grow, in your own way, right alongside her.

encouraged by you as she grows. You will grow, in your own way, right alongside her.

Offer your undying love, respect, and encouragement. Give gifts that transcend time and material things. Give gifts that honor, encourage, and support your child and his potential and seal your relationship forever. After all, who you see in your child affects how you parent him, his friendships and potential romantic relationships, and ultimately how he may parent. Who he sees in you is what he mirrors (or deflects). The daily gifts and lessons you live and learn from teach your child to become his future self in a big way. What you make important will translate. Think and behave wisely, as your attitudes, words, and actions teach him who you think he is and who you think he "should or could be." How you perceive and respond to your child will leave him figuring out who he is, who he feels compelled to be or resist, and mixes in with his own self-knowledge.

Your child has an intrinsic need not only to receive consistent love, affection, and support from you but to also sometimes seek your attention and approval in radical ways. You may find that your typically shy child develops an over-the-top, crude or bawdy sense of humor learned from a friend to test her new repertoire and also your reaction. Your typically emotionally expressive or dramatic child may become very silent around an important issue or person or develop new sullen behaviors that seem uncharacteristic. School performance, sleep patterns, choice of friends, daily habits, and personality shifts are some examples of what you should pay attention to. Notice what she is trying to tell or show you. Realize that while she is trying to find herself, she will do anything, whether positive or negative, to get your attention. This feedback and interdependent dynamic helps to set up her sense of personal identity and self-esteem over time and will define who your child is when she is no longer a child. After a while, as she moves through the teenage years and beyond, she will need your approval and validation less. If your child still needs your approval once she is in her later teens or adulthood, encourage her to find her truth, purpose,

How you perceive and respond to your child will leave him figuring out who he is, who he feels compelled to be or resist, and mixes in with his own self-knowledge.

and passion. By then, you often cross your fingers in hopes that she will do the right thing. You can only hope that she enjoys her successes or learns from her mistakes for the next time. By choosing to accept your child and cherish her for who she is, she will develop strength and security in her separate individuality and develop the courage to go out into the world with confidence, a genuine smile, and her head held high.

Much of our personal identity stems from the experience in the home and family. Smart parents leave room for interpretation, exploration, and recognition of a child's unique, emerging self. Despite any differences in communication or temperament styles between you, your child is precious and needs your enduring support and consistency as the loving, firm adult by his side.

Get to know who your child is and who she is becoming on a regular basis. Stay open and curious. Every moment creates an opportunity for your relationship to develop. Give both of you permission to be honest, accountable, and heal in the process of relating through life. Both you and your child's emotional armor will be stripped away, leaving more room for peace, understanding, and a true heartfelt connection between you. The melody of communication and connection will flow more gracefully, and the lyrics will be written as you dance together through life. The music will be fluid and open to interpretation and you will find new ways of relating. Suspend judgment until after the dance is over. Be the model of unconditional love, respect, and support. Your relationship is not preprogrammed or set to the tune of an old song. The past influences who you are and how you relate, but does not solely dictate the present or predict the future. Your parent-child relationship continues to develop as a work in progress while you each learn and grow together, apart, and along the way.

Welcome greater freedom of self-expression and life lessons to be learned in an open, workable dialogue as your child matures into middle school and high school years. That time

By choosing to accept your child and cherish her for who she is, she will develop strength and security in her separate individuality and develop the courage to go out into the world with confidence, a genuine smile, and her head held high.

does not have to be classified as a terribly difficult one, riddled with misunderstandings and hostile or conflicted power struggles. You may discover that it is a time for mutual self-discovery to build your relationship through personal insights and shared healing. You establish boundaries, natural consequences, and deepen your love. Learn to go with the flow as you evolve your lifetime relationship. Think of your lifetime relationship as a work in progress. Judgment and unhealthy patterns of relating should be replaced by honest living, with respect and openness to every positive and healthy possibility in each moment.

Embracing who a person really is helps him to feel self-worth and move forward in who he will become. Since you are the key model for your child, model self-knowledge and reinforce what you value and make important with consistency. Being honest means complete self-disclosure; this includes releasing pain from the past, releasing learned excuses for negative behavior, and releasing denial. When you reveal your authentic self appropriately (keeping the parent-child, not parent-friend, boundary intact while exploring limits and more mature subjects over time) and encourage this same authenticity in your child, your relationship becomes more honest. You will be consistently surprised by your child's nuances, growth, mistakes, and accomplishments. Give him room to live in a physically, emotionally, and spiritually safe environment. He will perceive you as a consistently loving, respectful, empathetic, and nurturing parent. The gift of love, learning, and acceptance will be forever shared between you.

Imagine reaching out to stop the hands of time. Today's events impact, influence, and create tomorrow's realities. Be fully present to observe what you see and hear in the moment while you imagine its future effects. Take the time to pay close attention to all of the cues, hints, and repetitive words and behaviors that your child shows you. She is showing you who she is. See someone uniquely beautiful, deserving, and separate from you, yet a part of you. Discover who your child is and who you are in each interaction. Pay attention to how you feel when

Since you are the key model for your child, model self-love and reinforce what you value and make important with consistency.

parenting and take note of what is easy or joyful for you and what areas feel more difficult, stifling, or just plain impossible. Remember that every age and stage is great. There is no best age or stage of development. You, as the parent have your own reactions, triggers, tools, and comfort levels with what your child presents to you each step of the way. As Marianne Williamson says, "The more room you give yourself to express your true thoughts and feelings, the more room there is for your wisdom to emerge."[43] Acknowledge and own your thoughts and feelings internally (or with someone you trust) so you can parent with as much wisdom and grace as possible.

Does your child remind you of someone else in your life? Does your child's temperament match yours or someone else who triggers you? Your child may be unlike anyone you have ever known before, or he may remind you of yourself, a parent, spouse, ex-spouse, sibling, friend, or family member. Keep feelings of hurt, anger, expectation, blame, or judgment separate from your feelings about your child. Release associated feelings based solely on similar personality traits that your child may trigger in you from previous relationships. Physical and behavioral similarities may also evoke strong feelings and responses. This could be true in any family, whether intact, dysfunctional, or divorced and blended. It depends on how cooperative or conflicted that co-parenting relationship is. If a child had the same pouty scowl or abrasive personality trait reminiscent of someone else, a parent could feel hostility, and then feel guilty about this hostility projected toward the child.

If and when you realize that your child reminds you of someone else and it is not a cheery or easily positive experience for you, own it. First realize this similarity. Is it the voice, hair color, dynamic between you or mannerism you could be seeing and responding to about someone else from another time? Your ability to take advantage of your growing powers of observation and building up your *insight moments and lifetime insights* (as described in Chapter 12) are part of the countless opportunities for your own healing. Learn to resolve your unmet needs and

> Remember that every age and stage is great. There is no best age or stage of development. You, as the parent just have your own reactions, triggers, and comfort levels with what your child presents to you each step of the way.

unresolved issues and feelings from another relationship or time and separate them from when your child came into your life. Work on recognizing, dealing with, and letting go—whenever you reach this insight. Your child was blessed with the gifts of her own identity, apart from and including all of her genetic predecessors. While you learn to see who your child reminds you of, work on seeing her for herself.

Consciously see your child, at every age, as a whole person who is continuing to grow every day. Choose to see yourself in the same light. Keep an open mind and heart; notice the positive ways you spend your time together. Abandon any preconceived definition of who you think your child is. Release static perceptions of what you think you know.

Get to Know Your Child's Temperament, Learning Style, and Spirit

> There is no one on this earth who is exactly like your child; allow him to explore, protect him from comparison, know it and enjoy that fact.

You know your child's personality, likes, dislikes, learning style, underlying spirit, and emerging individuality better than anyone. Your child's gifts, beauty, abilities, strengths, desires, personal expressions, feelings, aptitudes, and challenges are unique to him. Do not compare him to anyone else (to his face or behind his back), not even to a sibling. Get to know your child and remain open to learning more about what makes him tick and what makes him special. Grow your knowledge by observing, listening, and suspending judgment and forced expectations. The late and great Theodor Geisel, also known as Dr. Seuss, wrote to children and the parents who read to them in *Oh, The Places You'll Go!* He wrote, "You have brains in your head. You have feet in your shoes. You can steer yourself in any direction you choose. You are on your own, and you know what you know. And you are the guy who will decide where to go."[44] There is no one on this earth who is exactly like your child; allow him to explore, protect him from comparison, know it and enjoy that fact.

Enjoy the adventure of unconditional love and acceptance and pass that attitude on to your child. Your child may be a lot like you, may be a little like you, or may be nothing like you. Do not take it personally. There is no good or bad when it comes to individual style, preference, or soul differences. Enjoy the adventure of learning if your child is naturally more passive or assertive, introverted or extroverted, solitary or social, serious or playful, intellectual, physical, creative, practical, or spiritual. Understand how your child learns and remembers best. Her learning style may be visual, auditory, kinesthetic, right-brained, left-brained, or uni-brained. Notice your child's natural tendencies and encourage her natural aptitudes and personal style. Your child cannot be compared to anyone else. Recognize that she will adapt new aspects of her personal repertoire as she experiences walking the path of her life.

Enjoy relating, interacting, and observing your similarities and differences. Either way, you both are who you are. Fortunately, the world has lots of room for all kinds of people. Each style of learning and self-expression has its place. Know that whatever natural temperament, learning style, and spirit your child possesses, these traits can be acknowledged and engaged to yield the most positive results. Your child can learn to utilize his natural aptitudes and tendencies to his advantage with proper encouragement and consistent support. It is up to you to decide if the environment will provide that. You will find that a key in building a good lifetime relationship with your child is to actively honor who your child really is in the present and who he is becoming as he learns, grows, and develops into his future.

Allow for Trial and Error in Your Child's Learning Process

Allow for the natural process of taking one step forward and two steps back when learning and growing. There is no way around it. Your child (like you) will make mistakes and will, you hope, learn from them. It is natural to make mistakes while learning. Louise Hay in her book, *You Can Heal Your Life*,[45] expresses this sentiment with self-forgiveness, humor, making amends, and learning from the mistakes (as well as the successes).

Your child may be a lot like you, may be a little like you, or may be nothing like you. Do not take it personally. There is no good or bad when it comes to individual style, preference, or soul differences.

Mistakes are natural and to be expected. Expect blunders of all kinds to happen, so when they do you will not be surprised. They are inevitable. The key is to learn from our mistakes or oversights as quickly as we can. Sometimes the best and only way to learn and grow is when you have an *insight moment* (described earlier) with sincere gratitude and insight gained after a problem or mistake has occurred. Each *insight moment* builds the foundation for *lifetime insights*, which come around as often as the big, blue moon. Still, each insight helps you and your child to evolve on your prospective paths, improving as people in your relationship. We learn how to do something right or better by the wisdom earned from having made a mistake in the first place. The process of being a "student of life" requires the ability to be humble, open, and receptive. When you acknowledge gaps in your own knowledge, true self-awareness, introspection, accountability, and personal mastery begin. You can forgive your child's mistakes, teach her to forgive herself as you recognize and learn from your own. You know that you are both human, capable of naivety, fallibility, insight, and renewal. As a conscious lifetime parent role-model: show that you can learn from your mistakes (both big and small). Exemplify growth, maturity, truth, and integrity. Show a sense of confident pride mixed with receptive humility and make change happen.

To adequately offer encouragement and support, some self-discovery and inner reflection or personal introspection is required on your part. "Do the difficult things while they are easy and do the great things while they are small. A journey of a thousand miles must begin with a single step," as Lao Tzu so poignantly illustrated in the *Tao Te Ching*.[46] The more insight you gain about yourself, the more you realize the perfection of human imperfection. If through this introspection you discover the need for greater inner peace, motivation, knowledge, or uncover serious flaws and impediments to your well-being, then find the support you need and the courage to change.

Since your ultimate job is to love, protect, nurture, guide, and teach your child effectively, be as clear as you can be with

You can forgive your child's mistakes, teach her to forgive herself as you recognize and learn from your own. You know that you are both human, capable of naivety, fallibility, insight, and renewal.

your own tendencies and traits. Learn to create a temporary distance to become emotionally neutral if you realize you are feeling triggered or do not have effective coping skills in the moment. Explain your need for time or space and that you will reconnect at a specific time. Step back from habitual emotional reactions in order to see what is happening in the moment with your child. If your temperaments or momentary needs conflict, take responsibility for your own personal triggers, lack of focus or improper responses and your relationship can flourish. Pave the way for harmony to exist between you. With an open, emotionally neutral, and receptive attitude, you will automatically shift negative interactions. You will create more positive, growth-centered, solution-oriented, happy moments now and for the days to come. Hypocrisy and denial are not appropriate defenses for the conscious, mindful lifetime parent. Self-revelation, personal accountability, and effective communication serve this significant relationship much better. Know yourself, lay the foundation of your safe lifetime relationship, trust your child and get out of his way as he finds out who he is.

Your child's learning curve requires you to be a patient and compassionate caregiver. Your child needs to experience trial and error (like you do) and know that you support his natural process of a life under construction. Accepting and allowing for trial and error in your child's process correlates with the learning curve necessary for him to achieve and progress in the best way he can. Whether your child gets it right or gets it wrong, he learns about himself and the world. That attitude helps you to experience your child as a human work of art, gift of science, and a growing and evolving human being. Every person deserves to be seen, felt, heard and understood in each moment, for who they are and what they need to say. They deserve to express themselves—warts and all. Every person, including your child, deserves the chance to make progress, fall, and get back up again while being loved and accepted as the growing master of his own fate. Your job is to cheer him on, no matter where he is.

Hypocrisy and denial are not appropriate defenses for the conscious, mindful lifetime parent. Self-revelation, personal accountability, and effective communication serve this significant relationship much better.

Homework Assignment 13 ⚷

Parent Coaching Session—Examine Your Perceptions of Your Child

Describe your child in your *Parenting Journal* according to the following criteria:

- List at least five or six positive personality traits about your child.

- Of these personality traits, which ones do you like, love, and admire?

- Of these personality traits, which ones can you relate to, and which ones can you not?

- Now list at least five or six of your child's natural talents and interests. Think of everything.

- Notice if the last list repeats anything from the first list.

- Of these natural talents and interests, which ones do you admire and can you relate to?

- What are your hopes, dreams, and expectations for your child now and across his or her lifetime?

- What have you learned so far and are willing to continue to learn from your child?

- How do you convey your love, respect, empathy, and appreciation for your child? Notate changes in this skill over time.

- From a scale of 1-10, rate how well you listen to your child.

- Rate how well your child would say you listen to him or her, and "get" him or her.

- Record three Priority Focus Parenting Goals you have right now to improve your parental toolbox. Make sure these goals are important to you, clear, realistic, specific, and can be approached in manageable and proactive steps. These are the three most important, relevant, core priorities for you as a parent while you engage with, relate to, and think of your child.

- Next, write down three Obstacles that prevent or impede you to achieving your goals. Be as truthful and bluntly honest with yourself as possible. Do not hold back.

- Lastly, convey three Action Steps you will take to work toward accomplishing your Parenting Goals at this time. Give yourself a realistic Target Date to reach for, that is just past your comfort zone yet is absolutely doable.

- When you reach the date for your goal, check in with your progress.

- Choose to continue with your existing list or fine-tune your three Priority Focus Goals, three Action Steps, and three current Obstacles and set another Target Date.

- Become more aware of your perceptions of your child.

- Honor, admire, and enjoy your child when together and apart, as much as possible.

After the set period of time, check your progress and re-evaluate the steps necessary to achieve your goals or partial goals and how to fine-tune your future success. Record your findings in your *Parenting Journal* and check your preconceptions, over-reactions and judgments at the door.

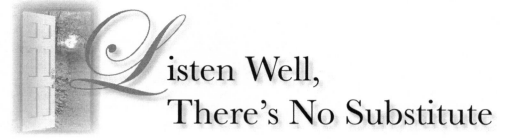

CHAPTER FOURTEEN

Listen Well, There's No Substitute

The first duty of love is to listen.

—Paul Tillich, Philosopher and Theologian

What Do Butter, Sugar, and Good Listening Have in Common?

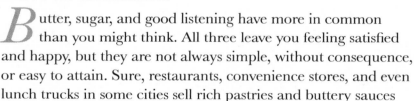

*B*utter, sugar, and good listening have more in common than you might think. All three leave you feeling satisfied and happy, but they are not always simple, without consequence, or easy to attain. Sure, restaurants, convenience stores, and even lunch trucks in some cities sell rich pastries and buttery sauces to tempt the most self-disciplined person. Still, all three are just occasional treats for many of us. Feeling truly heard by another person is deeply satisfying, necessary, and sometimes feels like a treat more than a regular occurrence. It feels appropriately fulfilling, and fills a hungry place inside with feelings of being loved, heard, respected, and known. Being listened to opens the heart and conveys a strong sense of being honestly seen, heard, valued, cherished, and understood. When you learn how to listen well, your child is acknowledged and you teach your child the same. Listening well and feeling heard should not just be a rare occurrence, or a periodic perk. Rather, it is best to be a consistent part of your everyday lifetime parenting practice. It is a requirement for you both to regularly and personally connect, one conversation, comment or silent moment at a time as you travel your relationship journey together.

> Feeling truly heard by another person is deeply satisfying, necessary, and sometimes feels like a treat more than a regular occurrence.

Consistently listening well to your child further secures a safe "home zone" when you listen with empathy and emotional neutrality. Create a cooperative household and family team. Take the time to stop, focus, put down your weapons (so to speak), and listen calmly with an open mind and heart. Drop your defenses and whatever you are doing to listen closely to your child's truth, ideas, wishes, hopes, dreams, feelings, fears, and conflicts. Sometimes, you need to switch gears that very moment to give your undivided attention and let everything else go for a time. If necessary, you can ask your child if the situation is urgent or if it can wait. Use your parenting intuition and observational skills to answer that question as well. You know the importance of being heard and the validation that it brings. It feels like a pleasure, treasure, and a joy that is lived in the moment. Your child needs and deserves to feel loved, heard, accepted, and respected by you and to take comfort in the fact that she can tell you anything. Your child, at every age, needs and deserves this basic respect as much as possible, so set your sights on offering your best every day. Do not think of listening well as an irregular indulgence. Over time, your child will savor the knowledge that your ears, heart, and mind are open to her each step of the way.

Butter and sugar substitutes on the market today are designed to mimic the "real thing," but so often they lack the rich flavors and ultimate joy that consuming the "real thing" offers. Some things cannot be duplicated and need to be enjoyed as-is. The same rule applies with the practice of good listening. There are no substitutes for deep listening, active listening, honest care, love and respect, receptivity and validation. Your child knows, as you know, when he is not being listened to fully and without distraction, judgment, or urgent time limits. How often do you as a parent (like all of us) pester your child about how he "never listens"? You have to tell him things 8.7 million times sometimes (or at least it feels that way) before you even see the tiniest flicker of acknowledgment in his eyes or improvement in his behavior. How many sentences start with, "How many

> Your child needs and deserves to feel heard, accepted, and respected by you and to take comfort in the fact that she can tell you anything.

times do I have to tell you…?" You expect, require and sometimes demand that your child listen to you. Yet, how often do you stop to ask yourself how well you listen to him? Give the genuine gift of good listening. There is no substitute.

To Listen Well is to Learn Well

We are born with two ears and one mouth so that we listen twice as much as we speak. There is perfect wisdom in what Oliver Wendell Holmes, Sr. said in *The Poet at the Breakfast Table*, "It is the province of knowledge to speak and it is the privilege of wisdom to listen."[47] You have wisdom and your child does too. Learn by listening (and make this a practice in all your relationships). In order to listen skillfully, put your own agenda aside to make room for your child's experience, needs, or point of view. Depending on your child's age and stage of development, as you listen you are better equipped to support your child, take care of her, and help her be herself. Teach and model the spirit of cooperation as leader of your family team. Part of listening well is to be willing to collaborate with the other person to meet their need. The same is true with your child as you ask her to cooperate and listen to you in return. Express mutual love and respect as an ordinary, everyday practice. This is a vital component of raising a child and developing the practice of parenting for life. You are steadily creating your lifetime relationship with your child. Where you both are at any given moment is real. However, as a parent you must have the wisdom to discern when your needs and perceptions matter less and your child's needs and perceptions (in youth and adulthood) matter more. Make sure that you listen far more, or at least half as much, as you talk with your child at every age and stage. You will learn and appreciate much more that way.

Teach your child, at every age or stage, the lessons of love and respect, personal accountability and responsibility, good communication, and empathy. Clearly share and teach what you value and what is important to you as a parent within your family culture that supports and nourishes family members.

You expect, require and sometimes demand that your child listen to you. Yet, how often do you stop to ask yourself how well you listen to him? Give the genuine gift of good listening. There is no substitute … We are born with two ears and one mouth so that we listen twice as much as we speak.

What matters to you is what you pay attention to. As Robert Brault said: "Enjoy the little things, for one day you may look back and discover they were the big things."[48] Whether memorable, exhilarating or subtle, enjoy the intricate process of life with your senses wide open. There is information and happiness available to you at every turn.

Develop a secondary awareness sensitive to the needs, experiences, and perceptions of the growing person you are relating to love, teach, and guide. It is often in your interactions together that your child learns the most. Your child learns from your example and consistent behavior. You are a model to your child in your conduct, and secondarily in your words. Posture, mannerisms, the way you walk, values and habits all play a role. However, when your words and behaviors match, you teach powerful lessons. By staying true to your word, you are a reliable mentor who models integrity, trustworthiness, and a sense of security that your word is your bond; you are someone who can be counted on.

There are four types of listening: 1) inactive listening—being present without active attention or absorbing shared information, 2) active listening—hearing what is said, repeating it back while concentrating on the message, and absorbing it, 3) selective listening—hearing only what you want to hear without hearing what is being said, and, 4) reflective listening—active listening, interpreting the information, and observing how it is being said. Active listening and reflective listening are the most effective and most complex but reflective requires more subtle receptive skills. Both require putting one's personal emotional response on hold while being fully aware of another's point of view and experience. To listen well does not require that you understand or agree for yourself, but that you do understand and revere someone else's truth and experience. You must place your needs aside and listen to understand, gather information, and enjoy. With wisdom and in time, you learn more about the importance of learning by listening; letting go of your own

> To listen well does not require that you understand or agree for yourself, but that you do understand and revere someone else's truth and experience.

agenda, judgment, or preconceptions. Over time, you learn how important it was, and still is, to simply listen.

Your sensitivity, listening skills, and devotion to the practice of acting as your best lifetime parent directly influence your child's self-esteem, self-expression, and self-honesty. You become the model for respect, empathy, good communication, and lifetime learning. Teach by positive example with clear and loving words, eye contact and relaxed tones of voice as you are able. Make agreements that you can keep, renegotiate agreements if necessary, and maintain emotional safety all the while. Encourage a closeness that is natural and not forced. Stop, look and listen with your ears and your heart. Your child will appreciate it and feel important. You will learn, this time as the student, while your child acts as the teacher, educating you about unconditional love and about him.

When reading a riveting novel, you are called upon to silently "listen to" the plight of its characters and make room for all the themes and voices to exist within your imagination. You observe with your mind's eye and listen with your internal ear. You discover each person's unique point of view and accept it as a part of understanding the character, theme, and plot. You learn to climb a metaphoric ladder out of yourself and into someone else's mind, heart, and life story. Watching your child evolve is similar to engaging in a novel as the characters develop and the plot thickens. You can read, listen internally, and process while you are observing. The difference is that, as a reader, it is not personal. You are like an innocent voyeur or a silent audience member as you can feel, yet remain disconnected. However, as a parent, you are not emotionally detached, nor easily able to coldly ignore, or step away from your child or your own triggers and reactions while you are listening and observing. You have a strong emotional attachment and a wide range of feelings and shared experiences to draw upon while witnessing who your child is becoming. Make sure you open your perspective to who your child (really) is, rather than who you want her to be.

Your sensitivity, listening skills, and devotion to the practice of acting as your best lifetime parent directly influence your child's self-esteem, self-expression, and self-honesty.

A good practice is to consistently employ "active listening" (as defined earlier in this chapter) and pay close attention to what your child says. Give her the floor then feed back to her what you heard (or thought you heard) by saying, "What I heard you say is..." Listen with love; suspend judgment, opinions, and emotional reactions. Ask your child after you repeat her statement back to her, "Is that I said what you meant?" or "Did I hear you right?" Any question that reflects the message back to the sender to clarify it is demonstrating active listening. This is done several times until as the listener, you get exactly what your child is trying to say. This system of active listening using neutral, open, and loving detachment allows you to listen well and develop the "ear of compassion" needed for your fertile, growing relationship. With this objectivity, you detach with love, allow for your child's experience and remain invested and emotionally connected within a safe distance. You are not necessarily stepping out of the situation, issue or relationship— you are simply processing your child's point of view without emotional co-dependency. You listen without the need to fix, rescue or react. Choose wisely when to respond and when to remain quiet, depending on the needs of your developing relationship. You will listen better and will be less reactive. This will result in increased understanding, an emotionally safe "home zone" and a path toward lasting health and peace between you.

> This system of active listening using neutral, open, and loving detachment allows you to listen well and develop the "ear of compassion" needed for your fertile, growing relationship.

The Best Present of All

When you provide your unconditional love, learn to be fully present and support your child's well-being, you show your child that you are "there" for him in a deep way. Show in behavior that you can put your own needs, agenda, or distractions aside and simply become present and open for your child. Turn off your cell phone, step away from the computer, iPad, Kindle, or reader and read the person in front of you. Be available in the moment and demonstrate loving and firm emotional support. Actively listen, self-correct, and convey that your care is endless. Keep your child as safe as you can while accepting his need to experience life and his need to have limits. Serve as a sounding board, mirror, and caretaker of the detailed components of his precious life.

This loving objectivity allows your child to evolve at her own pace and develop her own sense of self and the world in a natural and gradual way. When you practice the art of lifetime parenting, you choose to actively listen, offer unconditional love, support, and encouragement: basics that every child needs. You become acutely aware that *love and respect go together and respect is a two-way street.* You make time for communication, laughter, conversation, and fun in an intentional way, which develops your skills as a proficient lifetime parent. This is part of your job. Whether you like what you are hearing or not, you are required to simply listen, especially before you react or respond. Put your emotional reactivity on hold while you open your heart and mind to neutrality as a calm, open slate. If you are like most people in our modern world, you could do with less stress or drama in your life. As you stay less impulsive in your reactions and emotions, you create less stress and less drama. When you are more objective and neutral rather than reactive, you watch and listen as your child grows away from you progressively, which is her right and opportunity to seize when the time is right.

How to Process New Information Well

Your job as the parent is certainly a lofty one: you truly "raise" the body, mind, spirit, and consciousness of another. Once it begins, it never ends. What happens between you and your child now sets the stage for your future relationship (and your child's future relationships). Remember the influence you have as you relate to your child every day in each interaction. Take responsibility for what you bring to the table—your history, your skills or lack thereof, your attitudes, temperament, communication styles, stress levels, priorities, and distractions. The same is true for all other relationships in your life. Take responsibility for yourself. Capture opportunities to express

Be available in the moment and demonstrate loving and firm emotional support. Actively listen, self-correct, and convey that your care is endless. You exhibit care and that you always will care.

and enjoy an open forum for ongoing dialogue, mutuality, and respect when it comes to your child. Your lifetime relationship will benefit from focusing on good communication and knowing how and when to be loving and firm. When you signed up for this job, no matter how it happened for you, it was a lifetime commitment. You have been gifted with a life to nurture, encourage and support, and then let go. You are given a chance to have a huge impact on her world. You have been given the chance to change the world because of how you parent her for the future. You have been given a chance to let her change your world.

When you hear your child speak, take a moment to consider his new or repeated information. Your advice or comments do not have to follow immediately. You choose to react emotionally or become emotionally present and neutral. As described earlier, active listening by its very nature cannot be substituted by inactive or passive listening. It is the practice of purposefully hearing what a person is saying then repeating back the essential words and meaning to the speaker. The active listener asks the speaker if what she thought she heard was accurate or inaccurate. The speaker has the opportunity to clarify to make his words, feelings, and desires more clearly understood. It is only effective if the speaker responds back that the listener "got" what he said (or what he meant). To listen actively is to actively learn about another person or at least acquire their point of view.

As an active listener or active learner, you become a knowledgeable and trusted friend and a more revered teacher and guide. What better adjunct role to play when providing care to your child? Your ego is put aside and your child's emotional safety and sense of self is explored and protected. As Gerald Jampolsky sagely said in *Love is Letting Go of Fear*, "You can be right or you can be happy."[49] With that perspective, it is useless to routinely try to prove your point or need to be right; it is more important to be happy and healthy and inspire your child to be happy and healthy, too.

. . . it is useless to routinely try to prove your point or need to be right; it is more important to be happy and healthy and inspire your child to be happy and healthy, too.

The next step is the art of processing the information you heard or observed from your child. It could be new information or old, revised details presented in a new way. Wait for the feedback you receive and remain as objective as possible before reacting. Be willing to put aside personal projections and experience your child as a whole person, a clean and clear slate in the moment, worthy of exploration and expression. Gather information about your child's message. Be a good listener without judging or giving advice. The gift of patient listening sows a collaborative garden of acceptance and support. When you do this, communication will flourish between you. Discover that closeness sits next to understanding in your shared relationship.

Learn how to self-correct, if necessary, moment-to-moment. You will both be glad you did.

You possess the guiding power to reinforce strategies that help promote happiness and harmony, self-worth and inner security. As the leader of your team, you are responsible to lead well, build trust and provide workable interactions and solutions. Those qualities carry more weight than perpetuating conflict, power struggles, competition, and personal ego gratification. If you find yourself falling short of your ideal role as parental guide or role model, you have the power to learn the skill of self-correction. Learn how to self-correct, if necessary, moment-to-moment. You will both be glad you did. Be aware of your words and behavior. Choose to correct or re-direct your mistakes with the intention of creating win-win outcomes as much as possible. You may remember from way back in your early school days a teacher or little league coach saying, "It does not matter who wins or loses; it is more important how you play the game." The message then was to strive to do your best. The message now is exactly the same.

Since both your needs matter, negotiate for the benefit of both you and your child when you communicate. Take a breath and start over—when you need to—and model this behavior as leader of your family team. This means you may need to stop and breathe, take a walk, and find your inner calm as you wait to respond. This behavior teaches your child about self-control and personal discipline. You project a willingness to build trust, fairness, peace and cooperation. Teach your child to stop and take a moment before responding to a situation that may be challenging, too. Promoting calm when chaos occurs can prevent bad situations from becoming worse. Invite the skill of self-correction to be a part of everyday life, as mistakes (and learning from them) are necessary parts of the human experience. Allow mistakes as part of being mortal and imperfect in your family. This forgiving attitude allows you, your child, and your family to grow at individual speeds.

Communication becomes a limitless process defined by unlimited opportunities. Mahatma Gandhi said, "If we could change ourselves, the tendencies in the world would also change. As a man changes his own nature, so does the attitude of the world change towards him. ... We need not wait to see what others do."[50] I say, be the change you need in your life and in your family. Somebody has got to take a stand; someone has to take the lead. Be aware of your immense responsibility as a parent. Notice how your positive changes inspire positive change in your family. Someone has got to be the hero. Why not make that person you?

Choice is everything. Become clear about the nature and quality of the relationship you are circumnavigating. The degree of closeness you seek and the healthy boundaries you develop help you choose what to say and do. They also enable you to listen and respond as best as you can. Keep your triggers away from the conversation and deal with your child as a unique individual. Be proactive and learn to improve the interactions in your relationship each step of the way. Take responsibility for yourself and how well you listen. Notice when you fail to pay enough attention to your child. Recognize when your "hidden agenda" (stress and distractions) hinder how well you listen. When done skillfully, the way you relate to your child can transform your relationship. Since communication is one part intention and two-parts implementation, choose the path of conscious intention to best guide you.

> When done skillfully, the way you relate to your child can transform your relationship.

*H*omework Assignment *14*

Practice Active Listening

This exercise is an opportunity for you to flex your listening muscles. Practice letting go of your agenda and preconceived notions. All you have to do is ask the right questions and then be receptive to the answers.

- Find a time to connect with your child. This is preferable when done in person, but it can be done over the telephone or with Skype on the computer with an older adult child. The phone works best if prior experience with active listening has occurred while in person.

- Take this time to practice the acquired skill of "active listening." Refer back to earlier descriptions of listening styles in this chapter.

- Communicate in words and actions that this exercise is intended to give your child "the floor." You say it, you mean it, and you provide it.

- Keep the session brief, between 5 and 10 minutes, and not exceeding 20 minutes or so.

- Ask your child if there is anything that he or she needs to tell you, something important to him or her. If your child has nothing pressing to share, ask to share any topic, idea, goal, feedback, or fun fact for you to practice listening well as a parent. Assure him or her that he or she will have uninterrupted freedom and space to talk.

- Listen to what he or she has to say to you and repeat it back to him or her. Start by saying, "I heard you say" or "What I hear you say is" and complete the sentence or thought that you heard without any inserted value judgments or reactions as best as you can back to your child. Reserve judgments, reactions, or responses.

- After you repeat it back then ask "Did I get it right?" or "Is that what you meant to say?" Listen for your child's confirmation that he or she was heard correctly. If you misheard, ask for the message again and listen carefully, getting yourself out of the equation.

- When feeding back what you heard, imagine saying it from your child's point of view. You may develop greater empathy toward your child as a result of putting yourself more deeply in his or her place.

- When receiving your responses, remain open to hearing how well you heard what your child said in the first place. Continue this active listening role play back and forth until your child feels that you "got it."

- Thank your child for trusting you with something important to him or her. Thank your child for telling you his or her truth (even if some of it stung or shocked you). Allow the new information you received to linger in your thoughts and feelings and use it as a tool to become closer.

Over time, this exercise bolsters trust and can be used to resolve parent-child conflicts. When done with care, it can deepen understanding and empathy and will promote compromise in your lifetime relationship.

CHAPTER FIFTEEN

*P*ay Attention: Understanding Derived from Observation

Learn to see what you are looking at.

—Christopher Paolini, author

As a parent, your observational skills help you uncover your child's intentions, feelings, and uniqueness.

Be an Archaeologist or Behavioral Scientist

*Y*our relationship with your child is a work in progress. Learn to become aware of his emerging independence and "personhood." You can do this by waiting for the natural clues as you listen, observe, and then discover more of who he is as he develops. As a parent, your observational skills help you uncover your child's intentions, feelings, and uniqueness. You become an archaeologist, a behavioral scientist, and an informed parent while you promote open dialogue in an environment of trust, love, and respect. Search for new knowledge by accepting clues and data from what you notice. Allow a clear line of vision, a breeding ground for new insight and interpersonal learning. Learn what makes your child tick and what advances your special bond.

Put yourself back in school. Imagine sitting in your chair, listening to the teacher or professor at the head of the classroom. Be aware of your attitude about learning new information, integrating insight or knowledge, and your comfort and desire to incorporate new ideas. Notice what kind of learner you are and what holds your attention. Are you more of a visual, auditory, or kinesthetic learner? Remember this scene of being back in time, back in school when it was natural for you to watch and listen to everything around you openly and calmly. Remember that your task was to receive new information as significant, meaningful, and relevant, not to ignore, change, or veto the information you received. However you best process, retain, and recall information gives you a clue into the kind of learner you are. Your child has the same inherent tendencies and ways to learn, emote, remember, and express herself as you, but she just may do it in a different way.

Observation, listening, reading, and participating in relaxing activities, such as meditation or exercise all help to open the mind to new learning experiences. Seas of key lessons are available for you to learn every moment of your life if you are willing to simply pay attention. Navigating the relationships in your life requires understanding derived from dialogue and observation. Although it sounds simple, in time and with practice, developing the observational skills at your disposal will enrich your relationship with your child. You will be able to stifle your mental chatter and expectations by better exploring how to make more sense of your world and your child's world. Invite deeper levels of awareness in your life experience and allow your own perceptions and emotions to shift and evolve. With objectivity, you will no longer be at the mercy of your feelings and thoughts. Step out of the way, decide to let go of preconceived notions, and allow your mind to open to new and better ways of gathering data.

> Navigating the relationships in your life requires understanding derived from dialog and observation.

As you parent for life, simple observation can help you consciously develop deeper levels of receptivity and understanding for your child and where he is going. Welcome new perceptions of your amazing growing child. If you understand the multiple facets of your diamond-in-the-rough, closer feelings and better parenting ideas will result. Your relationship will improve and you will be able to offer greater empathy and understanding as a by-product. Mutual respect will follow naturally. You will learn in multiple ways when to let go and when to take charge of what (not who) you can control.

Parent with empathy, openness, tolerance, and appropriate humor as you teach those values in kind.

Hone in on your observational skills. You learn so much about yourself and the world around you by doing so. Patterns become clear, messages between you and your child are more easily received; closeness, conflicts, struggles and strengths reveal themselves. Similar to how a scientist observes data to support a hypothesis, secure a solid conclusion by paying attention through empirical observation, not emotional reaction. Your life and the life of your child (as you both emerge daily, weekly, monthly, and yearly) are worth watching in the ongoing experiment of your lifetime relationship. All healthy, close relationships require you to put yourself aside so you are truly present to receive what is happening in the moment. Be objective when you notice what someone else is trying to tell or show you; put aside your own defenses, perspective, or agenda. Just look, listen, and observe. Try to let go of judgment and keep breathing.

> Just look, listen, and observe. Try to let go of judgment and keep breathing.

Put on the hat of a behavioral scientist or archaeologist; you will find your personal expedition worth pursuing. Observe yourself, observe your child. Since your family is a unit of individuals, what everyone says and does matters. Live with the intention for greater awareness, knowledge, acceptance, and peace. Be grateful when that happens: notice and appreciate. You will discover that behavior teaches you a great deal about people and about yourself. You will see the benefit of slowing down enough to quiet the usual chatter of preconception or reactivity. Your child will welcome the feeling of being seen and heard for who she is.

When you develop your memory as you practice lifetime parenting, you will be tested. How many times have you thought you memorized something such as items in the corner of a room, a catchy jingle from a television commercial, the color of someone's eyes, an amusing anecdote, or an important fact or quote only to find that it has slipped your mind? That is natural and to be expected. As you develop your emotional and intuitive skills as a parent, you must also develop your mind and sensitivity.

In cognitive psychology, there are three parts of memory. The first part processes and combines new information, the second part creates and stores a record of this information, and the third helps you retrieve the recorded information. If you are tired, stressed or if the memory is not an important one (or is not associated with a significantly meaningful, dramatic or traumatic event), it may be forgotten or take time to recall.[51-54] Take time to develop your memory skills. You will want to be able to recall the many details you have taken the effort to observe in your child. Pay attention to what is going on in reality and also pay attention to your dreams. Some researchers have theorized that long-term memories are stored in dream format.[55]

Dreams involving your childhood or your child may be offering up memories of you or him from long ago. Although obscure, these memories can be added to your personal parenting arsenal. Also consider the powerful associations the senses have with memory. The feel of the warm summer air, songs or certain fragrances may spur memories from your best childhood moments at home or at camp, and may help you to plan a special upcoming summer experience for your child. The sound of a flute may remind you that your child has an upcoming school recital and may need help with practicing and stage jitters. The scent of gingerbread may remind you that your child was afraid of Santa and now that he is older, he is afraid of a new teacher or an intimidating boss at work. Offer support now, just as you did when he was young. All types of memory play into your role as a parent. In time, you are called upon to work on resolving your relationships and so is your child. Do your best to remember with all of your brain and keep your heart wide open.

Do your best to remember with all of your brain and keep your heart wide open.

You can see how significant and detailed memory is in your relationship with your child, as well as in all of your relationships. You need the whole trifecta of thought, emotional connection, and personal meaning to play the game well. Consciously thinking, feeling, and connecting emotionally to what you observe helps you understand the past and envision the future.

Showing vs. Telling: How Feelings and Needs Are Expressed

Consciously thinking, feeling, and connecting emotionally to what you observe helps you understand the past and envision the future.

Watch a mime, a television show, a presidential debate, or interview with the sound turned off, or watch babies and animals communicating non verbally. Recognize the unspoken language of the body and the face and how you feel while interpreting what is said without words. As explained earlier, young children in particular do not have the verbal or emotional skills to communicate well with words. They tell their story in other ways. When you pay attention well, you discover what they are showing you is what really counts. Your child is showing you in behavior how she feels and what she needs and wants until she has the words, skill, or readiness to articulate her feelings verbally. When she is able to communicate verbally, the scope of your communication with her can broaden. Throughout your entire relationship, you can best understand your child's feelings and needs by both watching and listening well.

With age, communication becomes more sophisticated. Your adolescent, teen, young adult and grown child continues to perfect his verbal communication skills, sense of self and personal self-expressiveness. When you listen, teach by example, love consistently, and care enough to openly "learn who your child is" throughout this lifetime, you keep the conversation between you flowing. As you deliberately practice parenting for life, you are doing a mitzvah, a very good deed indeed. You are giving the gift of perpetual love, positive reinforcement, and ultimate respect. These are gifts that truly keep on giving. When your child engages in significant relationships later on in life, including with his own child, he will know both the value of words and the power of silence.

Observation can help you heal your child, yourself, and your relationship. You can guide and negotiate with your child with more compassion and presence than ever before. Judgments, defenses, and power struggles are temporarily removed as you become more neutral and present in your role as "the observer." Receive your child's truth and your truth; speak to your child with great love, respect, and care. It is with this attitude that you reach your child and become a better guide and protector for her. Use the added insight of what your child has shown and told you (all along) to teach you how to love, protect, guide and progressively release her as best as you can all the days of your lives.

Be open to your child's natural developmental changes in behavior and learn to combine active listening with the observer role when you parent. When you fuse the two concepts and put them into practice, your choices and parental decisions emanate from a softer heart, a more open mind, and clearer forethought. You are inspired to be your best while in turn; your child is inspired to be his best.

Strive for Emotional Neutrality, Working Things out in "The Home Zone"

Recall your life before you became a parent. Reflect on when you were a child, teen and young adult. Remember the way you felt, the importance of your own parents remaining calm and emotionally neutral for you or not. You may have experienced a relaxed and nurturing parent, an emotional or reactive one, a distant, unavailable parent or a combination of the three at different times or in different scenarios. Your parents may have been capable of putting their needs, reactions, and expectations aside sometimes, often, or rarely. You were observed, understood, disciplined, and supported based on your parents' individual skills and what they saw, heard, and felt about you and how you presented yourself at the time. The level of calmness or drama in your "home zone" depended on

> Be open to your child's natural developmental changes in behavior and learn to combine active listening with the observer role when you parent.

what your parents knew and how they coped with life and the responsibilities of parenting. Your parents' emotional makeup, history and approach to life and to parenting, mixed with your relationship chemistry, determined how they parented. Either way, whatever emotional or energetic atmosphere existed in your "home zone" revealed a lot about your parents and less about you.

When you listen and observe well, the goal is to understand, empathize, and seek a compromise, solution, or resolution. Your job as a lifetime parent requires you to strive to lead your family culture toward tolerance, understanding, teamwork, harmony, and healing. Communication is best when open; all subjects that are age and stage-appropriate should be permitted. Offer a safe place and the promise of a safe, healthy, healing family legacy passed down when the time comes for your child to have a child of her own.

> The level of calmness or drama in your "home zone" depended on what your parents knew and how they coped with life and the responsibilities of parenting.

Invite Each Interaction, Positive or Negative, to Draw You Both Closer

Every interaction you have with your child at each moment in time has its value. Ultimately, both the positive and the not-so-positive moments offer you both the chance to be authentic, honest, and loving. Remember that when you feel upset or exasperated, your child still needs your love. By offering that love, you relax and the interaction (as well as the messages you send) can shift. As author Rodolfo Costa shared in *Advice My Parents Gave Me: And Other Lessons I Learned From My Mistakes*, "Learn to love someone when they least deserve it, because that is when they need your love most."[56] Whatever happens, do not take the unresolved conflict out on your child. Give him the safety and protection of your abiding love and respect. Show him by your example that life and growth are synonymous.

When you teach by example, you teach about accountability, respect, and empathy and create a safe haven for love, closeness, individual expression, and joy to thrive. Observe how you behave and how your child behaves. Notice your pre-existing attitudes; decide if you are willing to make some attitudinal shifts to draw you closer. Decide if you experience all of your interactions as gateways toward growth and connection or reasons to draw away. Some parents see and hear their child, but do not always "observe" her. It might be easier to see your little girl as innocently fixed in time well after she has passed puberty and is becoming a young woman on her own and dressing the part. Your growing boy or young man may have said some off-color remarks to a friend's parent or teacher in school as a joke, or to test the limits of acceptability but would never admit it in front of you. If observed, you would see another side emerge.

Either way, it is okay. You will have your turn to speak your mind, if necessary. Negotiate, step back, and let your child grow up. Let each interaction grow you closer, as you permit your mind and heart to use everything as an opportunity rather than a challenge.

When you see and hear evidence of your child's individuality, mistakes, and courageous acts you know her better. Your child is free to express her many aspects and free to be her best, when guided and supported by you to make smart choices. She can breathe easy that you still love and support her, no matter what.

All children need is a loving, firm, and fair parent. By showing these virtues consistently, you communicate your confidence in your child and encourage him to be his best. If you unintentionally negate, judge, ignore, disrespect, or over-control your child, you minimize your chance for closeness. Allow your child to be a human being who is learning as he goes. Learn from your mistakes. As mentioned earlier, "When you mess up, fess up." Make it a priority to improve your skills as a conscious and nurturing parent as you set a healthy example. Virginia Satir, in her book *Peoplemaking*, wrote "Feelings of worth can flourish only in an atmosphere where individual differences are appreciated, mistakes are tolerated, communication is open, and rules are flexible—the kind of atmosphere that is found

> Let each interaction grow you closer, as you permit your mind and heart to use everything as an opportunity rather than a challenge.

in a nurturing family."[57] Be accountable and remain open to "learning your child" with strength and grace as a parent. There is so much to be learned about your child. There is so much for you to learn about yourself. Even as individuals who are sharing a family, developing your relationship is key.

Though you may share similarities, you and your child are different as people and deserve to be treated as such. There is no place for comparison, blame or shame. Showing that you are responsible and accountable for your mistakes, can self-correct, and rejoin a healthy relationship between you and your child is majestic. You are human and imperfect. You make mistakes and get back up again. In doing so, you teach about humility, responsibility, faith, courage, gratitude, fortitude, and ultimately character. If you fall and have trouble standing afterwards, remember the words of Wayne Dyer, affectionately known as The Father of Motivation. In his book, *The Power of Intention*, he clearly teaches, "Be miserable or motivate yourself. Whatever has to be done, it is always your choice."[58] Each interaction your child has with you or witnesses you sharing with others plants the seeds for personal excellence or failure. No matter what separates or binds you, focus on encouraging strong, positive relationships for the future and start with the two of you.

> Showing that you are responsible and accountable for your mistakes, can self-correct, and rejoin a healthy relationship between you and your child is majestic.

*H*omework Assignment *15*

Heightened Awareness

Make it a practice to begin listening and observing your child without preconceiving, negating, judging, or immediately reacting for a period of time. Be sure to keep in mind your child's age, stage, unique abilities, and aptitudes. Be willing to stop, look, and listen to your child all day long during this period. Take the time, focus, and energy derived from your love for your child to motivate you to take this simple step toward gaining greater understanding of him or her.

- Using your *Parenting Journal*, as you develop your parental observational skills, write down important things that you see, hear, observe, and feel during this time.

- Include additional comments about what you have learned and can put into practice from your observations. Include some details that help you to remember what you have learned.

- Create a personal, parenting affirmation that supports you to be an "active listener" and keen observer of your child. Your affirmation is designed to heighten your awareness.

- Keep the affirmation positive, present, short, and to the point.

- Begin your affirmation with an "I" statement and rework it over time as your relationship with your child evolves and later resolves. Include your first name. The sentence best starts with I, (your name) am so happy and grateful now that (fill in your goals). Re-work your affirmation over time as your relationship with your child grows, evolves, and later resolves.

- Once you are comfortable with your reminder to listen and observe more regularly with greater awareness and neutrality, read, speak and even sing your parenting affirmation to yourself on a consistent basis.

- Post your affirmation in places that you will see it, include it on your vision board (or treasure map), bathroom mirror, car dashboard or simply remember to use it daily for a while until it becomes a new parenting habit.

- Remember that while you are observing your child, observe yourself. You will be joined by your child doing the same.

- Become an expert behavioral scientist in your family. You will be the leader with a clue.

Resolving Your Relationship

CHAPTER SIXTEEN

The Power of Positive Relationships

The quality of your life is the quality of your relationships.

—Anthony Robbins, motivational speaker

Positive vs. Negative Energy and How It Affects Relationships

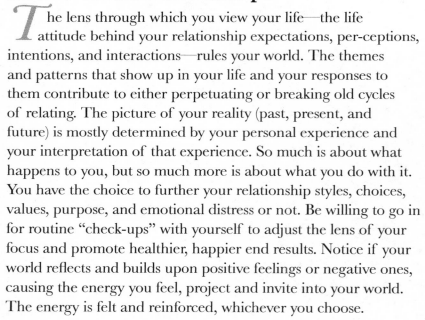

The lens through which you view your life—the life attitude behind your relationship expectations, per-ceptions, intentions, and interactions—rules your world. The themes and patterns that show up in your life and your responses to them contribute to either perpetuating or breaking old cycles of relating. The picture of your reality (past, present, and future) is mostly determined by your personal experience and your interpretation of that experience. So much is about what happens to you, but so much more is about what you do with it. You have the choice to further your relationship styles, choices, values, purpose, and emotional distress or not. Be willing to go in for routine "check-ups" with yourself to adjust the lens of your focus and promote healthier, happier end results. Notice if your world reflects and builds upon positive feelings or negative ones, causing the energy you feel, project and invite into your world. The energy is felt and reinforced, whichever you choose.

The quality of your life and the quality of your child's life with you depends upon your beliefs, intentions, actions, and the attitude you project. Your view of relationships colors

> The lens through which you view your life—the life attitude behind your relationship expectations, perceptions, intentions, and interactions—rules your world.

your perceptions, emotion, motivation, subsequent actions, reactions, and eventual choices. There is immeasurable benefit to living with alertness, maintaining an open mind and heart and being willing to learn a better way. In *Churchill By Himself,* Winston Churchill observed this when he said, "Attitude is a little thing that makes a big difference."[59] You craft, with your own consciousness, self-awareness, self-reflection, and intention, the energy you give and receive (with others). This results in the precise outcome you either dreaded or masterfully created.

When you become aware of the events on the news, the economy, keep up with pop culture, and live the hurried lifestyle that many people are facing today, it is no wonder that maintaining positivity can be challenging. Look on the bookshelves and at topics discussed on the Internet. Listen to the news broadcasts and talk show themes. Think about pop culture and the content in much of modern conversation.

We are trying to be more efficient while dealing with rapid change, technological advances, some moral breakdown and tough times for many. However for some, healthy, positive living has become an important part of not just surviving, but thriving in the modern world. Some people are seeking out alternate forms of relaxation and healing, like meditation and yoga. Due to this, they are realizing the importance of eating and sleeping well, not just trying to keep up with the rat race or project a false self to the world. Self and social awareness, or proactive activism, has become a tool to counteract and offset the stresses of living in today's world. We have the power to roll with the changes and deal better with the onslaught of information and pressure, by altering our perception of it. Wayne Dyer got it right in his book, *The Power of Intention,* when he said, "If you change the way you look at things, the things you look at change."[60] Keep your mind open so that your heart will follow as you relate to others. The good news is that despite and because of all the progress and stress, human beings are just that—and deserve to be self-preserving, while always striving to find the silver lining in all things.

Relationship wellness creates systemic wellness, a holistically positive approach through which you can feel better and live longer.

Relationship wellness creates systemic wellness, a holistically positive approach through which you can feel better and live longer. There is an increase in social awareness and acceptance of positive versus negative energy in the practice of maintaining a healthy body and spirit, living a balanced life, and fostering healthy relationships. More organizations are focusing on time, stress management, wellness, and work-life balance. At the same time, our society is dealing with global and political erosion, two modern topics that embrace positive solutions, health, and wellness across the board. While obesity and stress-related diseases are at an all-time high, some progress in terms of promoting health is being achieved in certain sectors and media outlets. This signals more social awareness in the arena of self-care to balance and offset mounting stressors. Included in this line-up is the eternal quest for satisfying, happy, and healing relationships. It all works together and all the parts make up a terrific whole.

Sometimes, in the quest for positive relationships, you find yourself taking a detour or two. You do what you must to express and heal yourself. You bring yourself into each relationship. You bring your history, personal background, individual baggage, unique beauty, and gifts. You bring the potential to learn, grow, and change with each choice you make in your relationships as you are ready. You know when you are ready to listen, learn, or adapt something new into your personal repertoire. Being ready is an essential, and much overlooked state to embrace where change is concerned. You bring your strengths and special qualities that balance your humanity, imperfections, tendencies, and emotional triggers. You learn as you go. You learn what you need to know. What you do and do not do supplies the groundwork for either positive or negative relationships in the days to come.

You have endless opportunities to think back over, learn from, and evolve. Given all of this pressure to change, you can either crumble or work toward repair. You can be inspired to learn and grow from all of your interactions and relationships,

> You do what you must to express and heal yourself . . . You have endless opportunities to think back over, learn from, and evolve. Given all of this pressure to change, you can either crumble or work toward repair.

whether they are positive or negative. Rise to the occasion, learn to adapt, elevate yourself, and change your life perspective. It starts with you and then radiates outward to how you relate with others. Self, interpersonal, and social awareness elevate you on your journey as you personally develop. People want to expand their lives, find peace and harmony, manage stress, connect with others, create success, and deal with the new reality that results from healthy change. Adapt to healthy change and go with the flow of life. See everything on your path as a vehicle to drive your purpose and evolution. As you do this, you manifest your best life and best relationships yet.

You live in your own reality, yet you perceive relationships and experiences as gateways to deeper understanding. See your relationships, including the one you have with your child, as vehicles to self-awareness, truth, transformational connections and opportunities for self-reflection. With this new insight, wellness between you and your child can begin to develop and you can move your relationship forward toward the goals of understanding and harmony.

Positive thinking and attitudes driven by feeling good create positive energy. Positive energy uplifts and connects people and all living things. This energy allows others of a similar mind and energy field to be attracted to you. Positive thinking, the healing power of thought, belief and intention, and the visualization of goals and outcomes are now socially welcome. The same is true for self-healing since more people have embraced the idea of holistic care making health and happiness really possible. Creating emotional, physical, and spiritual wellness has become more of the norm, rather than the exception for many people in some circles around the world.

Mindfulness, alternative therapies, and methods to dispel negative thoughts and emotions are now on par with Pilates and yoga. Meditation, spiritual practices, positive thinking, balanced living, personal affirmations, vision boards, and self-help books have become increasingly acceptable in the mainstream. Therapy, life coaching, business coaching, and training have

> Adapt to healthy change and go with the flow of life. See everything on your path as a vehicle to drive your purpose and evolution.

all become popular professions. Insurance companies and the corporate culture now recognize the need for work-life balance and wellness programs. Using these readily available tools enhances a balanced, healthy life that will result in the time and energy necessary to commit more deeply to mindful parenting. Health and wellness, positive attitudes, and positive, nontoxic relationships are in great demand. The goal of living a healthy, well-balanced life has come to the forefront of modern living. Living, thinking, and feeling well are pleasures and rights that we all want and deserve. These truths allow the practice of lifetime parenting to flow and allow parents to approach this practice with more to give and with more love and understanding for all.

With a positive focus, you are more relaxed and able to welcome healthy interactions, healing, and forgiveness.

Negative energy feeds on negative energy. It drags people down and stunts growth. Positive energy, thoughts, beliefs, expectations, and language create positive energy resulting in positive feelings and constructive change. Increased awareness, happiness, and new ways of living more effectively and harmoniously with other people, including with your child, is the ultimate goal. Positive relationships need as much positive reinforcement as possible. Align yourself with that goal and go for it!

As a parent, you teach your child to live, learn, and love with the focus on what is going well or how to make life better. Little things, moderate things, and big things all are worthy of positive reinforcement. Each person has the right to bloom in his or her own unique, vibrant fullness when the time is right—bit by bit—or in one fell swoop. Individuals deserve to know the special place they hold in their family. By focusing on positives, you can more readily learn from mistakes and life experience. With a positive focus, you are more relaxed and able to welcome healthy interactions, healing, and forgiveness. You stay aligned with the positive potential in each moment; a personally powerful growing evolution in your relationships then begins. By committing to create a positive relationship, your child sees, hears, and feels that he is valued and that the bond between you has a significance all its own.

Invite Gateways for Personal Growth and Healing in All Your Relationships

You are entitled to invite gateways for growth and healing in all of your relationships. Keep your mind and heart open to this growth and healing. The possibility for positive interactions and outcomes are real. Teach this by example to your child. Choose optimism over pessimism. Find precious positives: the hidden gems in your relationships. Include and prioritize your relationship with your child as one of the most highly regarded and important relationships of your life. Create space in your life to include all the people you love and who love you. See the possibility of relating in positive ways and creating positive win-win outcomes with everyone in your relationship radar.

Widen your emotional scope. The individuals in your life who matter most to you are what I term your *"Circle of Extraordinary People."* These are people who are co-creators of your world and you are co-creator to theirs. Some of these people are included in your lifetime relationships and others stay a while and then leave. Their purpose in your life for your personal evolution was served. Other relationships, including the one with your child, are lifetime relationships and their members are permanently included in your *"Circle of Extraordinary People."* Be sure to include yourself as a key member in this special group.

> Allow the idea of growth and possibility to be present in all of your relationships, especially your relationship with your child.

Allow the idea of growth and possibility to be present in all of your relationships, especially your relationship with your child. Be willing to be fully present and enjoy the positive experiences and areas of closeness in your life. Be aware of relationship stumbling blocks, especially the ones you have helped to create. Each relationship serves a different purpose and presents a different set of requirements for you to fulfill. Closeness, healing, and a deeper understanding of yourself and those you relate to grow over time and in a myriad of healthy ways. Some relationships are short-lived, others are meant to survive the test of time. Rest assured that all relationships, no matter the duration, are there for you to grow and learn from.

Since relationships drive much of your life, recognize the benefits of enjoying and building strong, positive, honest, forward-moving interactions. Be courageous to be your best, love your best and learn your best with all of the important people in your life. These relationships lift your spirits, boost your immune system, support you unconditionally, make you feel good, heal your soul, help you stand tall and feel equally cherished. Return the favor. Reciprocal generosity is contagious and the mutual benefits last forever.

Realistically, negativity, darkness, pain, and suffering exist and have their place, even in a healthy life. It is best if you can find meaning and learn from your challenges, as well as your triumphs, especially as a parent. Choose to meet these challenges by seeing the inherent gift presented in it. You grow as an individual and minimize suffering caused by fear and resistance. Within each challenge, opportunity for acceptance, transformation, and gratitude exists. Often times, it is mostly about your perspective and your choice to hold or shift it.

A woman in a workshop I taught at a local community college was struggling to deal with her adult daughter who lived with her. At the end of the program, the woman at first introduced her daughter to me as "her friend." She did this because she felt embarrassed and overwhelmed by her daughter's numerous issues and struggles, including anorexia, depression, and suicidal tendencies. There was palpable sadness between them. Their home was completely disorganized. The mother showed some hoarding behavior, as she had trouble letting go of her own unhealthy upbringing and habit patterns. She had smothering elderly parents who taught love by using control over her. Mother and daughter attended the workshop together initially as codependent partners in the process. They got the support they needed and sat quietly. Later, when they sought me out for a short, private consultation, they revealed their unhealthy codependency and need for immediate outside help. They agreed to live as co-creators in search of a new way of living and dealing with life together in a healthier, less enmeshed way and were grateful for some tangible strategies.

Rest assured that all relationships, no matter the duration, are there for you to grow and learn from.

I was honored to hear the mother tell me that she was ready to let go of her past and get help for herself and her daughter. It was a pleasure observing immediate "aha" moments for these eager life learners who craved more than just accepting crumbs. In this case, both mother and daughter had to learn how to enjoy the banquet and give up the crumbs. Each parent-child relationship, as they travel together through time has the potential to be adapted, recreated and parts of it healed. It helps when both people are on board and want health and healing between them.

Buddha is credited with saying, "Let us rise up and be thankful, for if we did not learn a lot today, at least we learned a little, and if we did not learn a little, at least we did not get sick, and if we got sick, at least we did not die; so, let us all be thankful."[61] Living life well takes a certain amount of courage, a good dose of humility, a strong modicum of gratitude and a great deal of letting go. That is almost always true when challenging your perspectives and adopting a new way of living. Change can become revolutionary and help move you to the next level of self-discovery, and to the next level of healthy, honest relationship dynamics. Personal self-mastery is a small method to begin to make a big difference in the world. With each person, each relationship, each family striving toward living a better way, the world becomes a better, kinder, and more honest place.

> With each person, each relationship, each family striving toward living a better way, the world becomes a better, kinder, and more honest place.

As you grow from each relationship, whether past or current, failed or successful, hopefully, you learn about yourself and have more to give. Ideally, if you can take responsibility for your part and release the urge to blame and shame from failings or impasses in your relationships, you will be all the wiser. It can be easier said than done, yet worthy of immediate and repeated attempts at mastering. All of your relationships, including the one with your child, can serve as catalysts for an improved, smarter, more loving you and subsequently, inspire a better life. That is a seed of integrity that can grow into much more.

Feel good about doing what is right. Believe in the vastness of possibility and the potential for closeness and happiness with the ones you love. At every turn, the potential for a healed heart and healed relationships exist, if only you believe. Beyond believing is the action that follows to make the magic happen. "Like attracts like," whether it be positive or negative energy, and then naturally generates more of the same. Hold a positive life attitude and envision the relationship you want with each person in your life. Use your head, heart and efforts when you think about, talk to or spend time with the people you love. They may be the easiest or the most difficult people in your life, but they are there and for a reason. Build upon your positive intentions, natural enthusiasm and energy that fuel your optimism and confidence. Believe in the power of truth, love and healing and share that with your child.

> Believe in yourself, the present moment, and endless future possibilities while you watch the power of positive thinking take shape.

Improve your emotional state and you are energized for the next round of lessons and challenges. Believe in yourself, the present moment, and endless future possibilities while you watch the power of positive thinking take shape. Your thoughts become your actions. Your emotions follow your thoughts and you begin to manifest your ultimate future. The force of your positive attitudes and relationships supports you to live happily with satisfaction, strength, and courage. This clearly positive attitude is passed on to your child, her children, and to all subsequent generations. You are responsible to choose what you believe, value, teach, and perpetuate. When choosing recurrent thought patterns and belief systems, choose ones that best serves you and the ones you love. As Judith Knowlton said in her book *Higher Powered*, "I discovered I always have choices and sometimes it is only a choice of attitude." [62] People are more important than things, making money, doing business or relentlessly keeping up with the rat race. In the business of relationships, the right attitude can change a life for the better—and all the people in it.

Close associations move you to act and behave in particular ways. Your parent-child relationship is a special one. It is one of the most deeply significant bonds in your child's present and future life. It presents you with many chances to expand yourself, to meet the needs of another while meeting your own needs. Multiple opportunities arise each day to help shift your awareness and experience and express love, respect, and empathy toward your child. As team leader, you navigate its course; your child follows your lead. As your parenting style develops, you will keep your relationship as positive and constructive as possible. The stiff and unbending style of the disciplinary authoritarian or old-school parent does not work. The permissive parent's approach is not strong enough to lead. Appropriate and balanced power (to some degree) from an authoritative/democratic parent evens the scales in a safe, loving, and firmly run household. You hold the privilege of having a deep impact on someone for life. You teach your values, have parental expectations and guide how to work as two individuals on the same team. Life is focused on what is happening now and what is possible later. Appreciate the power of positively reinforcing your special bond and realize how truly humbling, awesome, and healing it really is.

Continue to Do What Works, Let Go of What Does Not Work

Continue to do what works. Change what you can to improve what is not working in your significant relationships. Look at your life like a mirror. Engage your reflection. See and hear what others are telling you about yourself. Even if what you are hearing or reading is not the exact image you hold of yourself, pay attention to the feedback anyway. Develop and integrate your own inner wisdom with the truthful opinions of others who know you and spend time with you. You can devise an awareness booster along with insight moments while you are parenting, kind of like developing the art of lucid dreaming while engaged in a dream. Another awareness booster is to choose to pay attention to your child's perceptions and take note if two or more people in your universe give you the same or similar feedback. There may be some truth to what they say. That means that if what you are doing or saying is working in

> When choosing recurrent thought patterns and belief systems, choose ones that best serve you and the ones you love.

your relationships, continue to do it. If what you are doing or saying is not working, then change it. The feedback may be about your behavior, words, choices, or approaches that you need to look at and reflect upon. Sometimes people will give you feedback that is more about themselves than about you, so you need to assess and respond accordingly. In that case, the person is projecting a part of their disowned self and you know it is unrelated to you. Similarly, be open to feedback. Pay attention and make a deal with yourself that you will consider a percentage of everyone's impressions. Take this feedback as truth from your universe designed to help you learn, receive potentially important information, as you continue to evolve. This can be arranged on a daily, annual, or lifetime basis. The strategies of the past do not apply anymore when you are living in the present moment.

Look at your life like a mirror. Engage your reflection.

Whatever you do, your behavior tells others who you are, how you live, what you accept, and where you place your priorities. You show people rather than tell them who you are. Young children are particularly adept at this because they are less verbal and more creative. Adolescents and teens do not always want to open up or be transparent. Sometimes adult children need to assert their autonomy and keep their agenda far from view. It is okay because your child, at every age and stage deserves to be respected and all behavior can be quite revealing. If you pay attention, verbal and nonverbal messages in combination, especially when done consistently or with startling abruptness, convey everything.

You teach people how to treat you. Think of your life as an ongoing reflection of your self-esteem and self-love. The way that you feel about yourself expands to other areas of your life, including your relationships. It shows up in how you treat yourself, how you treat others, and how you allow others to treat you. Bring your relationship tools with you and feel free to continue to add to your relationship toolbox. Your behavior accepts, rejects, or enables the behavior of others. Who you are and how you see who you are when you look into your internal mirror is another story. Take the time to really see yourself. See who you are, always were, and need to become. Be real with yourself. Always be honest with yourself first and then include others, such as your child, in that humbling experience.

Notice and appreciate your parental stumbling blocks. These issues probably arise in your other significant relationships in some way, as well. They may not play out in exactly the same way as the relationships, roles, boundaries, personalities, ages, and genders all differ. The issues continue in your life until inner awareness, new choices, and eventual resolution occur. Find resolution; learn forgiveness for your own peace of mind. As you come to personal insight, shifts in consciousness and inspired epiphanies help you move forward in new and improved ways. True psychological shifts inspire permanent change in your awareness and naturally guide you to modify your behavior. The areas that require greater understanding must be welcomed and nurtured as gifts in disguise. Open them joyfully and with care.

Make your child aware of your appreciation for her as a person. Teach her to live with gratitude and freely give her specific, positive praise whenever possible about her strengths, values, and judgment are concerned. Always keep your child's needs, welfare, and well-being in the forefront of your mind. Get your emotional adult needs met elsewhere. Your child is not your buddy. This important truth can be difficult for some parents, particularly single parents or stressed parents with fuzzy boundaries of appropriateness, or who were raised with inappropriately sharing parents, to grasp. If ongoing and excessive, it is unfair of parents to trespass on their relationships with their kids by expecting them to be "buddies." It steals a piece of childhood by making a child feel responsible for filling a separate need for a friend or a confidant in the parent. That is not to say that you cannot fall into that tendency at times or "like" your child as a person (for all of her likable qualities) as well as love her as your child or share more as she gets older. It is to say that sometimes you can cross a line from parent to friend.

Notice and appreciate your parental stumbling blocks. These issues probably arise in your other significant relationships in some way, as well.

You know when you have crossed a line when the roles begin to reverse (who is parent, who is child?). If you suspect this might be happening at home, or you get feedback that you violated a boundary take responsibility for your misstep, apologize, and seek out an appropriate sounding board. Learn from your error so not to repeat it.

Be careful not to cross boundary lines when seeking greater emotional intimacy with your child.

In life, boundary violations cannot be taken back, only corrected and repaired, and no one is the winner. Keep it straight the majority of the time and self-correct if the lines become blurred and you are treating your child as your friend and confidant as a regular relational dynamic between you. This is often the case with divorced co-parents and some intact families. Keep those lines in the sand clearly drawn. Always think of the well-being of your child. She does not want or need to know about your personal life and struggles on a daily basis. It is your history, drama, and personal work, not hers. Be careful not to cross boundary lines when seeking greater emotional intimacy with your child. Guard and protect her from learning too much too fast or hearing the wrong information. Remember that one of your jobs as a parent is to protect your child, at all costs. Protect her from harm, which includes sharing too much information or demanding unfair expectations as best as you can. Free her to enjoy a happy life and happy, healthy safe relationships, starting with the one with you.

Homework Assignment 16

Parent Credos

Consider these parenting truths to be self-evident as you grow, evolve, and resolve your relationship:

- When you value and work on self-awareness, your child learns to be self-aware.

- When you are calm and calm down easily, your child is calm and values inner peace.

- When you are happy and grateful, you model happiness, and gratitude for your child.

- When you expect your child to succeed and do their own best, your child can.

- When you thank your child in advance for doing their best, your child will.

- When you seek wisdom and knowledge, your child is free to explore his or her own.

- When you listen well, your child speaks to you.

- When you respect your child, your child learns to respect you and him or her.

- When you are self-honest and truthful (with boundaries), your child values his or her own truth.

- When you are emotionally available, your child comes to you and feels safe.

- When you take care of yourself, your child has a stronger guide to lean on and learns the importance of self-care.

- When you make "family time" a priority, your child feels important and belongs to a special group that he or she can count on (and emulate later on).

- When you ask your child for their opinion and to participate (as developmentally appropriate) your child feels valued, heard and respected.

- When you laugh at your patterns and tendencies, your child sees humility.

- When you laugh as much as possible (not at anyone's expense), you all feel better.

- When you make positive changes, your child learns from a growing role-model.

- When you develop beyond your own negative limitations, your child understands that anything is possible when there is love.

- When you demonstrate unconditional love and support, your child knows that he or she is worthy of being who he or she is now and who he or she is becoming.

- When you emphasize positive behaviors, more positive behaviors show up.

- When you emphasize negative behaviors, more negative behaviors show up.

- When you have fun and enjoy spending time together, your child feels accepted and relaxed. Your child is free to be, try new things and enjoy you as yourself.

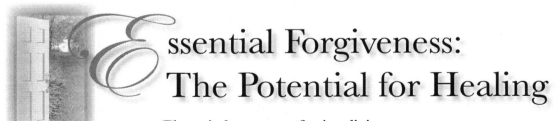 Essential Forgiveness: The Potential for Healing

To err is human, to forgive divine.

—Alexander Pope, Poet

Feel Your Feelings

As you travel through life, the ride can be rather tricky, dicey, beautiful, surprising, fantastic, painful, and challenging at times. The way you handle yourself in your relationships and during life events is an interesting challenge. Your natural reactions and immediate responses to interpersonal information and events are candid, obvious, and valid. You react and respond to your parents, children, friends, and everyone around you. Your style of handling another and managing your own feelings says a lot about you as you resolve the relationship patterns of your life.

As you develop your awareness as a lifetime parent and navigate your course, remember to enjoy the moments when love is expressed or felt. Feel the warm comfort that loving relationships bring and pass that experience onto your child. After all, relationships are at the heart of each life. Your best bet as family leader is to love and empower yourself as fully as you can, while teaching your child how to do the same. Acknowledge your own fallibilities, strength, and truth, and keep moving forward as best you can.

> Your style of handling another and managing your own feelings says a lot about you as you resolve the relationship patterns of your life.

The feelings you experience are real, even if they are subtly or highly emotionally charged, repeated from the past, or are just plain confusing. You may intellectualize, repress, deny, displace, suppress, and defend against how you feel, how you think you should feel, or how you have been told to feel. You then decide what actions to take because of—or in spite of—your feelings moving forward. You may also be unable to move beyond your feelings if you have been wronged by someone. You have feelings and you must decide what to do with them. Once you decipher how you feel, arrange your feelings in order of intensity...and then decide what action to take next.

You have feelings about the events and relationships in your life. Your child has feelings about these things, too. You have feelings about each other, especially when it comes to accepting positive and negative behavior. Like grabbing onto the end of a kite in a brisk wind, hold steadfast to your choice to hold steady, be brave and forgive (when you are ready) so that it does not blow away; otherwise, hurt, anger, bitterness, or resentment can take hold. Teach this principle and practice as you role-model how to feel your feelings and then deal with them. Once felt and recognized, hold on to your positive feelings for as long as you can and let go of your negative feelings as quickly as possible. Forgive either inwardly or outwardly when you are ready. That is not to say that offenses or wounds should be forgotten. Often, you will find that forgiving your parent, child, friend, or someone else can be a lengthy, solitary and rewarding practice. Learn to trust what you feel and experience as real, and respect what you acquire from your feelings. Think it through and find the lesson in it for you. Thomas Stephen Szasz, in his book, *The Second Sin*, pronounced "The stupid neither forgive nor forget; the naïve forgive and forget; the wise forgive but do not forget."[62] You decide which one you are with each opportunity you are given.

To understand how to process feelings and then forgive, you must determine what is forgivable or unforgivable. Your morality, family and life history, expectations, level of maturity, and understanding all weigh in here. Understand that you either choose to give peace to yourself and release blame, resentment, anger and hurt or hold onto it. Another person does not have to change for you to grieve, love, let go, forgive, or move past the

> Your best bet as leader of the pack is to stand tall inside yourself and acknowledge your own fallibilities, strength, and truth.

negativity that holds you back or binds you in heartache. You may receive a heartfelt apology, compassion, or resolution or you may not. The point is that when you forgive, but not necessarily forget, you release potent toxicity that buries your heart and soul and keeps you stuck in the past instead of giving love to yourself and finding a new way for the future. When you forgive and release negative emotions, your life experience changes, your health improves, and your child sees an emotional giant.

Awaken to the peace and power you can feel once you release the hurt, anger, resentment, or disappointment you hold inside. When looking at you, your child does not see an angel or tower of strength in every moment. Instead he sees a person humble and brave enough to press on, successfully negotiating hard feelings and challenging events. Show him that you are big enough to sustain healthy and happy present relationships and let go of the toxic ones. Lead the way by claiming inner freedom through choosing to resolve your feelings, forgive and learn what it means to choose wellness, harness inner peace, and move on.

> Lead the way by claiming inner freedom through choosing to resolve your feelings, forgive and learn what it means to choose wellness, harness inner peace, and move on.

Not all behavior is forgivable, and not all unforgivable behavior is worth making yourself sick. Choose to feel your truth and choose to forgive yourself and others (when you are ready). You know what you can live with for your own health and well-being and what you cannot. Sometimes when you choose to forgive, you need to negotiate a new way of seeing, relating to or processing information better. You may choose to forgive, change or end a relationship. Practicing forgiveness is somewhat of an art that requires a delicate balance of emotion and logic. Rather than denying your justified hurt, anger, resentment, or disappointment, embrace it. Take time to feel your feelings and, when ready, release the strong negative emotions as soon as you are able. That includes negativity about someone else or even yourself. Feel what is real in your experience. Set that stage at home so that your child can learn that her feelings are valid, too. Do not collapse away from your real perception, forgive blindly, or betray yourself out of a sense of obligation, self-delusion, or resistant denial.

Debbie Ford wrote in *Why Good People Do Bad Things: Stop Being Your Own Worst Enemy* that, "When we step into the tranquil state of forgiveness, we feel genuine love of our whole self...the parts of us that are flawed and weak as well as those that are confident and strong. Like turning on a light in a dark room, forgiveness brings the light of acceptance and compassion to all of our dark and disowned aspects."[64] To keep a healthy perspective in life, it is helpful to be self-honest, to soften hard emotions about others and about negative self-perceptions, and to learn to make peace internally. It is one of the greatest gifts you can bestow as a parent. It is also one of the best things you can give yourself.

Take time to feel your feelings and, when ready, release the strong negative emotions as soon as you are able.

Practice forgiveness with an open attitude from a genuine place inside yourself. Then, when ready, release the grasp that holds your anger, frustration, fear, sadness, rage, and bitterness that keeps you tied to the past and to your pain and suffering. You need to first acknowledge your feelings before you can move past them. As sure as rain, the only way out is through.[65] Be confident and courageous as you take yourself by the hand; ask for inner guidance or help from an effective professional and move through your pain so that you can get close to your peaceful pleasure.

When ready, grant forgiveness to whomever or whatever has caused you pain. Do it for yourself. According to Louis B. Smedes, author of *Forgive and Forget: Healing the Hurts We Don't Deserve*, he presents several stages of forgiveness. Smedes writes: "You will know that forgiveness has begun when you recall those who hurt you and feel the power to wish them well." He goes on to say, "To forgive is to set a prisoner free and discover that the prisoner was you."[66] As difficult as it may be, when your heart is ready, you will know and then let go. You deserve the healing that will allow you to find peace, feel the joy and gratitude in life, and move forward. Forgiveness does not mean you forget, stop feeling, or deny the lesson you learned by the painful experience. You will gain strength and wisdom from the experience. In your own healing, you can accept yourself and even learn to appreciate someone else's vantage point. Let go of the pain for yourself but also to set an example for your child.

Sometimes if you notice patterns in your life that are no longer working for you, it takes a good jolt to wake you up in order to grow, progress, and rise to the occasion to make things better. Taking stock—a *life inventory*—may cause you emotional pain, yet within the darkness, a chance for light emerges as you make new choices. Ultimately, you live according to your principles. Hopefully, feeling happy, satisfied, and proud of your life are on top your list. Human growth in all its forms, needs tending.

Growth can be described as awareness, discovery, and taking action toward positive change. This evolves from the desires to progress, move away from pain (receiving or giving it), and be inspired to grow. You rise to new levels of awareness, new directions, and new pathways that open your mind, heart, and life. By doing so, you feel more at peace and are free to express the most authentic and best parts of you. Once you do this, there is no turning back and that is a beautiful thing. Your wisdom leads you to do what you need to do. Establish what you are willing to let go of and cherish those that are dearest to you along the way. Cradle your lifetime relationship with your child. Hold it up as a beacon of unconditional love as you move forward. Think, act and speak in ways that make you proud. Your child will be proud of you and appreciate the act of commitment, courage, and valor you display.

When ready, grant forgiveness to whomever or whatever has caused you pain. Do it for yourself.

See the underlying gift of awareness that presents itself in personal and professional conflicts or struggles. See the potential to move through emotions and logic toward understanding and peace. The amount of energy invested when you hold on to something, both physically and emotionally, is far greater than the amount of energy it takes to let it go. The way you see your life unfolding and how you consciously co-create your existence stems from the power of your intention. Leave room for perspective, tune into the field of energy which is intention, and give yourself time to learn and heal. Be willing to learn a new way. Use your relationships as springboards for personal growth, maturity, and healing starting with the concept of essential forgiveness. Feel your truth and forgive yourself first. Then, be courageous and decide if you choose to forgive others (or not), learn from the pain, focus your intentions, and move on.

Appreciate Someone Else's Vantage Point

Appreciate someone else's point of view, including your child's perceptions. You do not have to experience, understand, or even agree with her vantage point. You merely need to acknowledge it; value her perception as valid and true for her. The same is true for you. You know what you see, hear, think, feel, and experience. No one can take that away. Since you cannot make another person experience something, empathize with you, or change, you must first start with yourself. That is the most powerful place to start. This will begin to free your emotional range and spiritual expansiveness as you model growth by example and consequently improve your relationship with your child. As you journey forward, find solace in your personal discoveries. As your child's ultimate guide and teacher in life's big classroom, your job description requires you demonstrate as many positive lessons shown by example as possible.

Insight about yourself or someone else is not something that can be forced. You are allowed to take time that you need to cycle through your feelings and integrate information. Your personal process of learning to assimilate insight has a direct impact upon your child and your future relationship. You discover, recover, and move forward in your own time. You have learned how to defend yourself or stay stuck in the past in order to take care of you and survive in an environment. Take the time you need to begin the process of accepting new ideas and finding inner resolution one step at a time. Walk the walk of love and peace, one step at a time.

Naturally, people need to retreat, become defensive, or counter-attack when hurt in some way. It is normal and a

Leave room for perspective, tune into the field of energy which is intention, and give yourself time to learn and heal.

necessary human response. It is a jungle out there. People are suffering from being over-stressed, over-worked, underpaid, unpaid, socially and environmentally ravaged, over-pressured, and out of time. While pressures mount, so do emotions. Sometimes people lash out and hurt the ones closest to them, the ones they care for and really love. Sometimes these are the people with whom we feel we can "let it all out." Discover healthy outlets and think before speaking instead of resorting to projection or displacement, aka human "dumping grounds." Ultimately, emotional and physical safety needs to exist in all relationships. When feeling "safe" with another person, you can express your true feelings and resolve any unresolved issues so that they are healed more quickly. New and better ways of relating and new, healthy relationships replace old, outmoded, toxic systems and unhealthy dynamics. Your future mental-emotional health depends on the way you parent you and your child now. Your past inspires your way forward.

Insight about yourself or someone else is not something that can be forced.

In conflicted, destructive, or "unsafe" relationships between parent and child, siblings, couples, lovers, friends, or co-workers positive solutions seem less attainable. Unhealthy relationships eventually self-destruct or destroy the people in them. The relationship either fails for both people or becomes damaging for one person. Underlying resentment, anger, hurt, and unmet needs come rushing to the surface whether you confront or deny them in your relationships. Sometimes in those conflicted moments, things are said or done that are unacceptable. Perhaps a repressed truth bubbles to the surface in a raw or inappropriate way. Truth expressed without censorship can cross the line of decency and is not constructive. Whether it is between you and your child or between you and someone else, become aware of your part in both the conflict and the solution.

Know yourself in your relationships, including the one you have with your child. It helps to be self-aware as you communicate with clarity and transparency, rather than delusion and concealment. Trust is either present or it is not. It is built over time with mutual honesty, respect, consistency, and truth.

Conflicts are inevitable, healthy resolution, however, is not. Only you can guarantee the final outcome. Separate the emotion from the problem. Invest the time and energy in resolving your own issues (from your past or present) to see the problem clearly, be accountable for your part, and seek common ground with the other person. The option to "agree to disagree" exists if a healthy resolution cannot be found. This gives grace and dignity to you both.

> Unhealthy relationships eventually self-destruct or destroy the people in them.

Think about the riches in your relationships, including the relationship you have with your child. Think about what you love and like about him. There is no one in the entire world exactly like him. Acknowledge your aligned and divergent perspectives. Get cozy with some of the comfortable, relaxed feelings and positive memories that you share with your child. What have you learned from him? What are you learning now? Ponder what life lessons exist for you because of and as a result of this special lifetime relationship.

Let Go of the Pain...for Yourself

When you seek to release difficulty, conflict, or pain in a relationship, start with honest, open, respectful communication to start the process of understanding and forgiveness. Try to resolve the pain between you, if possible. Say what you need to say and remain open to hear what the other person has to say. If verbal communication is stilted, agree to compromise in nonverbal active ways, write or e-mail each other. Do what is needed to keep the lines of communication open. Keep breathing and *stand up tall inside of yourself.* Make room for the other person to stand tall inside of him or herself, as well. Demonstrate mutual acceptance, respect, and empowerment. Behave and speak with the goal of honoring both of you in the interaction. By experiencing this level of awareness, natural respect will help shift emotional reactivity. Choose to be happy, rather than choosing to be right. Once emotions diminish, there is greater awareness and a greater capacity to move on, forgive, and negotiate a better way.

If you cannot communicate mutually or find common ground, be sure to identify and let go of the pain independently. The process of resolution can often be a singular one, yet it is just as powerful as if occurred between you and the other person. Either way, you come to insight organically and find a more healing way to deal with reality. If healing is necessary between you and your child; be sure to give both of you plenty of time and space to find a creative solution or compromise that works for each of you. It works best at a time when emotions are calm.

The human heart knows no bounds. It knows when it is hurt and when it needs healing. Since it takes time to heal, be gentle and compassionate with yourself, as you begin the mending process. To understand and then relieve psychic pain (which can also be felt as physical pain) as a whole is like eating an elephant, one bite at a time. In this case, it is one act of self-love, one act of forgiveness at a time that you get a real taste of.

To release your pain requires that you recognize it and then forgive yourself, another adult, your child, or someone who has hurt or offended you in some way. The essence of forgiveness is "giving" to yourself and to another person because you set you both free. You forgive someone an emotional debt. Forgiving is to give to yourself, freeing yourself from the chains of another, the chains of holding onto your pain. When you decide to "deal and heal," you grow exponentially. You may maintain the relationship or choose to let it go. Louise Hay said, "We may not know how to forgive, and we may not want to forgive; but the very fact we say we are willing to forgive begins the healing practice." In her book, *Forgiveness: Loving the Inner Child,* Hay crisply explains: "Many times we hold onto old hurts and punish ourselves today for something someone did to us when we were children. That does not make any sense at all. The past only exists in our minds. It is the inner child that really needs the healing, because the inner child is the one who has had all of the pain. Love, is the most powerful healing force there is, and the pathway to love is through forgiveness."[67] Release past hurts,

> Think about the riches in your relationships, including the relationship you have with your child.

> When you seek to release difficulty, conflict, or pain in a relationship, start with honest, open, respectful communication to start the process of understanding and forgiveness.

trust your faith in life, and let the process of moving onward take hold.

Most importantly, true emotional healing is done independently. Think of the process of discovering, understanding, and forgiving the pain you have suffered as a way of "giving back" to you. When you learn to heal your life, you give a beautiful gift of absolution and inner freedom, not permission or tolerance for unacceptable behavior to someone else. That includes tolerating your own mistakes and finding a path that helps heal those you have hurt. You learn to love and forgive from the inside out. Give yourself peace, calm, and quiet empowerment as you welcome more effective and compassionate relationships.

Your relationships serve the dual purpose of loving and learning. Use opportunities for personal growth as you love and learn. Depending on your personal history, family background, and comfort levels, learn to give yourself permission to continue your self-discovery. You are entitled to learn and grow all the days of your life. Embrace your right to achieve inner and outer harmony across your lifetime. If you have lost your way, you deserve to find your way back home to yourself and your life. Your child deserves the same quality of life. Everyone you know and care about, including yourself, is worthy of the introspection and self-exploration that leads to personal peace and happy relationships.

You remember, learn, and forgive what you can based upon your experience, understanding, level of motivation, and desire to heal. Forget the meaningless and remember the significant. Carry on and continue to grow at your own pace. You are not in your relationships alone, although what you feel is yours alone and is processed in your mind and heart alone. See what changes you can make to encourage a more positive relationship future. As you parent, you interact with and model for your child every choice regarding how to behave in relationships. Be forever mindful that he is learning from your lead.

> Release past hurts, trust your faith in life, and let the process of moving onward take hold.

> If you have lost your way, you deserve to find your way back home to yourself and your life. Your child deserves the same quality of life.

Parent as though your child's life depends on it. Parenting is a full-time, lifelong job; give it your best shot. When you make a blunder, your child will forgive you for it. When your child makes a mistake, you will forgive her more easily. Forgive yourself, forgive your parents, and forgive your child—all the loves of your life.

Uncontrolled expression, acting out, rebellion, hurt feelings, and disrespect cannot be taken personally unless your child is expressing honest wounded feelings that you need to hear. Love him with objectivity and compassion, and do your best to hear what he is trying to tell you, even if it is about you. Model self-restraint and maturity, and hold steady to receive your child's important message. You are here to help resolve his pain, not recycle it. Once heard, reflect back with "active listening" (as described in Chapter 14). Travel the path of loving responsibly, enhancing inner growth for both of you. With love and forgiveness leading the way, dicey waters become more placid. The potential for true relationship healing is real.

The potential for true relationship healing is real.

*H*omework Assignment *17*

Forgive and Live

In your *Parenting Journal*, write down everything in your life to-date that you are willing to forgive or have forgiven with your parents and within other significant relationships. Write as much or as little as you like. Take your time to complete this assignment. It may take some active introspection and release work before you can identify who and what you are willing and able to forgive. Write another list of what you would like your child and other significant relationships in your life to forgive you for. While you are at it, take some time to forgive yourself. Be compassionate with yourself as you continue to build your best life story.

Be sure to include the following:

- What I need to forgive you for is:

- What I need to learn and remember about our relationship is:

- I am grateful for knowing you because:

- What I have learned from you is:

- I feel strongly that:

- I see your perspective with:

- I am willing to release:

- The most important thing to me in my significant relationships is:

- I am ready to heal my:

- What I want/need you to forgive me for is:

Take time to reflect upon your insights and return to them as need be to reinforce new awareness and positive energy.

CHAPTER EIGHTEEN

What Happiness Is and What It Isn't

Most people are about as happy as they make up their minds to be.

—Abraham Lincoln, Former President, Civil Rights Activist

Love the Beauty and Potential of Each Moment

Each moment you have has within it the promise of a life well lived. Each moment is rare because it only comes along once and must be cherished—for it holds something special. The beauty and potential of all of life's simple and complex joys including what Joseph Campbell calls "Follow your Bliss" in his book, *The Power of Myth*,[68] are always possible in the present moment. You choose your focus and your feelings follow. Learn to see your world from a familiar perspective, safe or courageous. Look outwardly and capture life's awe.

No matter what has transpired so far, your momentary perspective reigns supreme. Remember that when you are happy, your child is happier. As you become more peaceful, joyful, and positive, so will your child (at least he sees the road you are paving for him). You set the stage as the family leader to create the emotional and mental tone of your "home zone." Your parenting purpose helps you define the quality of life you promote. Take a couple of long, slow deep breaths. Feel the air

> Each moment is rare because it only comes along once and must be cherished— for it holds something special.

going in and out of your lungs and your chest rising and falling like a refreshing breeze. Take another deep, slow breath, this time with your eyes closed for a moment. Then open your eyes when you feel most relaxed. Be here and now in this present moment in time. Find a quiet and calm place within yourself. Ask what you cherish, value, and what makes you feel happy gratitude in your life right now. Listen to the answer. Next ask, "Am I happy now?" If you answer is yes, then find out what the specific reasons are. If the answer is no, ask if you have ever been happy. When have you felt pure joy and happiness in your life? What conditions had to exist for that wonderful feeling to happen? In your life today, do you give yourself permission to enjoy the beauty and potential of each moment? Do you take opportunities to receive simple pleasures that align with your values? Have you known profound satisfaction, acknowledge personal blessings, and found beautiful gifted moments in time? If so, wonderful! If not, what is stopping you?

Whether you know it or not, everything you experience can be translated into a positive or negative spin.

Life lessons continually present themselves and are perceived differently according where you are in your life. Wherever you are, strive to be happy. Max Ehrmann's poem *Desiderata* illuminates this point by saying, "You are a child of the universe, no less than the trees and the stars; you have a right to be here. And whether or not it is clear to you, no doubt the universe is unfolding as it should. Therefore be at peace with God, whatever you conceive Him to be, and whatever your labors and aspirations, in the noisy confusion of life keep peace with your soul. With all its sham drudgery and broken dreams, it is still a beautiful world. Be careful. Strive to be happy."[69] Since the moments that define happiness vary with each individual in their life experience, a shortcut approach to find happiness is to be happy for what already works in your life and in all your blessings. You are the master of your own fate. Start now with where you hold your focus and energies. Whether you know it or not, everything you experience can be translated into a positive or negative spin. Consider Wayne Dyer's keen insight that *if* you change the way you look at things, the things you look at change.[70] Life happens to you while you also choose so much along the way. Your interpretation of all that happens to you, how your relationships go, and the choices you make help you to learn or continue your patterns, facilitate learning your life lessons or not. What you choose to focus on adds to your happiness, inner pride, and bliss. You choose how to process your thoughts and resulting emotional reactions creating your ultimate happiness or unhappiness, your personal heaven or hell.

You deserve to be happy and to feel special, worthy, confident, successful, and peaceful inside. You deserve to feel comfortable with yourself and your life choices (as long as you do not hurt yourself or anyone else). That is your birthright. Your child shares the same right to happiness and feelings of being loved and lovable as you do. She deserves to feel deeply happy just for being alive on this earth and for being who she is. Be introspective and nurture yourself with love and self-care; take responsibility for your own life, your own process, and ultimately your own journey of self-discovery and inner peace. Whether you know it or not, like with Dorothy's emerald slippers, you have *always* had the right and the power to enjoy the beauty and potential in each moment, all the days of your life.

You have the power to be happy in each moment, no matter what is going on outside of your control. You may have needed your parents to teach you that or at least help point the way. Maybe your parents felt and expressed gratitude and joy easily and maybe not. Now it is your turn to teach the secrets of how to live a happy life to your child and learn that same lesson from your child in return.

> You choose how to process your thoughts and resulting emotional reactions creating your ultimate happiness or unhappiness, your personal heaven or hell.

Where Does Happiness Come From?

Everybody just wants to be happy, or at least they say so. The question is how do you find happiness, hang onto it, and pass it on? You explore little and big ways to conjure up a sense of peace, joy, achievement, and gratification. After all, in the human condition, we live in an intangible and also physical world. Because of life's complexities, we are programmed to experience both pleasure and pain. When you break it down, you grasp love and happiness when you can and when you are ready. You feel a deep appreciation for life as you become aware of those special, close, tender, sweet, happy moments that are components of a bigger picture. What you think about, are grateful for, and pay attention to expands or shrinks your happiness factor. As you continue the practice of lifetime parenting, you figure out that you either welcome or repel true happiness as a natural, comfortable state. Whatever your *life attitude* is will dictate who you are and how you live. Similarly, whatever your parents' *life attitude* was or is has had a strong bearing on yours. Individuals, families, couples, siblings, communities, and societies collectively benefit from genuine states of well-being. These happy places emanate first from small places within, then translate outward and are shared with others to make the world a happier place.

When shared, happiness is contagious, just like laughter, tears and emotional energy. The specific, elusive search for inner peace and happiness can be equated with outside sources that feed the ego and the pocketbook, such as career, monetary or superficial success, public attention, and achievement of power or status. The happiness derived from these sources can be fleeting and unstable, perhaps unreal. It is a sense of reeling in happiness from the outside in, from your efforts and disciplines and your connections, rather than from your heart and mind. You feel good and want more. However, if you engage in outside sources reinforcing your self-worth, you get the support of others to bolster you and recognize your gifts and contributions. That is fine. You feel noticed, validated, complimented, relied on, empowered, and possibly loved. The trouble is that you cannot count on real, sincere, joyful feelings that way. True happiness and peace come from within. Learn to relax, laugh, and choose to be grateful and happy. Do it while your child is still watching.

When you stop comparing your life to another's, you do yourself a great service. Another part of Max Ehrmann's *Desiderata* poem states, "If you compare yourself to others, you

What you think about, are grateful for, and pay attention to expands or shrinks your happiness factor.

will become vain and bitter."[71] You walk your path your way and in your own time. You prepare yourself with sturdy walking shoes or topple over with spiked heels. You wear dark glasses or let in the light. You hum a few songs, grumble loudly, or suffer in silence as you travel your road. It is all up to you and how you walk down the path of your life. You feel you deserve to be happy and search for ways to claim your divine right to happiness or you kick it away like an old can on a street corner. Your life is calling and your child is still listening. She is following in your footsteps or running down her own path away from yours. Watch what you are doing as you teach what you know and what you do not know starting now.

When you focus on *external happiness prompts* or outcomes, approval from outside sources can bring unhappiness. As you grow, you learn that real success starts and ends from within. It is your *internal happiness prompts* that matter and last. Your feelings, faith, hopes, and attitudes predict your success or demise. Failing happiness is associated with losing something or having less than someone else, when in fact it is really just missing your own potential. If your internal mindsets and emotional states are repeated, reinforced or paired with either positive or negative feelings, this can cue your expectations from then on about your happiness or unhappiness. So, focus on what makes you feel happy within your value system and have fun sharing your happiness at home and when out with your child.

Learn to relax, laugh, and choose to be grateful and happy. Do it while your child is still watching.

Temporary and permanent happiness fulfillments are separate things. *Temporary happiness fulfillment* is a sensory or emotional dependency linked to something or someone outside of you. It does not fill your heart or a genuine emotional need. It is often without meaningful emotion, is rushed or fleeting, and lacks a sense of security or permanence. The happy feelings are dependent upon the other person or event. Rather than searching inwardly for good feelings, the good feelings are generated by and dependent upon what happens outside of your personal range of control. Rather than enjoying peace from within, a blast of positive feedback is sought from without, a habit of looking for the next "happy fix," positive reinforcement from someone or someplace else. Conceptually, it makes sense to feel good about yourself when you get attention and accolades outside of yourself. Inner kudos is the greatest feeling to generate and keep with you, along with appreciating the simple treasures of being alive. You create a sense of permanent happiness and fulfillment when you live a life of accountability and integrity that makes you feel proud.

Permanent happiness fulfillment stems from what is lasting and within your personal locus of control. You feel good because you like and love yourself; your choices reflect your self-worth and your life has depth of meaning. This simple truth has profound permanence, no matter what happens outside of you. Your real happiness and underlying self-worth have nothing to do with anyone or anything else. That includes external and temporary feedback, material acquisitions and real emotions about your life. You, not the factors in your environment or your fleeting emotions, are responsible for the way you feel your everyday journey already in progress.

> You feel good because you like and love yourself; your choices reflect your self-worth and your life has depth of meaning.

Not everyone defines happiness in the same way, nor does everyone have the same opportunities, gifts, desires, motivations, or intentions. Further, not everyone feels deserving to receive joy and bliss. If happiness is a new concept or habit, it can be difficult to adapt to at first. Recycling old patterns of repeating the past and making unconscious choices that do not serve you to feel happy now (living a victim's plight, comparing yourself to others, being selfish or competitive instead of cooperative) are traps that sabotage your current happiness. Another trap is ignoring the things that you already possess that make you happy. Small things, moments that capture your heart and soul, connections with significant people, being grateful and laughing across the journey will make your expedition happier and more deeply satisfying. You are here in life's open classroom as a soul whose real destination is about love and learning. Remind yourself that your child at all ages, from birth to adulthood, is a blessing in your life. You are a blessing to her, too. The only trap there is if you forget that.

Comparing yourself to others is risky because your perception is based on outer differences, not necessarily privileged inside realities. Do your best to enjoy your life and deal with your own successes, goals, dreams, and reality. Evolve yourself on your own merit and claim your own divine right to find happiness. The formula for happiness is individual, and while you and your child aspire for more, you may realize all is already well in your world right now.

Look at the range and complexity in your palette of emotions. What moves you to feel happiness despite or including real emotions about your life? Emotion is like fluid water, it moves, flows and changes in waves, sometimes powerfully and sometimes gently. Emotions flow and change as you process what you feel and define the degree to which you feel it. Because you and your child are multifaceted, emotions play a part when you intentionally choose to feel happy. Find true moments of happiness that stretch across time, starting with a curious attitude of self-discovery. Finding happiness is an acquired habit, a personal commitment, and a journey that fulfills your unique requirements. When you find your bliss, individual peace and happiness becomes your guide, and you guide your child to do the same.

Permanent happiness fulfillment grows from what is good for you and feeds your soul and general well-being. It derives from what and who makes you feel happy, from the inside out or the outside in. Feeling good in a permanent way comes from knowing and honoring yourself well. Know and affirm your inherent right to be happy. Give yourself happy thoughts and feelings and create happy experiences that align with your values while you experience other realities of life. As you tell your child, tell yourself, "As long as you are not hurting yourself or someone else, do what makes you feel proud of yourself, happy, and peaceful inside." You will make mistakes and learn from them. Learn to focus on your accomplishments, large and small, and keep generating more. By doing this, you inherit a positive attitude and your growth, progress, and personal evolution continue, thus making you happy. There is essentially no other

Small things, moments that capture your heart and soul, connections with significant people, being grateful and laughing across the journey will make your expedition happier and more deeply satisfying.

way as you realize the wisdom and security in permanence.

Happiness also comes from special lifetime milestones, positive interactions with others, the practice of daily gratitude, parenting for life, and appreciation for life's wonderful surprises. Material success and external conquest often trump emotional and interpersonal success in modern life. The outside world can affect your inner state but does not necessarily define or dominate it. To learn and master the art of creating a happier state of being, self-awareness, self-acceptance, and self-discipline are required. Strive for self-development and sincere well-being as your guideposts.

> When you find your bliss, individual peace and happiness becomes your guide, and you guide your child to do the same.

Remember, as you experience the practice of parenting for life, develop your vision, clarify your intention and purpose, and put into practice the daily art of putting your money where your mouth is. It is not enough to talk alone, it is necessary to walk the walk. Dalai Lama, the leader of Tibet and worldwide spiritual teacher teaches us that, "Happiness is not something ready-made. It comes from your own actions." He goes on to say in his book, *The Art of Happiness: A Handbook for Living* by Dalai Lama and Howard C. Cutler, "When we speak of this inner discipline, it can of course involve many things, many methods. But generally speaking, one begins by identifying those factors that lead to happiness and those factors that lead to suffering. Having done this, one then sets about gradually eliminating those factors which lead to suffering and cultivating those which lead to happiness. That is the way."[72] Make your happiness as well the happiness attitudes you pass on to your child, your responsibility, a high priority, and a conscious choice on your to-do list.

You Have a Right to Be Happy; Your Child Has a Right to Be Happy

You have to want to honor yourself and then acknowledge and release your fear, sadness, anger, doubt, and pain. Know that you are lovable and worthy, and always have been, without having to do anything. Knowing this, you acknowledge that you deserve and choose to feel happy about who you are and about life's grand potential.

Listen to the sound of your heart and soul's calling. Honor your core values and live in a way that supports your highest good. You have a right to be happy and so does your child. Encourage a positive life attitude in both of you and *internal happiness prompts* that lead to *permanent happiness fulfillment.* If the focus is on fitting in or standing out based on external feedback and reinforcement, the opinion of others becomes the barometer and source for feeling happy and contented. It is more important however, to impress yourself—reach in and then reach out with confidence. When you focus on being yourself, loving yourself and your child, your world opens up. When you stand for love, anything and everything is possible.

Connect to the most important source of your love: you. Connect to your inner child and love him or her now while you also love your child. You must take care of both of you. You teach your child to take care of his own health and happiness. Make balancing love for all a high priority. Ensure that the heart of your home is love. Take the time to enjoy learning and teaching about healthy self-respect, self-worth, and self-love. Value your independence and goals, and deal with the stress in your life while taking time to relax and become introspective. Factor in time for fun, family time, date nights, and time with friends. Take care of your physical and mental-emotional health. Eat, sleep and exercise well. Get plenty of hugs if you like and need them. Find ways to de-stress and un-clutter your life. Find your life's purpose. Re-create happiness that you have missed before and create joy now for yourself in your own way. Share the joy your feel in your interactions with your child, including your child's joyous expressions. Build upon these precious moments. You will be happier and your child will be happier. Remember that your child, young or grown, is always watching you. This helps you to watch yourself. This helps you to watch both of you grow.

In many families, underlying messages suggest that it is selfish, negative, and wrong to feel or maintain a prolonged sense of pride or happiness. Somehow, the message from the parent leader to the family team connotes that feeling good,

Encourage a positive life attitude in both of you and internal happiness prompts that lead to permanent happiness fulfillment.

Make balancing love for all a high priority. Ensure that the heart of your home is love.

moving ahead, advancing with glee or rising above the parent's limitations is unacceptable and threatens the family's emotional status quo (or some facsimile). In an ideally healthy family, the dynamic sets its members up for success and ongoing support and equally values, supports, and encourages each person. Accomplishments of all kinds are noticed and celebrated. Unfortunately, all too often conflict, denial, blame, shame, patterns of abuse and neglect, personal projection, and lack of awareness become the hallmark of what life is, and therefore define what happiness is and what it is not. How can you feel the beautiful grasp of a happy life when the culture you emerged from and reside in does not recognize or support it? We all know a toxic person who seems to thrive on creating emotional turmoil for him or herself or others and also lives by the credo that drama is the name of the game and misery loves company. How do you sustain joy without knowing deep down inside that happiness is preferable to suffering? How do you teach by example that your child deserves to feel well? She deserves to know that.

> The key is to nurture yourself. The more you have within you, the more you have to give to your child.

The key is to nurture yourself. The more you have within you, the more you have to give to your child. Find windows of hope and faith by seeking out healthy ways to love yourself, and deal with stress, change, or loss, and build a healthy support network. This clears the way for love and light to begin to emerge in yourself and your life. Shine your light outward; invite your child to beam his own beautiful light right alongside you.

Your life attitude defines how you cherish or ignore single moments, passages, and periods in your lifetime. Your life attitude offers you the potential to experience life consciously with enthusiasm or with blinders, thereby causing self-sabotage and destruction. The choice is up to you.

Actively unwrap the joy, healing, and life lessons that unfold in each moment. Reveal these virtues in your relationships and in your experience of parenting. There is a gift in each moment. Let that teach you about the meaning of life: to love and to learn. Choose to enjoy the moments, overall process, and lesson in everything (whether positive or negative). See the silver lining of life; in your days and relationships, and learn to be thankful.

Change takes time. Over time things slowly morph, especially if you work on inviting positive transformation into your life. You may defend against the change that it takes to live consciously all the moments of your life or you may welcome it. You may prefer to repeat what is familiar and therefore safe, not necessarily doing what is best for you or your child. Only you know what your pattern is. True happiness requires awareness that it is chosen; each insight, each joy, is an exquisite gift. Decide if you want to live as a victim or a master of your own fate. Choose which messages you want to pass on to your child about discovering happiness in life. Select and appreciate golden opportunities that help you grow and evolve. Ultimately, you decide which steps to take, where you are going, and where your child is following you.

Whether you are the hero, victim, martyr, or something else is entirely up to you. That, by definition, helps you to clarify what happiness is: be alert and awake, live courageously, make yourself proud, and see the bright silver lining that wants to shine through.

> True happiness requires awareness that it is chosen; each insight, each joy, is an exquisite gift.

Like a child on Christmas or Chanukah morning, dig in and unwrap life's special magical gifts with innocent excitement! Look inside of the behaviors around you. Reach inside your own thoughts, and without excess emotional drama, but with rationale and forethought, pull out meaning for what life is all about for you. Be willing to get "unstuck" from a feeling of inertia or persecution. Understand the gift you give to yourself when you awaken to organic insights simply by finding ways to heighten your awareness. You live your best life when you are ready to understand. You know when to you must accept reality as it is, and find the best ways to intentionally move into your future. It is with understanding and compassion (for yourself as well as others) that you live consciously. Think about the most directly meaningful questions of your life. Ask yourself how do you define the purpose, meaning of your individual life? What is your wish for your lifetime relationship with your child? What emotional/attitudinal/spiritual legacy do you want to teach your child by your example, words, and actions? What do you allow your child to teach you about life and about being happy? Whenever possible, re-kindle the excitement you once felt as a child of wonder. That is when you will allow love and learning to come in to your life, by being open, receptive, and unbiased.

Enjoy That Which Gives You Joy; Seek Inner Peace

When layers of experience are uncovered and examined with honesty and an open mind, over time, a sense of peace and satisfaction can result. When you unveil your life to yourself, your deep, authentic inner peace as well as your misery and suffering belong to you. Only you can feel your feelings, learn from them, and if necessary, release them. I recommend holding on to your positive feelings for as long as you can and let go of your negative feelings as quickly as possible. As you begin to reconcile the darkness in your life, lightness emerges and shines in its place. Happiness (as well as misery) propagates and can be shared with others. As this place of inner knowing and inner contentment grows, relationships are more satisfying, harmonious, and peaceful, too. You are a calmer person and parent whose love and joy are at the core of your lifetime parenting practice. You grow your self-worth, actively chose and improve all of your relationships. You become a good student, find your lessons, live with integrity, and accept the flow of life and all its potentials. Your wisdom shines brightly with a wellspring of peace, joy, and confidence. Happiness that was there all along is finally realized.

You can learn anything. Make your experiences work for you. Look for the gems of life there for you in each moment, including, during, or after mistakes are made. As quickly as possible, apologize from your heart and self-correct. Take care of the aspects of your world that you can control. Learn to let go of the facets that are beyond your control and find peace in that.

> When you unveil your life to yourself, your deep, authentic inner peace as well as your misery and suffering belong to you.

Be your best self and live with faith. Let go of the rest. Take all experiences and see if you can put a positive spin on them. Enjoy the sunshine as well as a crisp and light rain. Enjoy a beautiful song, a shared smile, helping hand from a stranger, or a positive and affectionate interaction with a friend or loved one. Enjoy divine solitude and expansive experiences in groups. These are moments of inspiration. Without reserve or resentment, enjoy the act of giving to your child. Acts of kindness stimulate the brain and brain chemicals that bring feelings of gratification, joy, and true happiness. In Paul J. Zak's book, *The Moral Molecule*, he reveals through studies that the brain chemical oxytocin is released when someone is nice to us. This mammalian experience tells mothers (and in some species fathers) to care for their young. It is the chemical basis for parental love. The feeling of empathy and emotional connection can also exist between strangers performing acts of kindness. Those same chemicals are released and make us feel good. It feels good to be human, to be connected by our humanity, and to give without gain.[73] Use your heart more than your intellect to drive experiences that bring more love, joy, and happiness into your life.

Use your heart more than your intellect to drive experiences that bring more love, joy, and happiness into your life.

Look for the beauty in life. Enjoy the awesome intricacies and grand complexities around you. Appreciate a great song, book, movie, concert, play, walk in the sunshine, or belly laugh. Feel the wind against your skin, each breath in and out of your chest, or a big bear hug with someone special. The promise of prolonged *permanent happiness fulfillment* is guaranteed when you remember the simple, sacred value of life and all its blessings. Value and honor significant moments and relationships in your life right now, and claim your right to peace. Imagine how much happier you will feel. Begin with this moment, breathe it in deeply.

Be present and relax. Stay as positively focused as you can during your practice of lifetime parenting. Be alert—then transmute tendencies that recycle negative habit patterns. Stop catastrophizing, over-dramatizing, bullying or living with an emergency mentality or victim-scapegoat role. Even with stress, learn your triggers and solutions. Know that stress itself is not all bad; it can serve as a catalyst for positive change and expedited progress. Learn to relax and release unrealistic expectations or aspirations for perfection. If you need professional support, by all means, go and get it. Take care of yourself because you deserve and so you can be there for others. Stop waiting to be happy. Decide to be present in the moment, envision hope for the future, and relax into a state of happiness that warms your soul and makes the corners of your mouth turn up.

Find productive ways to solve your problems, release stress, and reach out for needed emotional support from people you trust. Give yourself permission to get the care you need to resolve your issues and then move forward. Love yourself and find people who you trust to be on your team. They can be friends, family or trained medical, psychological or educationally- based professionals. Those people can be in your current inner circle or may be new contacts that are professionally trained in the healing arts and services. You are resilient and can spring back quickly with greater wisdom and peace into a state of greater resolve and comfort. Put on your coping tool belt, the curiosity to solve problems with creativity and courage, your sturdiest boots, and go!

> Know that stress itself is not all bad; it can serve as a catalyst for positive change and expedited progress.

Throughout your life, enlightening opportunities to practice attitudinal shifts will continue to appear to you, requiring your awareness and self-honesty. Enlightening epiphany moments are windows into true lifetime happiness, as long as you remain open to them. It is akin to internal flashes of wisdom turning on inside your mind and deep within your soul. When that happens, pay attention to when the switch of insight turns on inside of you. What conditions prompt you to want to move forward, learn and grow? With practice, you pay attention to the spark of genius within you; the gift of wisdom that your higher self and divine inspiration supply you. What you focus on creates your reality. What you think about, you then feel. Your thoughts, words, and actions generate feelings. From that, your behavior and outcomes follow and you attract more of the same. Seeing that connection helps stimulate your life experience and eventual insight.

The path to inner peace and enlightenment is not easy; it requires doing the work, letting go and can be fraught with surprises, challenges, and obstacles. With each phase of increased awareness and personal development, you see that it is worth the effort, and your life begins to reflect that.

The path to true happiness requires that you remain an open vessel for the simple joys in your daily experience and significant relationships throughout your lifetime. In the moments you have deep calm within you, you create a well-constructed loving home for your soul. Once built, it is a great place to invite others to come and join you.

Since parenting is for life, welcome all information that helps you and your child relate, feel happy, and evolve. Good lives contain the life skills that move you forward, keep your significant relationships working well and help make a positive difference for others. A good life gives you joy, personal insight, and supports your personal growth and overall success. Stay open as you work on the close bond you develop with your child over time at every age. Recognize sparks of wisdom, humility, clarity, and insight that you glean as a parent. Celebrate the victories with your child, as you work through issues together. Reward each other and gain closeness in the process. You learn from your wisdom—and your child's wisdom—what works best between you. Since you are both student and teacher in the universal classroom of life, take a seat up front and do your best work to discover what true happiness really is.

> Celebrate the victories with your child, as you work through issues together.

Homework Assignment 18

Happiness Requirement Chart

This exercise is designed to help you sort out the basic needs of your individual happiness requirements. In your parenting journal, create a self-care list, a clear path to find your bliss. Write down your key requirements for happiness. Write down the key elements of what makes you feel happy. Make your list about your both inner and outer worlds. Consciously reinforce your words with behavior day-to-day. By taking care of yourself, what you need to feel happy will increase your awareness, parenting toolbox and overall happiness quotient.

Use this exercise to learn (more) about love, peace and happiness to empower both you and your child. Write down each question and then your answers without too much thought or force. Let your heart guide you.

- The key elements necessary *for you* to feel peaceful, self-loving, proud of yourself, contented and happy are:

- The key elements for your child to feel peaceful, self-loving, proud of him or herself, contented and happy are:

- Create list titles that support your key elements. Make them creative and empowering.

- After your lists are created, post them somewhere visible that you can see every day.

- Post them in places like your bathroom mirror, car, or *Parenting Journal*, where you read or can see (unconsciously) them in the background and affirm them daily.

- Add visual images, such as a treasure map/vision board if you want to, especially if you are a visual learner.

- Create an affirmation that you can read, sing, or speak if you are an auditory learner.

- Repeat when you are showering, bathing or exercising as a moving meditation if you are a feeling-sensing-kinesthetic learner.

- You can suggest any combination of positive reinforcement that works.

- Share this homework with your child and make it a family project. You can work on it separately or together. Decide as team leader what is best for your family, or hold a family meeting. Choose to do what works best in your family system to evoke cooperation, introspection and participation.

- Hold a family meeting to share both your lists when completed. If your list is too mature, personal, private, uncomfortable or inappropriate to share with your child, then create a simple, more family-friendly list of self-care goals, objectives, or affirmations to share with your child. Keep your more extensive private list private. The list you create about your child does not need to be shared, unless you want to compare his or her list with your perceptions of him or her. Respect your child's wishes. Most importantly, it is an individual exercise that you both share what you are comfortable sharing.

- Hold a follow-up family meeting or informal discussion to check-in if need be at the right time. If it is necessary, schedule a time a few days, one week or two weeks away.

- Positively reinforce you and your child's positive *Life Attitudes, Internal Happiness Prompts and Permanent Happiness Fulfillment* as you become witness to each of your happiness potential being fulfilled.

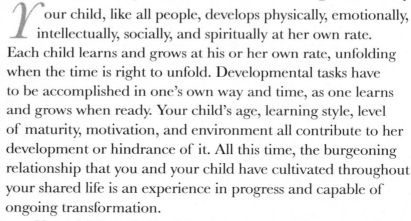

CHAPTER NINETEEN

Know When to Hold On and When to Let Go

*Consider the trees which allow the birds to perch and fly away
without either inviting them to stay or desiring them to never depart.
If your heart can be like this, you will be near to the way.*

—Zen Buddhist teaching

Know Where your Child is Developmentally

Your child, like all people, develops physically, emotionally, intellectually, socially, and spiritually at her own rate. Each child learns and grows at his or her own rate, unfolding when the time is right to unfold. Developmental tasks have to be accomplished in one's own way and time, as one learns and grows when ready. Your child's age, learning style, level of maturity, motivation, and environment all contribute to her development or hindrance of it. All this time, the burgeoning relationship that you and your child have cultivated throughout your shared life is an experience in progress and capable of ongoing transformation.

Your child's individual developmental pathway starts in infancy and continues throughout adulthood. It requires that you accompany your child (at important times and ways) as you travel both difficult and easy paths together as parent and child. Depending on where you are in your respective developmental journeys, you experience both struggle and flow together. Familiarize yourself with where your child is developmentally

> Your child, like all people, develops physically, emotionally, intellectually, socially, and spiritually at her own rate.

246

(as discussed in Chapter 1) and which developmental task or milestone she is working toward achieving at each stage. This process continues into and beyond adulthood. You know your child's personal development and witness milestones conquered (or not). Parent for life by being aware of the stages you share with your child. Keep them in mind starting now while the future is always in the front of your mind. You both learn about who you are as individuals while you grow lasting love, respect, trust, and joy. Realize the importance of enjoying the time you spend with your child all along the way, no matter what events or feelings may be in the forefront or background on any particular day.

Do not take those basic joys and skills for granted. The time you share is invaluable and irreplaceable. Cherish those in your life while you can. Let them know how much you care. Build upon that practice with your precious child.

Parent your child as you continue to heal your own life. Live and learn alongside your child as you share paths on your walk of life. Guide, teach, and learn the best that you can. The fact that this relationship transforms and teaches you both over time is fundamental. At first, you grow your relationship. Next, you evolve your relationship. Lastly, you both need to somehow resolve your relationship. Your unique lifetime bond has many facets and purposes that only the two of you can discover. If you have more than one child, you teach and learn with each of them. You need to learn, understand, and accept where you and your child are on the developmental continuum while moving into your future. Discover where there is room to grow and learn while resolving the stories of your shared life. You become witness to your child's growing aptitudes; encourage her potential, and support her as she faces her stumbling blocks. Advocate for your child's potential; look forward with optimism, and look back to learn and remember.

Now that you see the importance of educating yourself as you educate and guide another, you can parent lovingly with

> The fact that this relationship transforms and teaches you both over time is fundamental. At first, you grow your relationship. Next, you evolve your relationship. Lastly, you both need to somehow resolve your relationship.

awareness, a clearer purpose, and improved communication. Once you recognize which developmental stage your child is in, understand that you must shift gears and adapt to your child's specific (youthful and adult) needs. Empathize with his struggles and celebrate his triumphs. You must constantly adapt, be ready to react or respond, and take action. You must process a thought or emotion, change your schedule, change your mind, lose sleep, and gain so much love—whether you are ready or not. That is the unspoken knowledge about parenthood that you figure out fast. Awake or not, ready or not, and at a moment's notice your child or you (at every age and stage of life) might inspire action, a reaction, or a response. Your time, energy, and love are shared with another, and you are secured together for life. That is just the way it is when you are a parent. There is no doubt that a loving parent is kind, mindful, able to acknowledge the truth, and has to be resilient. You have got to be sensitive and strong to be a parent.

Be strong enough to do what is right and sensitive enough to work on healing what is wrong.

Be strong enough to do what is right and sensitive enough to work on healing what is wrong. Deep love can exist along with the conflicts of struggling wills, egos, perceptions, developmental tasks, and temperament challenges. Despite the clashes, you maintain the love and respect you have for your child, since day one, and encourage the same in return. You must be mindful to take good care of yourself so that you can take care of your child. Be sure to fortify yourself with adequate self-care. Get sleep, eat well, take your vitamins, exercise, enjoy your support system, and have fun to maintain your balance. Do what calms and empowers you. You will be better prepared to parent from a full well from which to give love and understanding rather than from an empty one with barely anything to offer. Your child will do the same for himself and feel happy and full.

During adolescence, teenage years, the onset of adulthood and beyond, another part of the necessary process of parenting presents itself. You recognize that your baby has developed into the young adult you have helped her become. This person, who has grown before you, has an increasing self-knowledge and has others in her life but still needs to connect with you at times. You have to understand and allow your child to mature and live life on her own terms, make her own decisions, her own mistakes and successes, and be her own person more and more.

In *The Psychological Birth of the Human Infant: Symbiosis and Individuation,* Margaret Mahler created the Separation-Individuation Theory of Child Development. She worked with unhealthy children but also wrote for healthy children with secure attachments to encourage adequate coping skills later on in life. She identified the importance of a child experiencing healthy separation and individuation. The Margaret Mahler Psychiatric Research Foundation describes the importance of her work by saying, "Individual attention is essential in helping children to grow up to become the kind of creative, flexible and adaptable people, capable of utilizing their talents and fulfilling their individual potential. Empathetic understanding gives rise to child rearing practices that promote emotional, intellectual, and physical growth."[74] Ultimately, your child needs to separate and individuate away from you, needing you less than ever before once the last stage of childhood development—adolescence (ages 13-18 years)—takes hold (as discussed in Chapter 1). Trust your child and how you have led her. After that, you are relating to an adult. Ride the waves of honest recognition. Be a guide who is also an ally and build sails of peace.

> Your parenting role begins to change as your older adolescent or young adult child's developmental milestones force your relationship to change—again.

Your parenting role begins to change as your older adolescent or young adult child's developmental milestones force your relationship to change—again. It will settle into less of a separate, rocky roller-coaster experimental parent-and-teen relationship and into a more seasoned, reasonable, and mature one. Whatever the dynamics have been will remain unless you value and convey the importance of working on things to improve your relationship and change negative patterns between you. Your growing young adult needs your encouragement and permission to be free and to emerge as he truly is—a separate, unique individual in the world thinking, feeling, functioning, and experiencing life apart from you. Your evolving child is becoming or has become an adult and needs you to let go. You need to allow him to request that, so do your part and release the strong hold. When you give emotional or physical space, you hope that he is safe while away from you. The good news is that when that happens, he comes back to you with appreciation for your release of him as you recognize his natural desire to explore and be independent.

Your child always prefers your attention, acceptance, and encouragement to your rejection, absence and lack of support. She wants you to wish her well, have faith in her abilities and desires, and let her go when necessary. When you do this, you can enjoy your time together more throughout adulthood. You can understand what it felt like to grow up and know your child is standing where you once were. So, with sincerity and compassion, develop your ability to become a calm, benevolent parent. When you learn how to let go and hear your grown child's wishes for you to do so, she will be more inclined to want to spend time with you and feel more confident when apart. She will feel understood, respected, and more like an equal. Ray Bradbury wrote in his book, *Farewell Summer*, "Learning to let go should be learned before learning to get. Life should be touched, not strangled. You've got to relax, let it happen at times, and at others move forward with it."[75]

> You can understand what it felt like to grow up and know your child is standing where you once were.

A Reciprocal Relationship

The relationship you have with your child over time parallels your own lifetime learning experience. You both learn and grow, to the degree that you can. You have the privilege of impacting the life of another while you experience and heal your own life. Keep in mind that whether your child is more like you or less like you, all of his unique gifts and abilities shine and help to create a balance to yours. Your relationship contains many elements that are experienced mutually, shared, and interchanged. You can both enjoy a ball game, dinner, a concert together or a conversational meeting of the minds. You may also bring out qualities in each other that are difficult to deal with, yet are signs of reciprocity in that you are both feeling the same complaint and both want things to improve.

You can each acknowledge the conflict, and can each agree to take responsibility for your parts. Sometimes your child's qualities or temperament may seem reminiscent, thus challenging for you further, so ask yourself a few questions. Ask if this similarity is a reflection of someone you had difficult or negative feelings or interactions with. Perhaps there is a projection of a part of yourself unseen or unexpressed that is triggering you with your child's mannerisms, attitude or behavior. Either way, you have unconsciously associated bad feelings between you. Whatever the issue, it points to a reciprocal investigation. Both of you feel the impact of the challenge and need to participate in its solution. You may approach it from different angles, but remember that the goal is to engender understanding, empathy and peace. If only one person is motivated or capable of active resolution, positive change can be initiated, albeit in a less effective way. If that is the case, then the reciprocity is not literal but merely symbolic.

Understand that a difference of opinion is not a breach of respect. Since perceptions often vary and are a cause of misunderstandings and hurt feelings, know that you will need to negotiate that terrain. Be open. Be willing to hear your child's perceptions about how you parent and how he feels. After all, as in any reciprocal relationship, room must be made to accept both points of view. Listen to your child's deepening voice along with your own.

When you consciously parent for life, you come from a calmer, clearer mind and see the relative cause and effect outcomes that result from human synergy. Your synergistic (not co-dependent) relationship with your child concludes that people with different complementary skills can cooperate and create better outcomes. In co-dependent or other unhealthy relationship patterns, family members disenfranchise each other and the joy is stolen from the time you share. She can learn

> You can each acknowledge the conflict, and can each agree to take responsibility for your parts.

from you and you can learn from her as separate beings. In co-dependency, the enmeshed and often boundary-less dynamics create less favorable results and more psychological drama and trauma.

In Melody Beattie's bestseller, *Co-Dependent No More: How to Stop Controlling Others and Start Caring for Yourself,* she describes co-dependency as form of control and emotional over-involvement often disguised as rescuing and enabling both which are destructive to healthy relationships for the child's eventual self-mastery. Co-dependents, according to Beattie, "...rescue, persecute and then feel victimized."[76] During your lifetime relationship with your child, understand that you do not need to change each other or continue to act out old patterns from your family of origin; you just have to accept and adapt to one another as you both keep on living. Taking personal responsibility and finding ways to become personally empowered is where the truth and subsequent peace and happiness lie for both of you. Allow your strengths and your child's strengths to complement each other, accept your differences, and create the best version of your lifetime bond that you can.

> He will know it is safe to explore and be independent and that he can count on the lessons of his youth and the lessons about relationships starting with you.

Your task is to build up enough trust and safety along the way as you and your child grow together so that when released, your child can leave the cocoon of home, spread his own wings securely, and fly out into the world. He will know it is safe to explore and be independent and that he can count on the lessons of his youth and the lessons about relationships starting with you. Find ways to increase your natural synergy. Create better ways to connect, relate, and solve problems, misunderstandings, and long-standing issues between or within each of you. The time you have is precious. See your child emerge as he finds himself away from you. See him as a grown adult and more able to relate as one. As you learn to let go, bit by bit, you both grow more into yourselves. The strength of each individual becomes clear and the process of finding peace begins to make more sense. Ironically, by respecting individual wholeness and separateness, your relationship connectedness deepens in a transformational way.

Remember What It Felt Like to Be a Child, and Then Grow Up

Remember what it felt like to be a child. Take a moment and allow your mind to drift back in time. Allow yourself to easily regress to a time when you were a small, trusting, vulnerable, and powerless child. Remember that you needed consistent kindness, love, care, affection, empathy, and encouragement. You may have had your needs met or may have gone without. For most people, the experience of growing up combines some sort of mix between heaven and hell. You required your caregivers to realize the importance of your needs (some of your wants) and your drive toward having them fulfilled. You were an innocent and helpless child, learning about who to trust (who not to trust), what your perceptions and roles were (and what they were not), and how to become empowered (or disempowered) in your life as you grew. You moved from having been a child with all of the innocence, hopes, dreams, and needs you felt at the time, searching to validate your perceptions and gain gradual independence. You needed your parent to know when to hold you tight and know when to let you go. You knew the importance of learning from experience, achieving your developmental tasks as you were able, and seeing where you could go from there. You knew it then, and you know it now.

> You know what it felt like when you did not get the understanding, empathy and support you needed.

You know what it felt like when you did not get the understanding, empathy and support you needed. Because you know how that feels, and how she may feel if you do not—give that to your child. Only ask, teach, and expect your child's best to emerge with love and respect, without the pressure of perfectionism or low expectations. Both can be a crushing blow to your child's self-esteem. You are doing your child a big favor by being present and reasonable, while cheering him on as he does his best.

Remember what it was like when you were younger. At some later point in your history, you grew into a young adult forging a life of your own. Whether you matured gently or were hurled into adulthood by some striking or traumatic events and choices you made or were made for you, you developed into an adult. Your physicality, emotional range, intellectual focus, and spiritual development all are at the core of who you are as an adult. Those elements, the choices you make, and the responsibility you take for your life all factor into your being a full-fledged and well-rounded functional adult. The process of maturity can take a lifetime to master. Remember that for yourself and your child.

Depending on your attitude about lifetime learning and healing your life, your perspective can cause you to externalize or internalize your experiences. You develop the richness of your self-knowledge and gratitude for all of the detailed chapters of your life story. Your identity became known to you as you transitioned into adulthood by chronology, developmental mastery, rites of passage, choice, and life experience. Depending on your personal process, your family and social environments have provided you with the space to work, play, and experiment. You knew when you felt ready to be yourself in a realm unknown. Your hopes, dreams, pain, and interpretations led your way, and your future was only a stone's throw away. Life, especially to the young, exists in each moment in time, and the future remains distant and unwritten. Live as though life is still your classroom and also your playground. Treat yourself with the love and respect that you give to your child and vice versa. Trust that you will learn your lessons well, be true to your own personal ethics, take safe risks, and enjoy your time along the way.

You have got to know where you have been in life in order to know where you are going, where you begin to lead another, and trust yourself while doing both. Realize as you think, feel, parent, work, and relate to others what parts of your younger life experience are still with you now and what parts you have released. Embrace the truth of your personal story and the history that still influences you today. Consider what you have been conditioned to think regarding what it means to be a child and what it feels like and means to you now to live as an adult.

> Remember what it was like when you were younger.

> Embrace the truth of your personal story and the history that still influences you today.

Knowing When to Hold On and When to Let Go Brings Benefits

As you practice your skills as a lifetime parent, learn when it feels right to hold on and why, and when you need to let go, and to what degree. Learn to release some control over your child's life for each passage and situation. Understanding when to hold on and when to let go is one of the most necessary and challenging of all parental skills. When to do so combines wisdom gained from knowing your child, knowing yourself, and being aware of the necessary progression of your relationship evolution over time. You gradually release the privilege of being involved in or having control over all aspects of your child's life. When your child is young then grows into being a teen and adult, you take care of him in different ways.

Over time, your child integrates your support so he can take care of himself without you. Eventually, he will use that knowledge to care for himself, and others, including with his own child (if he decides to become a parent) when the time comes.

Understanding this balance requires sensitivity to the familiar trapeze act that only a lifetime parent can fully understand. As Deborah Reber wrote in *Chicken Soup for the Teenage Soul*, "Letting go does not mean that you do not care about someone anymore. It is just realizing that the only person you really have control over is yourself."[77] Your job as your child's advocate is never-ending, but you must release the importance of your influence especially as your child is learning to stand up and advocate for himself.

You need to learn to let go almost as fast as your child enters your arms, your world, and your life. You see your child develop and risk, succeed, fall, and get back up while you decide if it is appropriate to hold on or let go during each one of those times. You and your child need you to learn this complex and delicate balance. Readiness and receptivity are king. You know when you are stretching outside of your comfort zone or are making a change when it comes to your parental hold. Your child deserves her earned autonomy and independence, even if

> Understanding when to hold on and when to let go is one of the most necessary and challenging of all parental skills.

she is your princess, her personal kingdom starts with you both trusting her.

Be sure to hold your child's hand in your heart of hearts, while releasing your grip when necessary. You will be sure to always have love and reason as your guides as time passes and your relationship continues to mature and blossom. An unknown author articulated beautifully, "Parents hold their children's hands for a while… their hearts forever." Walk beside your child with love, no matter what, how, why or when.

At different times as a conscious parent, knowing when to hold on and when to let go reflects the highest forms of unconditional love, respect, trust, and fairness that you can bestow upon your child. Love is expressed in both active and passive ways in words and behaviors. You cannot stop the flow of life, only ride the waves of it. Your loving intentions are tapered with restraint as you learn when to hold on and when to let go.

Your job as your child's advocate is never-ending, but you must release the importance of your influence especially as your child is learning to stand up and advocate for himself.

Bless and support your child on his journey, allowing his natural process to unfold gradually. Remain nearby as situational protector, guide, encourager, role model, and parent who is a part of his past, present, and future. Become a positive force in your child's life, someone who demonstrates love, support, empathy and compassionate listening. Let go and move with the flow of life and accept these natural changes that accompany maturity. Be willing to embrace new, healthy, adult ways of relating when the time comes as you both grow.

As you parent your child, there are millions of opportunities every day when you will be required to choose whether to hold on or let go (symbolically or literally) of your child, her behavior, or your reaction in some way. Some of your choices may be unpopular, but if you are clear and have conviction, step up as a strong parent. Know that your choices to let go or compromise a new way are successful when you are ultimately both happy and the negotiated outcome is positive, or at least tolerable for both parties. Lessons will appear and reappear until you learn them. Your child may have been screaming important feedback to you for years (in word or behavior), but you will not learn or grow until you are willing to hear and recognize the truth. As you learn from your mistakes and successes, you learn to make better choices and control your reactions. With practice, you respond with calm and clarity necessary to be your child's best parent for life. Strive to keep your hearts close while giving you both healthy room to live your own lives.

Once your child enters the teen years and adulthood, your relationship takes on a new form—as an adult relating to an adult. Some aspects remain intact and other facts must be taken into account. The connotation of what it means to be a parent and a child in relationship together changes. Boundaries, needs, expectations, and even conversations differ and require new parental attitudes and responses. Perceptions evolve as you and your child adapt to new aspects of your relationship, as you bring facets of your former parent-child relationship with you. You begin to understand and know (through experience and instinct) when to lend your opinion and active encouragement, and when to observe, respectfully disagree, and quietly support your child.

Jane Isay also asserted in *Walking on Eggshells* that whatever issues, patterns, feelings, and styles of relating or communicating you have shared up to this point will continue to replay between you and your adult child unless changes are consciously made.[78] Therefore, the sooner you can address unresolved conflicts and stumbling blocks that exist between you and your child, the better your shared future will be. Deal with what is happening now in order to help create what will happen between you later. There is hope that healing and new ways leading to shared peace are available at any time.

As your lifetime parenting relationship shifts from "adult-child" to "adult-adult," the dynamic is redefined. Sometimes you will be able to resolve the patterns between you, and other times, the peace, forgiveness, and resolution reside solely within you. The same is true for your adult child. He may never reach agreement with you on something that is important to him, or feel understood or resolved regarding a long-standing

Bless and support your child on his journey, allowing his natural process to unfold gradually.

issue with you and will then find his path to inner healing without you. Resistance can appear within one of you but does not have to determine the other person's commitment to improving communication between you or find understanding and resolution. Either way, you each make peace as best as you can. As you resolve your patterns and hurt feelings, you both stretch some earlier relationship dynamics resulting in greater communication, equality, and freedom. As you each find peace, you pave the way for increased understanding and compassion in the days to come. Your interactions soften and your style of relating transforms into a better way. Discover as you practice the art of lifetime parenting, what it means to be present and accounted for all the days of your parenting life.

> Deal with what is happening now in order to help create what will happen between you later.

Lead with the Power of Your Heart

As family team leader, you have the ultimate power to lead and follow with intelligence and heart. You have the power to sustain or relinquish control, talk less, and listen more. Lead by deepening the mutual love, respect, trust, and admiration that exists between you. When you consciously agree to grow alongside your child and release what no longer works, or what never worked, you both win and feel happier. Improved communication and sustained connectedness will result. When unresolved difficulties and wounds remain, so too do dysfunctional and unhappy dynamics between you and your child. Memories of years gone by, both the sweet and the sour exist within and between you. Allow those memories to inspire a better way as you move forward. Lead with the power of your heart and make the heart of your home about love.

There is always opportunity in every moment to create a new vision and work toward a better future. Over time you and your adult child will continue to relate and you can potentially elevate your relationship to a deeper level of mutual love and respect. The experience of symbiotic, highly attached interactions and dependencies as parent leading the way comes to its natural end, morphing into something else while your child comes to you as an adult. This process of separation and individuation starts in late adolescence (ages 12 to 18 years), giving you a striking clue into what this journey was all about in the first place.

When you parent well, your child feels secure, strong, and confident in the world. The relationship between you does not vanish in a puff of smoke. On the contrary, it simply takes on a new and different form and meaning. Your child feels sure about herself, sure of who she is and who she is allowed to become, without you, because of you, or in spite of you. This kind of confidence is a good thing. It is better to have a willingness that supports growth and empowerment as this developmental stage of your child's maturity unfolds. You cannot stop the process, just like the process of your own maturation is still unfolding as it should. You can be proud when your child feels capable and self-loving when she steps out on her own. When you parent well, she takes her secure upbringing with her.

Lead with the power of your heart and make the heart of your home about love.

You constantly adapt, from the beginning to the end of your parenting experience. You and your child both experience growing pains: imperfections that give your relationship depth, wisdom, and character. Like a sculpture that stands for a thousand years, it is the crafting, molding, and careful chiseling with time that creates the end result: a beautiful work of art that stands the test of time to value and enjoy. If you acquire the same philosophy about parenting and tend to the lifetime garden of your parent-child relationship by feeding it well, you and your child will thrive. Take responsibility for what you bring to the family table and notice what values you place upon both of you.

Let Go and Learn: Invite Understanding and Resolution

When you begin to understand the nature of all relationships and the overall development of each individual in it, what transpires between you transforms. You keep some of your relationships and grow with them. Some relationships last a lifetime, others remain for a few chapters of your life, and many exist for mere moments. You alter or release the relationships that no longer feel good, make you grow, hurt or no longer serve you. Lessons are learned and you realize that it is time to move on, flowing into the next chapter of your life. Deepak Chopra explains in his book, *The Seven Spiritual Laws of Success*, "Whatever relationships you have attracted in your life at this moment, are precisely the ones you need in your life at this moment. There is hidden meaning behind all events, and this hidden meaning is serving your own evolution."[79] Be willing to understand the purpose of your relationships. Unlock the mystery and see what lessons are in store for you. You help each other to love, learn, and grow, or repeat patterns from the past. This depends on the relationship themes that present themselves and your ability to deal constructively with them. Begin to clarify who you are and the necessary next steps in your evolutionary process. Be inspired to inspire and see what positive change results.

Working things through using honest insight and mutual dialogue offers great lifetime lessons for both you and your child. Walk the road of your personal truths bravely and with integrity. Be strong and courageous as you discover your own revelations and hear your child's feedback. By doing so, you will heal your life and teach by example how to survive, thrive, and be authentic in life. By inviting understanding and resolution, you learn your parental lessons and accept the innocence of youth as well as the wisdom of maturity. Be gentle, strong, fierce, vulnerable, and triumphant. Do what it takes to be happy and live in harmony. After all, that is the bottom line. Make peace with yourself and do all that you can to make peace with your beloved child. You must value personal responsibility and insight, as they are important life skills to teach your child. When combined with the courage to take appropriate action, you can inspire him, too.

Learn to observe and understand where your child's level of functioning is and support her evolution into personal authenticity and self-reliance. Remember to expect that once you learn one aspect of your child's growing needs, you will be

> You can be proud when your child feels capable and self-loving when she steps out on her own.

> Be willing to understand the purpose of your relationships. Unlock the mystery and see what lessons are in store for you.

required by the laws of parenting to adapt to the next set of needs (as the process will never end). Put on your seatbelt and do not expect a smooth ride all the time. When you are prepared to adjust, learn, and enjoy as you travel the journey, the time you spend together is more enjoyable. With your support, your child will bloom and give you parental pride that is unequal to anything else you will ever know.

When you were blessed with the gift of your child and your child was blessed with the gift of you, you were both given a great opportunity. From the very start and with endless moments thereafter, you clearly hold the power to express unconditional love and acceptance, respect, and belief in another person. Your influence lasts a lifetime. However long a time you have with your child here on earth, enjoy the passage of joint experience that builds your lives rich in history shared with the ones you love. Love your child more, hold him a little tighter, and ask him to hug you back. Love your parents more, too, whether they are near to you or not. Each relationship is an opportunity for you to learn, love and heal your heart. You are given a free education to learn to give and receive as much as your heart can hold. Close relationships in this hectic, chaotic, and ever-changing world are a gift worth appreciating and cherishing, so treat them accordingly and hold them close.

Choose to live with the door of healing and insight open forever. It is never too late to love your inner child, find joy in life, and repair, heal, or enjoy your time together with your own child. Recreate your relationship; redefine, deepen, and resolve wounded hearts or broken dynamics, if necessary. This can be done at any age. It can be accomplished to varying degrees, as long as you are both breathing and willing. Do not let anything stop you. There is always hope and possibility when love is involved.

The love between a parent and child lasts a lifetime, even if there are painful shared life experiences. There is no greater gift than to build the foundation for a spectacular lifetime

> When you were blessed with the gift of your child and your child was blessed with the gift of you, you were both given a great opportunity.

relationship with your child, knowing that the tools are always in easy reach as you stroll side by side. Invite the chance for understanding and resolution at every turn while you walk your mutual path.

Every child's wishes are fulfilled or put on a shelf depending on his parents' level of awareness, priority, and ability. Figure out what you can realistically provide and what is outside of your comfort zone and control. Take charge; do what it takes to get it done so that you can be your best self as a parent. Your child may not always get what he wants but you should strive to ensure that he gets what he needs. Make adjustments. Welcome each age and stage of your child's development, while you attune to your own, as well. How you feel, what skills you possess, and how you practice your parental obligation move you toward or away from relating well. Each experience reminds you of your parenting purpose and goals and whether you are on track or not. You come face-to-face with yourself as you provide your protection and loving comfort, own your challenges and limitations, and encourage your child's essential freedom.

... be the change you need in your life and in your family.

As you parent for life, it is significant that you recall your experience as a child and a teen growing into adulthood. The direct experiences that remain in your consciousness, whether known or buried, carry you forward and help establish the kind of parent (and role model) you become. Indirect experiences serve as valuable tools with which to carve out your most comfortable role as a parent moving forward. Remember if your needs were met (or went unmet), how you felt while growing up, and what you needed as far as closeness and independence. You learned about trust, intimacy, and love one way or another. You were encouraged to stand after falling and supported to strike out on your own. Or perhaps you weren't. Whatever you learned, you pass on what you know. You can repeat the past or continue to pass on new knowledge with a heart full of love and commitment all the days of your life. The way you parent impacts your child's life, your grandchild's life, and future generations to come.

Reflect in the vast mirror of love beginning with your child looking up at you. Over time, your eyes connect at equal levels and in many cases, the roles reverse as you are the one looking up. Care for the emotional health of your family system and allow softening of rigid roles, increased understanding, so that mutual respect can emerge. Remember the powerful visual reminder of your child getting bigger over time. The symbolic and literal merge in the phrase "growing up." The relationship between you and your child never ends. Your bond can always be reconnected or recreated as it is one of the most powerful evolutionary relationships that transcends time. Even when letting go, you both hold onto what connects you. It has been said that even when family branches are everywhere, their roots are in one place.

The way you parent impacts your child's life, your grandchild's life, and future generations to come.

Even when letting go, you both hold onto what connects you.

Homework Assignment 19

Hold On, Let Go!

An interesting way to understand the concept of holding on and letting go is to make it a physical exercise.

- To demonstrate this concept in simple terms, make a tight fist.

- If possible make two tight fists.

- Do this as hard as you can. Hold, squeeze, and tighten.

- Do so for as long as you can and tighten your grip incrementally. Continue to hold, squeeze, and tighten.

- Put all of your strength and energy into clasping your fists tightly so that you are aware of nothing else in the moment.

- Hold on a little longer, then release. Just *let go*. Release your grasp and allow your hand(s) to relax and do nothing.

- Feel the relief in simply letting go.

- Notice what you feel.

Realize what it feels like as you compare the two sensations of *holding on and letting go*. Notice how easy it was to actually release your grip and simply let go. It took no thought, no energy as you realized you had nothing forcing your grip. Notice the energy it took to maintain your grip and how effortless it was to release that same hold.

When dealing with feelings, power struggles, and your own resistance to giving your child the space and respect he or she deserves, it is not always that easy. However, moments in parenting can be compared to this physical metaphor.

Notice how this simple exercise can become an analogy or physical metaphor for other struggles or relationships in your life. Many opportunities exist to help you choose whether to hold on or let go in your life. Sometimes that choice makes all the difference. Often, your child's lifetime relationship with you depends upon it.

CHAPTER TWENTY

Create a Lifetime Relationship with Your Child

Love begins at home, and it is not how much we do . . .
but how much love we put in that action.

—Mother Teresa, Humanitarian, Nobel Prize Winner

Treasure Every Moment, Every Stage

When you bring a child into the world and into your home you agree to protect, guide, teach, and above all else, give and keep on giving your love. Every moment counts, and every moment is special. The joyous and difficult moments deepen emotional connection and create memories, inspiring you to parent without reserve. Whether your cup is full or empty, realize the essence of giving all that you can, and do your best. Realize the tremendous, endless epic potential for your lifetime relationship. Treasure every moment and every stage. Cherish the positives between you and your child in the moment. Look forward to create more wells of peace, joy, and hope in the days to come.

Realize the awesome power of your parent-child relationship at every turn. Your connection sparkles and dims as your relationship is born, transitions, and resolves over time. Your heart is uplifted, touched, wounded, bewildered, challenged, awakened, healed, and strengthened as is your child's. When you are aware of your parenting purpose and

> Realize the tremendous, endless epic potential for your lifetime relationship. Treasure every moment and every stage.

266

resolve the painful parts of your history, you take responsibility for what you create with the child you love. You are changed for having become a parent. Find joy in connecting well with your child. Work through the obstacles and your own emotional triggers, however difficult, because your child is worth it. Notice natural changes, the way your child is growing and maturing, and relate accordingly. Take time often in your harried life to stop and spend time with your child. Your love is special and your time together is irreplaceable. The lives you lead are made rich with history, substance, and a lifetime commitment that you both value. What makes it all worthwhile is to live life with the ones you love, to let the ones you love live life and shine in their own way. When you do that, nothing important is ever lost.

Your connection with your child spans a lifetime. The urge for your child to connect well with you is deep and significant. Your instinct to connect well may vary, especially when you feel emotionally triggered, exhausted, or distracted by life pulling you in different directions. This is based on your family history, your ability to love, nurture, and account for yourself as you deal with everyday life. As time moves on so does the need to resolve the unspoken feelings between you. Your relationship can flourish and you can refuse to remain stagnant, limited by the past, or allow current challenges to impact your interactions.

You must meet your child's basic needs for him to feel that he is worthy, that he belongs and that he receives enough love, protection, and proper guidance from you. Your child needs to connect, disconnect, relate to, be loved by, be separate from, and ultimately learn from you. Remember that "no effort that we make to attain something beautiful is ever lost."[80] Find yourself deep in the muck or soaring above it, but keep on loving. Parenting is the hardest job you will ever love. Because of that truth, your lifetime efforts promote the next generation, which also affects future generations. Settle into the realities of your life and keep forging ahead, exemplifying the ultimate in parental consciousness and self-care.

A real key to enjoying the moments of child-rearing and

Work through the obstacles and your own emotional triggers, however difficult, because your child is worth it.

267

beyond revolves around your self-awareness and sensitivity toward your child. You are building a relationship designed to endure the test of time. Your gift of lifetime love and all that comes with it promotes growth, healing, and close ties that last forever. When you become more aware that you are parenting for life, anything becomes possible in your shared expedition.

Face it, in a whole lifetime there are tough parenting moments. No matter how hard you may try to avoid them, power struggles and conflicts of all kinds emerge between you. It is natural and inevitable, like the sun rising in the morning and setting at night. Do not be surprised, just be ready. It is in these moments that thoughtful strategies work best. It is better than making a choice that you will not be proud of or that could hurt your child. The same is true when you parent multiple children. Siblings have their own dynamic and parents often have great difficulty witnessing their children in conflict. Mothers and fathers want to protect their children from danger or harmful predators, not from a sibling. They do not wish to watch their children fight or argue, even though it is typically unavoidable.

> You are building a relationship designed to endure the test of time.

The Zuckerman Parker Handbook of Developmental and Behavioral Pediatrics for Primary Care notes that when children are three years apart or greater in their age spacing, there is less sibling rivalry. However, when siblings are spaced less than three years apart, and depending on their birth order and gender, there tends to be more rivalry between them to gain parental attention, exclusive parental love and to gain dominance. [81]

The sense of lack of control and upset, inner conflict about who to support, or how to inspire effective resolution can be a source of great frustration (in both parent and child) if children are not given the skills to resolve conflicts on their own. Learning how to empower children to resolve their own conflicts or disagreements is an invaluable (and sometimes mystifying) gift that benefits everyone.

Keep your love and humor handy, you will need them both often.

Listen to your child's point of view with a loving, open heart and receptive, open ears. Put your defenses on the shelf, along with your ego and need to be right. If problems escalate, self-preserve by taking a "time out" while keeping your child's safety, self-esteem, and dignity intact. Absolutely refrain from setting consequences when you are angry, overly stressed out, emotionally out of control, or tired. Never victimize, demoralize, diminish or aggress upon your child. If you have been aggressed upon or mistreated, get help and stop the cycle of violence and abuse. When your child is old enough, allow her to voice her opinion when setting appropriate consequences. Be willing to take some for yourself while you recognize that many consequences can be positive and rewarding, rather than negative and demeaning.

Cool yourself down and remember that this person is your child for life. "Time outs" for everyone offer a way to distance yourselves emotionally from power-struggles, behavioral challenges, personal triggers, and inappropriate consequences as you preserve your relationship. Recognize the unresolved emotional or trauma triggers from the past that have you responding irrationally and work them out away from your child. Relax and think through reasonable and rational responses. This mindful approach allows you to regroup and respond better to conflicts or communication breakdowns. By being intentional you behave in appropriate and responsible ways, keep your child safe, and are a stronger role model for her. Your display of empathy, healthy limit setting, creative problem solving and benevolence with conscious intent will be greatly appreciated.

Over time, you have the opportunity to examine how the roles in your family team have played out and whether various interaction styles, themes, adapted attitudes, and expectations have worked or not. Awareness and wisdom are "supposed to" come with age and maturity, although maturity does not always come with age. We all know someone who is "old enough to know better" but still says or does the wrong thing anyway,

> Keep your love and humor handy, you will need them both often.

perhaps time and again. It is very exciting to realize that learning is a lifetime process. It comes in both little and big ways; you just have to be open to each lesson. You are never too old or too young to learn. The learner just has to be ready. There is always more information (within and around you) to bring into your awareness, your relationships, and your overall life experience all the days of your life.

Despite a lifetime of opportunities for closeness between you, do all you can to reconcile any conflicts that separate you in your present lives. Your time together has a beginning, and you share a physical ending, but not an emotional or spiritual conclusion. Because the way your child is parented and what his experience is (or was) during childhood (and the teen years) lasts a lifetime, be aware. This ripple effect can easily move across future generations. Your grown child may choose to copy how he was parented or rebel against it, so always keep that in mind. How he felt as a child, teen, and young adult may cause him to parent in the exact same or exact opposite way later on. Your consistent love and mindful parenting helps ensure positive results. If imitation is the sincerest form of flattery, then make your lead count.

> You are never too old or too young to learn. The learner just has to be ready.

Caring for your child gives you the chance to give more than you receive and develops you both in different ways in the process. You get the pleasure of giving without gain and an invitation to teach, guide, and encourage using unconditional love, support, respect, and trust as your guides. As you practice the art of parenting for life, accept personal responsibility for yourself and blame your child less. Blame, shame, fault finding, or labeling ought to be replaced by acceptance, tolerance, appreciation, and honoring your child's personal dignity. Begin to understand that to release ineffective parenting, you must let go of what does not work and continue to relate lovingly and respectfully. This is a vital part of the whole formula. For both of you, psychological and behavioral personal evolution is possible each day, each month, and each year of your lives. Both individuals fill an important role in the development of the other at very different stages in your parallel lives.

While you relate to your child, a fundamental aspect of the unfolding moments to enjoy is to find the truth, beauty, and meaning within each experience. Persevere, give all that you can, self-correct, self-preserve, and increase self-care in your routine. Modify your habitual reactions to your personal triggers by being present in the moment and work on your own issues away from your child. Intentional self-correction enables you to regroup, open yourself to insight, and create better ways to relate with love as your guide. It is your honor and duty to seize the endless opportunities available during your time together; teach and learn from your child as much as you can. Harriet Lerner, author of *The Dance of Intimacy*, crystallized it well when she wrote, "Intimate relationships cannot substitute for a life plan. But to have any meaning or viability at all, a life plan must include intimate relationships."[82] Find the intimacy in your shared moments and become comfortable with the necessary role of separation. This balance helps to secure an overall healthy connection. The resulting impact of both will connect you and set you both free. As family team leader, your attitude about how you value this important relationship will naturally build the chapters of your lifetime story together. Make sure that it is a good story, with a healthy and happy beginning, middle, and end.

Remember that Knowledge is Limitless

When you plant seeds in a garden, you make sure that they have all of the elements necessary for growth. You nurture the plant as it grows and blossoms. As you learn about your child and yourself, your lives remain open to new information that support and nurture everyone. You continue to learn and study as you can. Your child finds herself bit by bit, and you hold steady as the observant nurturer. Experience and sense who your child is becoming as she undergoes her personal metamorphosis in her own time. Observe, keep learning, and encourage your child to embrace self-discovery, healthy self-esteem and relationships, and lifelong learning.

As you continue on your life's path, know that you can awaken to a more conscious way of living, one that gives

> While you relate to your child, a fundamental aspect of the unfolding moments to enjoy is to find the truth, beauty, and meaning within each experience.

you limitless knowledge and the ability to heal your life and relationships. Even during times of conflict or uncertainty, when limits are tested, and your time and patience are wearing thin, love and respect must prevail. Love and firm limits are instituted and life is kind, fair, and in balance. Remember that the impact and aftereffects of how your child is consistently parented during childhood and beyond, lasts a lifetime. Over time and with careful diligence on your part, wounds and unhappy memories can mend. This pattern of cause and effect can move across future generations. Like throwing cooked spaghetti against the wall, more sticks than you may think. If not before conception, then certainly after birth and all of the years to come, the recognition of how significant this relationship really is begins to sink in.

Observe, keep learning, and encourage your child to embrace self-discovery, healthy personal boundaries, and lifelong learning.

When you are given the chance to parent a child, you have to think of someone else's needs. You love unconditionally, give more than you receive (at times), nurture and guide, must be strong, humble, and encourage someone else's growth. You grow alongside your child and it is good. Otherwise, you are alive, but not fully living if you cease to progress. You face your own demons and angels when you realize how you want to parent and how you were parented. You then decide if you want to parent the same way or create a new way of relating.

Embrace your parental life's purpose and live accordingly as best you can, day-by-day. Sometimes you need to heal your own childhood wounds before being the best parent your child needs you to be. As long as you continue to work on yourself and grow, learn from your mistakes, and stop the urge to repeat the negative cycle, you will be ahead of the game. Make "learn from it" your mantra. Replace negative habit patterns with positive ones. Your child will forgive you as long as you are accountable for your words and actions and apologize with sincerity, when it is called for. This will demonstrate your willingness to reveal your humanity and be accountable for it. You are parenting responsibly when you acknowledge your part in each dynamic. It is a dance between you and each of you have your parts. Take care of yourself and your child as you model how to heal wounded places with honesty and courage, and then thrive in life.

Thich Nhat Hanh, Zen Buddhist spiritual leader and author of *From Peace is Every Step: The Path of Mindfulness in Everyday Life*, encapsulated this point well when he said, "I have heard many stories about parents who have hurt their children so much, planting many seeds of suffering in them. But I believe that the parents did not mean to plant those seeds. They did not intend to make their children suffer. Maybe they received the same kind of seeds from their parents. There is a continuation in the transmission of seeds and their father and mother might have gotten those seeds from their grandfather and grandmother. Most of us are victims of a kind of living that is not mindful, and the practice of mindful living, of meditation, can stop these kinds of suffering and end the transmission of such sorrow to our children and grandchildren. We can break the cycle by not allowing these kinds of seeds of suffering to be passed on to our children, our friends, or anyone else."[83]

In the book, *A Lifetime of Peace: Essential Writings By and About Thich Nhat Hanh*, he reminds us that, "If you look deeply into the palm of your hand, you will see your parents and all generations of your ancestors. All of them are alive in this moment. Each is present in your body. You are the continuation of each of these people."[84] This being said, your connection to family members is your chance to expand or contract wells of knowledge, love, respect, trust, and tradition as well as to break cycles of pain, dysfunction, and isolation that remain for you.

Self-discovery is an outgrowth of fierce introspection and a conscious parenting practice for you and your child. Over time, you develop your relationship. You both become accountable and responsible for yourselves, free to fall, and encouraged to stand. Limits are set as proof of valuing family rules, personal boundaries, and safety at home. Let your child know how important he is to you and how important his well-being,

. . . your connection to family members is your chance to expand or contract wells of knowledge, love, respect, trust, and tradition as well as to break cycles of pain, dysfunction, and isolation that remain for you.

health, and happiness are. Express your positive feedback and observations about your child's unique gifts, natural talents, individuality, and personal growth. Raise and then release your child when the time comes. Ultimately, his happiness, life skills, and character originate from the integration of his early and holistic experience within the family combined with his life experience in the world. This is reflected in who he is and how he handles life's successes, trials, and tribulations. Make your unconditional love and support for your child available and accessible until the end of time. Be a parent who is trustworthy in word and action. Develop your character so that your child can develop his.

> Think about what you believe your child is here to teach you . . . Expect great things from yourself, your child, and your relationship.

Trading Places: What Your Child Can Teach You About Yourself

You have so much to learn about your child. Similarly, you have much to learn about yourself. Often, your child brings out aspects of you—sometimes the best of you and other times perhaps the worst. Your child by virtue of being around you so much and requiring a great deal from you, makes you aware of areas in which you have grown in your life and areas that still need development. If you pay close attention, your child shows you more of who you are through direct and indirect feedback than you ever thought possible. At times, the feedback you receive practically slaps you in the face. You cannot avoid it, even though you may try. In the easiest and most difficult interactions, there are always many lessons you can learn. Think about what you believe your child is here to teach you. Take a moment. Better yet, take a lifetime.

Instead of being defensive, letting your ego and need to be right lead the way, be open to feedback and the accompanying life lessons that your child brings to you. Whether you think you know it all, are similar to one another or vastly different, or at different places in life, there is always information to help you grow. When you appreciate a new point of view, you see the situation or your role in it differently. Rather than pushing away feedback as potentially new knowledge to help you to learn and love better, you take it in. You welcome discussion, personal, and shared exploration. You absorb experience like a sponge, observing with emotion and neutrality. You use it as viable information for you to live with the greatest level of awareness possible. As you live this way, you eagerly point the way for your child to do the same.

Walk the daily and yearly path of your lifetime relationship with the desire to love, learn and grow. This attitude helps to build the foundation of closeness that family members need. Release the urge to make excuses and blame your child for what she brings out in you. Hold your parenting responsibility in reverence for its massive impact on the life of another. Expect great things from yourself, your child, and your relationship. The potential is limitless. Cherish your shared moments and reflect on times apart with awareness and gratitude.

When you parent as both teacher and student, transformation naturally occurs, like a million rebirths throughout your lifetime relationship. You both grow and growth is life. Since knowledge is limitless, be willing to be accountable for what you know and what you do not know. Acknowledge the accuracy about you, at least from your child's perspective. Recognize what you know about your child from your own vantage point, too. Own your life as a living example and humble guide teaching and showing how to use your history to inspire your future. Be receptive to finding peace within and between you and be comfortable agreeing to disagree. When the mutual love, respect, and empathy follow you all the days of your lives, your relationship is successful. You deter success when you get caught up in excuses, blame, and avoiding responsibility for the life you create. It is you who determines your success in life, in all your relationships, and everything else. Mark these words in your mind and make them a permanent tattoo on your heart.

> Whatever time you have been given together is a true gift and an intricate lifetime love story waiting to unfold.

Your Heart Knows No Bounds

Your heart shares a beat with your child's heart. Whether you are relating to and loving a biological, inter-generational, adopted, or foster child, the love for your child is never-ending. The parental job you hold is an awesome one: all-encompassing, life-giving, and life-affirming. You define your love in feelings that words may or may not be able to describe. The love between you is reciprocal, powerful, and endless, no matter what challenges befall you along the way. When it comes to love for your child, there is no end. Your heart is already parenting for life. Your head is learning how to do so.

To care for another person is to give one's heart unconditionally and without reserve. The task of loving another is made real by the commitment to do so once the heart has realized that love. It is timeless and eternal.

> Your responsibility is to try to understand what your child is both saying and showing to you, all the days of your lives.

In your lifetime relationship, both you and your child enjoy the gifts that unconditional love, acceptance, self-awareness, mutual respect, trust, and good communication bring. Over time, your child will learn to reciprocate and show you the earned respect and trust you give him. Your high ideals mixed with high behavioral standards will translate to him. You have generously offered the gift of a lifetime love to your child from infancy into adulthood. Whatever time you have been given together is a true gift and an intricate lifetime love story waiting to unfold.

As a guide, protector, and observer, apply and adapt what you know as you learn about who your child is. Nurture, encourage, empower, and support her. Inspire your child as best as you can by being your best self. You may not understand your child's thoughts, behaviors, and motivations, but that does not matter. Your child is imperfect, as are you, and always needs you to love and accept her no matter what. You are your child's advocate and ally, not adversary. Recognize that moments of identity crisis or "acting out" mirror her inner world and that she will find herself as best as she can. Be gentle in that knowledge, remembering never to betray or leave her and never to diminish her value and feelings. To do either of those things would be a terrible betrayal, a loss beyond measure that your child never deserves.

Your responsibility is to try to understand what your child is both saying and showing to you, all the days of your lives. Even if it comes out wrong, your heart still loves your child and you still need each other. After all, if there is one thing that you can count on in this uncertain, ever-changing world it is having a reservoir of love that may sometimes dim, but never runs out. With that in mind, teach about healthy loving relationships, starting with the ones at home. Work on yourself. Your home environment needs to be a safe haven for all its family members. Home is a place that supplies the means to learn lifetime habits, foster healthy intimacy, and creates the potential for a spiritual sanctuary for the soul. Strong individuality and the tolerance for differences, along with the good habits of mutual p ersonal accountability matter. Healing hurt feelings and resolving conflicts with respect and empathy are prized in your home. No matter the question, love is the answer. Remind yourself daily that it is a new day and a new way and love is the answer. Learn from living. Live every day as though your life depended on it; your child is depending on you to help reveal its deeper meaning. He needs to learn from you how to do it for himself.

You parent a life outside your own. You parent for the rest of your life in new and emerging ways.

Use your love for your child as your guide. It is an honor, privilege, and duty to take advantage of the endless opportunities you have to advance your parent-child lifetime relationship. Work toward healthy interactions as you teach your child and learn from her every day. Use this understanding while you look at yourself, your patterns, and your past. Become an expert at loving without conditions, pairing love and respect, active listening, and self-correction. Keep your ego and need to be right or in constant control in check. Like any dance, know when to lead and when it is best to follow. The dance of your parent-child relationship is life-giving and life-changing. Be the parent your child needs you to be. Be the parent to the child you once were who still resides within you. Be a good mom or dad to yourself. Listen, love, respect, empathize with, and observe both of you.

Define Your Legacy, Your Ultimate Message

Parenting for life is an immense undertaking. It is made all the more significant when you consider the complexity of the individuals forming the relationships that define it. As family leader, it is incumbent upon you to pass along aspects of yourself, and values you hold dear—hopefully the best that you have to offer. The underlying task you have is to lead the way with love and wisdom. It carries with it the enormous potential of a well-loved, well lived life that creates your personal family story. You parent a life outside your own. You parent for the rest of your life in new and emerging ways. Naturally, you are opened, closed, pushed to the limit, transformed, and forced to be the older and wiser guide, role-model, and caregiver. Choose to see your parallel lives as a blessing, whether your relationship is easy or challenging. See your relationship as a guiding force, an interchange of two souls whose lives serve to inspire growth, and who will never again be the same because of your connection.

Like a gifted artist or writer, respect your perceptions, receive your ideas, and let them inspire your next work of art. Take each of your *insight moments* and with patience and a sense of creative intent, build upon your *lifetime insight* experience. Keep them available to use as tools throughout your life. Use your love and wisdom to make magic and remember what is really important in the grand scheme of life. Think before you act and speak, and be wary of emotional outbursts and unresolved attempts to define you or your true purpose. Welcome the gift that true understanding brings. Put down the dark mask of illusion and pick up the light of truth instead.

At the end of your time together, and along the way, you draw your own conclusions. Gloria Steinem, feminist, journalist, social and political activist wrote in her book, *Outrageous Acts and*

> Welcome the gift that true understanding brings. Put down the mask of illusion and pick up the light of truth instead.

278

Everyday Rebellions, Second Edition, "Happy or unhappy, families are all mysterious. We have only to imagine how differently we would be described—and will be, after our deaths—by each of the family members who believe they know us."[85] For many, the memories, wishes, and bonds closest to the heart mean the most. Your life is gifted to you, so live it wisely with clarity, intention, and purpose.

Cherish your child and all you hold dear while you can. Let all whom you love, including your child and yourself, know how much you care. You are in it for life—so seize the opportunities to enhance, transform and build an incredible happy life. You deserve it and so does your child. Hopefully, you leave your loved ones feeling loved, valued, and more fulfilled for having known you. Your presence and contribution to the life of another human being has made a meaningful difference. Your child's life is forever enriched because of your life and the ripple effect of your relationship continues indefinitely.

Barbara Bush was quoted in the book, *Barbara Bush: Matriarch of a Dynasty,* by Pamela Kilian, from the former First Lady's commencement address to Wellesley College: "But as important as your obligations as a doctor, a lawyer, a business leader will be, you are a human being first, and those human connections with spouses, with children, with friends, are the most important investments you will ever make. At the end of your life, you will never regret not having passed one more test, winning one more verdict, or not closing one more deal. You will regret time not spent with a husband, a friend, a child, or a parent."[86]

Invest in yourself and your child so that at the end of your shared journey, you are both skilled in the human art of giving and receiving love and respect. Even though you have other relationships that need tending to in your life, the one with your child is irreplaceable. It validates the power of true love and the stunning potential of personal growth for both of you. Make improving current moments in your life a high priority. Memories last a lifetime, so why not choose to create the life you

> You can choose to transcend the repetition of history, refuse to live with unawareness or mediocrity, and strive to create a memorably healing, happy, and extraordinary life.

> Your presence and contribution to the life of another human being has made a meaningful difference.

and your child deserve and desire most of all? You agree to love partially and with conditions, or fully and unconditionally, and without hesitation. You can choose to transcend the repetition of history, refuse to live with unawareness or mediocrity, and strive to create a memorably healing, happy, and extraordinary life.

When all is said and done, it is all about the relationship with yourself and the significant people in your life that matters most. If we are here to love and learn, heal and connect—then the time to open up to this way of living is now.

In a real sense, the course of action you choose to take as you relate to each person and as you relate to your child makes your life worth living, meaningful, and truly your own. Enjoy your time together. Make it a prototype for other significant relationships in your life where unconditional love, support and respect (and all the good that goes with each) is practiced. Similarly, model appropriate roles and boundaries and support mutual accountability (at the appropriate developmental stages). Revere and honor these values and those that mean the most to you. Remain aware of yourself, your child, and all of the learning opportunities in your life as a vital part of your daily parenting practice. You both deserve to find peace and empowerment in your lives.

Remember that parenting is a journey of love. Cherish your relationships, especially those in your "Circle of Extraordinary People" (including your child, children, special friends and loved ones, and yourself). Trust the wisdom of your heart. Claim the permanence of your relationship with your child as you grow, evolve, and resolve your lifetime bond. Know that whatever happens, you have made a significant contribution to someone else's life and your own, and it is an unforgettable adventure. In the end, be grateful and humbled that you had the privilege to love another person in such a special and enduring way.

*H*omework Assignment *20*

Your Final Words of Wisdom

Imagine that you have the ability to step into your future, as you envision what can be. This is a chance to contemplate your entire life's impact upon your child. If you have more than one child, keep each one in mind. While there are so many aspects of life and the parent-child dynamic to consider, this exercise gives you supreme clarity about what you can control. This will help direct you to living the messages of your heart.

- Get into a comfortable physical position in a pleasant and private room. Sit quietly with your *Parenting Journal* and a pen or pencil. Make sure that you are uninterrupted for a few minutes.

- Close your eyes for a few moments. Wash away the contents of your mind, your emotions and your day. Sit quietly, relax, breathe deeply, clear your mind, calm your heart and be still. Allow yourself to relax as fully as possible in this moment. When you are ready, open your eyes.

- Ask yourself one simple question, "When I am at the end of my life, all that I have lived, learned and with all the love that I feel for my child, what is my greatest, wisest teaching? With all that I want for my child's future, what is the most important message I want and need to convey to him or her at the end of my life?

- What is the most important message I need my child to know, and I need to share before I die? What "straight to the heart" expression of love, encouragement, wisdom, legacy, empowerment, and inspiration do I plan to leave behind?

- Make sure that you write down your answers in your *Parenting Journal*.

- Make especially sure that you convey in words and actions your lifetime message of love from now on.

- Live the messages of your heart. Do not wait until the very end. After all, all that really matters is love.

Afterword

If you have parented with this kind of vision and discipline while traveling on your shared lifetime relationship ride together, great! If not, how come? What is stopping you? If you have just begun, that is alright. Start from where you are, and live the deeply felt messages of your heart. Come from a place of love not fear. Envision the brightest future, one that is transformative and restorative. Make this world a better place while you are here. Be reflective and take stock of the dynamics in your relationships. Make peace, reconcile all that you can within yourself, and between you and the ones you love.

One definition of a well lived life is that at the end of your journey, you have lived a life full with love, meaning and rich experience. You are the person you were destined to become, the parent your child needs, and the best role model you could be. Your lifetime parenting practice influences the parenting practices of future generations to come. You have chosen wisely and can live in peace with your choices. Enjoy the benefits of consciously creating your lifetime relationship with your child better than you thought you ever could! Make yourself and your child proud.

Learn how to make peace with yourself—and your child—for life!

Remember, *Parenting for Life* holds parents accountable, helps children forge their own paths, and strengthens the parent-child bond through love, respect and empathy.

Live Inspired!®

Nina~

What's Next?

- To order more copies of *Parenting for Life* go to: Amazon US, Amazon Europe, Create Space, and Kindle. To contact Nina for speaking engagements, therapy, and coaching visit her on the web at: **www.LiveInspiredwithNina.com**

- Read and comment on Nina's blog at: **www.LiveInspiredwithNina.com**

- Like Nina on Facebook at: Nina Sidell, Inspiring Lives: Psychotherapy & Life Coaching

- Find Nina on LinkedIn

- Follow Nina on Twitter at: @Nina Sidell

- Watch Nina's videos on YouTube and Vimeo at Nina Sidell's channel

- Sign-up for Nina's eSeminar Series *Learn to Live Inspired!*® **www.LiveInspiredwithNina.com**

Live Inspired!®

Nina~

Bibliography & References

1. Koenigsberg, Richard A.: *Symbiosis & Separation: Towards a Psychology of Culture*, Library of Social Science, 1989

2. Chopra, Deepak and Tanzi, Rudolph: *Super Brain*. Harmony; 2012.

3. Lerner, Harriet: *The Dance of Intimacy*, Harper & Row, 1989.

4. Kindlon, Dan and Thompson, Michael: *Raising Cain—Protecting the Emotional Life of Boys*, Ballantine Books; 2000.

5. Hoffman, Martin: "Power Assertion by the Parent and Its Impact on the Child," *Society for Research in Child Development*, 1960.

6. Iacocca, Lee; Novak, William: *Iacocca: An Autobiography*, Bantam, 1985.

7. Eighteenth century English proverb.

8. Robbins, Anthony: Awaken the Giant Within, Simon & Schuster, Inc., 1991.

9. Whitman, Walt: "There Was a Child Went Forth," *Leaves of Grass*, Fulton Street Printing Shop, 1855.

10. Gottman, John; Schwartz, Julie: *Ten Lessons to Transform Your Marriage*, Three Rivers Press, 2006.

11. Bronfenbrenner, Urie: *The Ecology of Human Development*, Harvard University Press, 1979.

12. Maslow, Abraham: "A theory of human motivation." *Psychological Review*. 50(4):370-96, 1943.

13. Satir, Virginia: *Peoplemaking*. Science and Behavior Books; 1972.

14. Hedges, Donna

15. Luskin Biordi D., Nicholson, N.R.: "Social Isolation in Chronic Illness: Impact and Intervention, Eighth Edition by Ilene Morof Lubkin and Pamela D. Larsen." Jones & Bartlett Learning; 2013. pp 97-126.

16. Hall-Lande, J.A., Eisenberg, M.E., Christenson, S.L., Neumark-Sztainer, D.: "Social isolation, psychological health, and protective factors in adolescence." *Adolescence*. 2007; 42 (166): 265-286.

17. "Effects of Social Isolation Traced to Brain Hormone," *Science Daily*, November 15, 2007. Available at: http://www.sciencedaily.com/releases/2007/11/071114121316.htm

18. Baker, K.: "Causes and Effects of Dysfunctional Family Relationships." Available at: http://EzineArticles.com/3454968

19. Hay, Louise: *You Can Heal Your Life*, Hay House, Inc., 1984.

20. Byrne, Rhonda: *The Secret.* Atria Books/Beyond Words; 2006.

21. Huxley, Aldus: *Texts & Pretexts, An Anthology with Commentaries*, Chatto & Windus London, 1932.

22. Crary, Elizabeth: *Love and Limits: Guidance Tools for Creative Parenting.* Parenting Pr; 1994.

23. DeGeneres, Ellen: Interview with Katie Couric, Glamour Magazine, 2010.

24. Cummings, E. E.: "A Poet's Advice to Students," *E. E. Cummings, A Miscellany*, Argophile Press, 1958.

25. Turkle, Sherry: *Alone Together: Why We Expect More from Technology and Less from Each Other.* Basic Books; 2011.

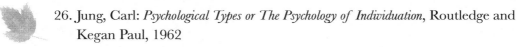

26. Jung, Carl: *Psychological Types or The Psychology of Individuation*, Routledge and Kegan Paul, 1962

27. Nin, Anais: *Children of the Albatross*, Dutton, 1947.

28. Dalai Lama and Cutler, Howard C.: *The Art of Happiness: A Handbook for Living*, Riverhead, 1998.

29. Jung, Carl: *The Essential Jung: Selected and Introduced by Anthony Storr*, Princeton, University Press, 1983.

30. Ginott, Haim: *Teacher and Child.* Macmillan, 1972.

31. Lesser, Elizabeth: *Broken Open: How Difficult Times Can Help Us Grow*, Villard Books, 2005.

32. Covey Stephen R.: *The 7 Habits of Highly Effective People: Powerful Lessons in Personal Change.* Free Press, 1989.

33. Carlson, Rachel: *The Sense of Wonder*, Harper, 1956.

34. Dennis, Patrick: *Auntie Mame: An Irreverant Escapade*, Vanguard Press Books, 1955.

35. Williamson, Marianne: *A Return to Love: Reflections on the Principles of a Course in Miracles.* Bantam Books; 1975.

36. Isay, Jane: *Walking on Eggshells: Navigating the Delicate Relationship Between Adult Children and Parents.* (Reprint) Anchor; 2008.

37. Rumi: *Art as Flirtation and Surrender*, 1207-1273.

38. Einstein, Albert: To J. Dispentiere, March 24, 1954, AEA 59–495.

39. Vaillant, George Eman: *The Wisdom of the Ego*. Harvard University Press; 1995.

40. Excerpted from Virginia Satir's lecture at a 1986 conference of 600 Los Angeles-area psychologists, psychiatrists and other mental health professionals.

41. Freud, Sigmund: "The Origin and Development of Psychoanalysis." *American Journal of Psychology.* 21:207-8, 1910.

42. Erikson, Erik: *Childhood and Society*. Norton, New York, 1950.

43. Williamson, Marianne: *A Course in Weight Loss: 21 Spiritual Lessons for Surrendering Your Weight Forever*, Hay House, Inc., 2011.

44. Geisel, Theodore (Dr, Seuss): *Oh, The Places You'll Go!*, Random House, 1990.

45. Hay, Louise: *You Can Heal Your Life*. Hay House, 1984.

46. Lao Tzu: *Tao Te Ching*, translated by Stephen Mitchell, Frances Lincoln Limited, 1999.

47. Holmes, Oliver Wendell: *The Poet at the Breakfast Table*, G. Routledge, 1872

48. Brault, Robert: *The One Year Alive Devotions for Students*, 2009, Tyndale House Publishers, Inc.

49. Jampolsky, Gerald: *Love is Letting Go of Fear*, (Thrid Edition) Celestial Arts, 2010.

50. Gandhi, Mahatma: VOL 13, Ch 153, "General Knowledge About Health," Page 241, Printed in the *Indian Opinion* on 9/8/1913 From *The Collected Works of M.K.Gandhi*; published by The Publications Division, New Delhi, India.

51. Baddeley, A; Eysenck, MW; Anderson, MC: *Memory*. Psychology Press; 2009.

52. Willingham, DT: Reframing the mind: "Howard Garner and the theory of multiple intelligences." *Education Next.* Summer 2004/Vol. 4, No. 3.

53. Baddele, A: *Working Memory, Thought, and Action*. OUP Oxford; 2007.

54. Miller, G. A.: "The cognitive revolution: a historical perspective." *Trends in Cognitive Sciences*. Volume 7/No. 3. 2003:141-144.

55. Tarnow, E.: "Why The Atkinson-Shiffrin Model Was Wrong From The Beginning." Webmed Central NEUROLOGY 2010;1(10):WMC001021.

56. Costa, Rodolfo: *Advice My Parents Gave Me: And Other Lessons I Learned From My Mistakes*, Author House, 2009.

57. Satir, Virginia: *Peoplemaking*, Science and Behavior Books, 1972.

58. Dyer, Wayne: *The Power of Intention,* Hay House, 2005.

59. Churchill, Winston: *Churchill by Himself: The Definitive Collection of Quotations,* Edited by Richard Langworth, Public Affairs, 2008.

60. Dyer, Wayne: *The Power of Intention,* Hay House, 2005.

61. Buddha: Unknown origin from the Buddha's teachings founder of Buddhism, 563-483 B.C.

62. Knowlton, Judith: *Higher Powered,* Crossroad, 1991.

63. Szasz, Thomas Stephen: *The Second Sin,* Anchor Press, 1973.

64. Ford, Debbie: *Why Good People Do Bad Things: Stop Being Your Own Worst Enemy,* Harper Collins, 2008.

65. Hunt, Terry; Paine-Gernee, Karen: *Emotional Healing: A Program for Emotional Sobriety,* Warren Books, 1989.

66. Smedes, *Warren: Forgive and Forget: Healing the Hurts We Don't Deserve,* Harper Collins, 1984.

67. Hay, Louise: F*orgiveness: Loving the Inner Child,* Hay House, Inc., 2004.

68. Campbell, Joseph: *The Power of Myth,* Clarkson Potter/Ten Speed/Harmony, 1988.

69. Ehrmann, Max: *Desiderata* prose poem, 1927.

70. Dyer, Wayne: *The Power of Intention,* Hay House, 2005.

71. Ehrmann, Max: *Desiderata* prose poem, 1927.

72. Dalai Lama and Cutler, Howard C.: *The Art of Happiness: A Handbook for Living,* Riverhead, 1998.

73. Zak, Paul J.: *The Moral Molecule.* Dutton Adult; 2012.

74. Mahler M, Pine F, Bergman A: *The Psychological Birth of the Human Infant: Symbiosis and Individuation,* Basic Books, 1975.

75. Bradbury, Ray: *Farewell Summer,* William Morrow, 2006.

76. Beattie, Melody: *CoDependent No More: How to Stop Controlling Others and Start Caring for Yourself,* Harper & Row, 1988.

77. Reber, Deborah: *Chicken Soup for the Teenage Soul,* Turtleback, 1997.

78. Isay, Jane: *Walking on Eggshells: Navigating the Delicate Relationship Between Adult Children and Parents.* (Reprint) Anchor; 2008.

79. Chopra, Deepak: *The Seven Spiritual Laws of Success*, New World Library, 1994.

80. Keller, Helen: *The Story of My Life*, Doubleday, Page & Co., 1903.

81. Augustyn, Marilyn; Zuckerman, Barry S.; Caronna, Elizabeth B.: *The Zuckerman Parker Handbook of Developmental and Behavioral Pediatrics for Primary Care*, Lippincott Williams & Wilkins, 2010

82. Lerner, Harriet: *The Dance of Intimacy*, Harper & Row, 1989.

83. Tich Nhat Hanh: *From Peace is Every Step: The Path of Mindfulness in Everyday Life*, Bantam, 1991.

84. Willis, Jennifer Schwamm: *A Lifetime of Peace: Essential Writings By and About Tich Nhat Hanh Everyday Life*, Da Capo Press, 2003.

85. Steinem, Gloria: *Outrageous Acts and Everyday Rebellions*, Second Edition, Owlet, 1995.

86. Kilian, Pamela: *Barbara Bush, Matriarch of a Dynasty*, St. Martin's Griffin, 2003.